UNDER CADER IDRIS

Alienora Browning grew up in Oxford and studied at Aberystwyth University, gaining a degree in English Literature and a PGCE in English and History. She subsequently taught at a secondary school in North Somerset for thirty years.

Now retired, she has six other books published. In this seventh book, she returns to the magical landscape of West Wales.

Her hobbies include playing various musical instruments, singing, reading and drama.

Divorced, with a grown-up son, she lives in Glastonbury.

Also by Alienora Browning/Taylor on Amazon:

Long-Leggety Beasties

Come Laughing

Riding at the Gates of Sixty

My Esoteric Journey, Volume 1

The Lyre of Logres

Booby Fellatio's Lockdown Diary

ISBN: 9798592405112

Dedication

This one is for Lisa Lipman and Mark Halper, wonderful, supportive and inspirational friends.

Author's Note

'**Under Cader Idris**' was originally written in 1984, the first three chapters winning First Prize in a South West Arts' Writers in Progress Award that same year.

Full-time teaching and motherhood delayed its publication by some three decades.

Now, partially rewritten and carefully edited, it is finally ready to be born, after what must be one of the longest literary pregnancies in recent history!

CONTENTS PAGE

'UNDER CADER IDRIS'

ALIENORA BROWNING

PART ONE: SEPTEMBER 1980

THURSDAY 4th

Cader Idris unclouded. Its north face was purple, craggy brow jutting out, bright green bryophytes forming stubble on the jaw. Rain bristled. A few drops moistened the marshlands, landed on village roofs, lingered over Pritchard's Farm.

Two leverets, scut-to-scut like cased dueling pistols, lay in front of the farmyard's inner gate. Miriam Forrest's face appeared at an upper window, red hair sleep-tangled. Anxiety narrowed her throat at the sight of the vulnerable pair. Danger stirred, as nearby predators – men, dogs, foxes – sniffed the air. Their warning shades moved in about the creatures.

Each of the baby hares was surrounded by a rough horse-shoe of pebbles and mud cast up, Miriam presumed, when the animals leapt into their uncanny position. She saw hares frequently, flitting across fields in the tawny mid-evening, or lying in gory heaps along the roadside; but never before like this, so open and trusting. They were quick, restless creatures, born of prey surviving long enough to mate - and with instincts to match.

Miriam could not understand their passivity, feared myxomatosis.

Their ears lay flat and low against their heads. Body fur, darkened by the rain, appeared to run so that they resembled spongy old shoes left out for the dustmen.

As the girl gazed, the gate creaked open. She craned her neck round, and out into the upper farmyard. Heneghan stood there, gun under his left arm, an English setter on each side, furry rabbit corpse hanging from his belt.

She held her breath.

One of the dogs pointed and stiffened; the other whined low in its throat. Heneghan's hat tensed back as he lifted the gun.

"Oh, please go, little hares," Miriam said, and found her hands pressed together in early childhood's praying position.

As if hearing her, the leverets leapt between two gate struts and made for the back fields, streaks of last-minute survival.

Heneghan shot, once, twice, just missing them. One bullet dug a groove in the side wall. The second came to rest, with a damp plinking noise, in the ditch. Blood dripped onto the packed mud surface from the gun's earlier victim. The younger dog sniffed the bloody patch with its snout and howled, knowing that it had missed out on the kill. Heneghan barked at it.

He tightened the string tying the dead rabbit to his belt and then, whistling, sauntered off down the track.

Throat dry with shocked relief, Miriam climbed back into the bed she shared with Flora – and moved close, wanting comfort. But her lover slept on, oblivious.

Miriam feared and loathed Heneghan. They both did. He was a bully who killed or maimed because he wanted to. It seemed to give him a savage, borderline-sexual thrill.

Flora, in one of her more stridently anti-male phases, had said that the man's gun was an extension of his cock, and that his unerring accuracy with the former probably meant a correspondingly trigger-happy use of the latter.

He cast a shadow wherever he walked among the villagers. It seemed that he could throttle living conversation into strangled silence with one vicious comment. Angela, his wife, was a virtual recluse. Village gossip had it that she tended the children and dodged his moods.

When the girls had moved here, nine months earlier, just before Finals, they had seen the man striding down the tracks bordering the farm on their second day.

Flora's smiling, "Good morning," had been met with nothing but an incredulous scowl.

Now, with eight weeks' teaching observation at Pwll-Coedwig Primary School lying ahead of her, Miriam's natural anxiety was heightened both by the little dead rabbit hanging from the man's belt, and how close he had come to adding two more deaths to this frighteningly-casual tally of violence.

And yet, within that cavern of fear, dark fires of guilty lust occasionally sparked up – as inappropriate, in every sense, as they were threatening. She preferred women, was happy living with Flora.

Perhaps it was simply the lingering memories of those first sexual fantasies – times, in her early teens, when she would lie under her bedclothes, in a lather of lust, and imagine Heathcliff poised above her, grinning nastily.

Aroused by the very thought, she put an arm around the girl lying next to her and started, gently at first, to kiss her.

The fact that her eventual loud orgasm reflected imagined contact with the man, as well as the reality of sex with the girl, was instantly buried in her chest of forbidden erotic thoughts.

***

Heneghan flung the rabbit down on the kitchen table. He took his hat off and then jammed it back on again, feeling edgy for some reason. What if Caradoc Pritchard found out about this morning's little business and stopped his shooting rights? What if one of those lesbian bitches living in the farm cottage had spotted him or heard the shots? Say it was a mistake? The gun went off accidentally?

He took his sharp hunting knife and, making a slit in each tendon, slotted one back leg through the other and then hung the rabbit up until he had time to deal with it. There was no smell. It was fresh.

He'd get Thomas to gut it before he went to school. It would be a good learning experience for the lad, teach him a few things about preparing dead animals for food.

The two dogs sat at his feet, quiet and eager to please. They were devoted to him. He took their affection and, occasionally, gave it back in grudging half-measure, ruffling their fur or balling his fist at them. They were hungry now.

He laughed, liking the sound of their teeth scraping the remains of previous morsels off the plate, hinting. He took the chopping board and grabbed the slab of unfrozen meat from the fridge. With precise movements, he cut it into small pieces and then slid some onto each dog's plate. They watched him intently, but did not move.

Walking to the larder, he took out a large sack of dog meal, heaped a dusty mound on top of the meat then mixed the lot together with a bent fork.

The dogs knew what to expect next. Plyn, the younger, moved his tail slightly along the floor and then stopped apologetically.

Cupping each hand, he let the dogs sniff the five vitamins nestling there. Their noses tickled his fingers as they tried to get at the yeasty tablets. One fell. Plyn swooped after it.

He held a flat hand out to each dog and then put their bowls onto the floor. They ate. His hands smelled of dog.

It was seven-fifteen. Through the small kitchen window he could see a black teddy, lacy and fine, on Gwawr-who-pulled-the-pints-at-the-Farmers-Arms' washing line. It gave him quite a start to think that the barmaid, with her long dark hair and tired face, could be hiding sexy undies under her normal clothes, and wondered who she wore them for.

"*Iesu mawr,*" he whistled to himself. Mind, she gave all men the look and a bit of cleavage – and, though not exactly beautiful, had the kind of wide mouth that promised much ("...and probably delivers bugger-all," he thought cynically).

A stray dog had once leapt from behind a bush in the lane and mauled her leg badly. Alerted by her screams, he and Angela had gone out to help, administering First Aid and phoning 999.

He remembered her eyes as she looked at the blood on her thigh. He had tracked the dog for days and had seen nothing – only, in his mind, the gradually healing wounds on Gwawr Jones' legs.

He had wanted to kill that dog; to have it as a trophy, a symbol of his dominance – and, simmering behind faux gallantry, had been the image of Gwawr's wide mouth, the thought of fear and the way it made a woman into sexual putty, to be molded into a shape that gave huge pleasure.

She would owe him. The echo of the killing shot would stand as a constant reminder between them.

The animal's disappearance had thwarted him – but he could see, in her eyes, that she had got the message: that the unsaid semaphored flags between them.

He scared her, and her fear made him glad.

***

Thomas walked into the kitchen to fetch his boots for the early morning stint helping Caradoc Pritchard's son, Iestyn, with the farm chores. He liked to drive the tractor. It made him feel like a giant to be so far above the ground - and he liked the grinding of the gears, more throaty than those in a car.

He saw his father, leaning back in the chair with his hands on his thighs; he took in the gun, broken now, which leant against the table leg.

Tom felt the usual gripping of adrenaline in his stomach. His father affected him as no one else did. There was an element of fear. Most things he would not say to his dad, yet he felt physically at ease with him. James, by contrast, chatted away with complete spontaneity. He felt envious of his younger brother at times.

Despite this, Dad's male power thing was easy for Tom. All you had to do was to let him be top dog, allow him to see that he was the boss in every situation, and everything would be fine.

All was fine now. The wordless moment of tension had passed as the father gnawed on the gristle of his son's uncertainty and, sated, fed it through his own muscles. He felt great. Sun climbed in at the window and, laughing, Heneghan rippled it up and down his leg. The boy watched. His father passed him the knife.

"Gut that rabbit for me, Tom. Don't you puncture the stomach, now, or we'll be gassed-out by the smell. Rabbit pie tonight."

Tom liked blood - both the colour and the faintly metallic smell – but his hands trembled as he held the knife over the cooling abdomen. His father was watching – therefore it mattered. He could not rip, whistling, through the skin as he normally did.

He sliced out the guts with care, pushing the shudders back up his arm each time. He was breathing lightly, floating along.

Entrails lay on yesterday's *Cambrian News*.

Heneghan flexed away the arthritis in his right forefinger and watched every movement.

The lad scraped out the clinging pieces of tissue with the sharp point. His shoulder blades were jumping and juddering. He wiped the knife and put it down on the table next to the emptied rabbit.

Man and boy smiled at one another. Tom had done a good job. His hands were firm and confident.

Heneghan felt proud of his firstborn.

"Always put a knife back," he said. "All weapons have their place."

"Yes," said Tom, though it was hard to see whether he was agreeing or obeying.

**

Tom pulled on his boots and left, closing the door after him. Heneghan did not move.

Tom ran down the fields, over the stream and on toward Pritchard's Farm. The wind was warm in his face and the buildings blurred through his squinting eyes. He could see Iestyn opening the big barn doors to get the tractor out.

Iestyn was large and strong, with wiry dark hair; his English was guttural, its inflection upended, making it obvious that he was translating direct from his native tongue as he went along. He found the boy strange. Tom tried hard, but the work did not come naturally to him - and Iestyn was baffled by this.

There often seemed to be an invisible third person between them, a messenger who translated more than the occasional language difficulty. Iestyn was amused by Tom. The boy was rough and stained as an old Brillo pad and he made the man laugh.

They came from widely-differing cultures. For Tom, the peaty land down the track was just springy marsh to bounce upon or be swished at with a stick. He struggled to understand Iestyn's meticulous approach, the way he walked quietly and carefully, watching, picking up pieces of wool and cow-horn along the way.

The boy would not have dreamed of questioning, let alone criticising, Iestyn's way of doing things. Each stood on one side of the cultural battlefield, waving a white flag.

"Better feed the bullocks, Tom. Come on, get up behind. Dad left the gate open last night when he came to check that sick sheep."

Tom climbed up behind Iestyn on the tractor and stood with his arms out-stretched. The farm dogs ran alongside the machine, nipping in and out, barking madly. The vibrations caused his teeth to rattle.

Something leapt across the ditch and ran for the triangle of trees bordering the back fields. The water level was low. Cracks had appeared in the mud by the side. Weeds grew from them.

The bullocks stood under a tree. Their knobbly polls were blood-stained from yesterday's dehorning. Pieces of bale-string, sticky with tar, hung from the wounds.

The animals moaned with hunger and discomfort. When Iestyn fed them, they crowded him, pushing each other clumsily out of the way. One stepped on the man's left foot. He swore loudly and limped out of their way.

At the corner of the track, a dead sheep floated in the ditch. Iestyn got down and poked it with a stick. The distinctive brand-mark came into view. It was one of theirs, not a wandering stray from Jones' small-holding. He'd get it out later, if he had time. It was not urgent; things disintegrated quickly in the brackish water.

At ten to eight, they shared the sweet tea from Iestyn's flask, sitting on the stone steps in the sun, not talking. Tom untied the rope from the moribund sheep's hind legs, checked its wound, rebound the rough blanket and tied it up once more. The creature was comatose. Iestyn put in clean straw bedding and, carefully, they put the sheep back into the shed and padlocked the door.

It was getting late; the school bus would arrive soon. Tom had to hurry home, change into his school uniform and then join his sister, Rachel, in the usual place, trying to pretend he didn't know her. He thought of the injured sheep as he dressed. It would probably die. He wondered if it would be dead by the time he returned in the evening.

Rachel stood by the broken stile. She ignored him. They could hear the bus rumbling round the bend, then down past the chapel and into view. They were the first ones on today. Sharon and Melanie from the village must be skiving again. They got onto the bus and sat on opposite seats. The vehicle moved off once more.

***

James Heneghan realized he had forgotten his reading-book half way along the lane. He told his mother, and Angela sighed but said nothing.

James got out of the car and ran back to the house. The slam of the door alerted Dr Wyn Jones's horses. They turned and looked at James from their field at the bottom of The Grange. He did not like them. They frightened him. He imagined them trampling down the thin wire of the fence and charging him.

It was the second week of school and James had been put up a year. He hadn't told his mum yet. He didn't think Mrs Roberts, who taught the top class, liked him much, perhaps because his older brother had been so naughty at school.

James was only just nine and the youngest in the class. He missed sitting next to Aled; the big children ignored him – and Rhodri, with whom he'd been made to sit, smelled big-boy-sour and was enormous.

In James's fantasy world, his mother would not find out. That way he could spend two years in this class and still go on to the big school with his friends. Perfect.

In the playground before school, James told Aled he'd wait for him to go to Glyndwr Comprehensive. Aled promised to keep it a secret.

The hymn was in Welsh that morning. There was a strange woman standing next to Mrs Roberts in the teachers' line. She was having trouble with the words.

James looked hard as the woman's mouth opened and closed like a sucking loach, out of time with the rest of the school.

A tiny girl, in the infants' line, was sharing her upside-down hymn book with another little child. James felt embarrassed for her. Fancy not being able to read!

The woman next to Mrs Roberts had long wavy rosy-gold hair and pale, fragile-looking skin. She was smiling to herself and didn't seem to mind the snarls of Welsh all around her. James was puzzled.

After the prayer, Mr Lewis, the Headmaster, stepped forward to face the children and, switching to English, announced that this was Miss Forrest who was going to be with them, helping, for the next few weeks.

Miriam smiled.

***

Angela Heneghan glanced at the joints of rabbit on a plate at the bottom of the fridge. Once she would have recoiled, but she had hardened over the years. As long as she was not required to wrench their small bodies apart herself, she did not mind the raw-looking remains.

Besides, Mike took pride in his shooting and Angela hated to dampen his enthusiasm through fastidiousness. She did not like the taste of rabbit, but had never said as much to Mike. He would be angry and, at a deeper level, hurt.

It was the vulnerability rather than the violence in his make-up that constrained her. Hitting her was at least an outward show of something. It was a link of sorts. The formlessness of most of his communication saddened her. She felt he was like a shapeless jelly searching for a hard mold. The soft substance flowed, unseen and bitterly resented, eroding all it touched – but hurting Mike himself the most, an endlessly-repeated cycle.

All this she sensed. She knew what people in the village thought. They did not say, but it was obvious in their eyes for all that. She grew hot and ashamed even thinking about it because, after all, these people – with their surface impressions and snippets of the district nurse's gossip – did not know the full story.

She experienced their assumptions as a kind of treachery, a betrayal of Mike – and he was the least able, of all the people she knew and loved, to explain.

She took out the large Portmeirion pie dish and greased it carefully, rubbing the paper around the corners before she noticed her compulsive behavior and stopped. The meat was cool and she handled it as little as possible. There was pastry over so she made another pie. She'd take it over to Gwawr Jones later.

One large butterfly wing stubbornly resisted the pastry no matter how much she pressed, pushed and wetted the sides. The finished product looked strange, sloppy at the edges.

"Not good enough," grated the harsh voice in her head.

Angela usually enjoyed these rare still moments, times when the house was silent and she could wander about, enjoying her own space. She liked the texture of things in her everyday life, especially wood. Visual stimulus always came second for her.

She took her solitary walks head down, searching for particularly fine specimens of bone-like wood or drift wood or, if nothing else were available, simple whittle wood. These she peeled like recalcitrant bananas, then ran her fingers up and down the newly-smooth edges.

The simple act of touching was not enough today. She was restless and wanted to be out and about. Normally she took the car to the beach and walked from there; this time, she decided to walk the whole way. It was a challenge, something she had never done before. She put on trainers and set off.

The road was completely flat for most of the journey. With the hills in the distance, it felt like travelling in a straight line along the bottom of a china bowl.

Beyond the ditches, the marshland steamed and squeaked; bulrushes lined the waterside.

Once out on the main stretch of road, she could count the houses on the fingers of one hand. The surface was sticky where tar had bubbled up from the depths in the heat. In some places she had to pull her shoes out of every step.

To left and right she could see, through the heat haze, tiny men on tractors wheeling back and forth across the fields. The smell of hay, and manure, was strong in the air; minute insects flew into her damp face repeatedly. She spat them out and slapped them off in vain. There were always more; the air hummed with them.

It should have been easy walking but was not since one had the enervating illusion of endless travel. The district nurse's house, and a tiny camp site on a hill, bisected the two long stretches in an elbow bend which Angela had learned to approach with care because cars, scenting another long uninterrupted drive, inevitably accelerated at that point.

The placing of the district nurse's house was fortuitous. On several occasions she had been required to deal with the victims of minor road accidents. Once, a girl and her pony had been dragged several yards by a thundering great trailer. Matt, the handyman who tended the nurse's few chickens and cows, had shot the dazed and broken pony straightaway.

Angela remembered that day. The girl had been Rachel and she had escaped with nothing more serious than cuts and bruises, but the emotional wound caused by the slaughtering of her pony remained as fresh as ever.

There was no sign of Imelda, the nurse, though her chickens were wandering about the roadside as usual. They squawked at the sight of Angela and ran around in crazy, pointless circles. The ridiculous thing, to her, was their amazing road sense. Not one of the silly, fluttering creatures had ever been road-killed.

She walked on, past the huge house with the goats and up towards the estuary. The slats of half-finished barn were slimy from morning rain.

Aberdyfi appeared, from this distance, ready to step into the water on the other side of the channel. The tide was far out, no more than a tiny moat around the harbour walls.

Angela could see the ridges of sand where the sea had rolled back, and imagined the scattering of shells, the small lakes and pools of warm briny water. The air was thick with salt. She could walk over to Aberdyfi if she wanted. She chose not to, however, because the times of the tide were too uncertain on the way back. She had visions of being swept away in a great rush of returning water. For a spontaneous moment, it needed too much checking.

She climbed round and up. Sheep lazed on rocky plateaus. A bull rattled his nose-ring on the gate post and Angela stepped back instinctively. Twin half-grown lambs jumped over a small gorse bush and careered on down the hill unable, it seemed, to stop. She leaned on the gate and smiled at the small animals.

The slopes were surprisingly tiring and she rested often, feeling the shiny warmth of gate bars beneath her elbows.

She told the time, twelve-ten, by the lumbering by of the midday bus. People knocked on the windows and waved. The bus hit a pot hole and she could see three girls in the back row being thrown up against the roof. She could imagine their laughter, spiked that little bit by fear.

She felt timeless and rested by the very act of travelling in the opposite direction to her home and commitments. Walking like this, nothing was expected of her.

At the fork in the road, she waited for a while by the telephone kiosk, thinking and deciding. She could do whatever she wanted, and that increased the difficulty. She was rooted in obedience and the decisions, often unspoken, of others.

She turned left in the end, towards Borth, and walked along the road next to the sea wall, facing oncoming traffic.

At the first set of steps, she climbed and then jumped, landing on the pebbles next to the slimy groyne.

Straightaway she realized she'd chosen the perfect day. There had been a storm, of some severity, the night before and the beach squares, checkered between the wood-and-stone-built groynes, were like scrapyards overflowing with junk. Looking at it all, Angela was aware of an acquisitive side to her nature that she did not normally show.

Few people were about. It was too late for holiday - makers and too nondescript a part of the day for anyone else.

The groyne was gaping at points, the result of many a winter storm. Clumps of seaweed hung from rusted nails; crustacean warts disfigured the smooth surface of the dark wood. The outer curves of Aberdyfi were visible way off to the right, ringed now by midday gold.

Angela looked and luxuriated. Crates and tree trunks, picked clean by the salt, lay in her path. She knelt and touched the cold clear surfaces. Nothing dropped away from her fingertips as was customary with land wood. All was white and clearly-defined as bleached bone. She inhabited an arboreal graveyard.

Down below the layer of pebbles, the sand stretched for miles, with sea faintly visible at the furthest point. This was how she liked it best.

The tatty beachcomber, a figure familiar to Angela, was busy collecting in the next square. They had spoken on several occasions, and she had been astonished to find that the man was a retired professor of Mediaeval Literature from Wadham College, Oxford. He'd talked about his lecturing days, while she drank in the sound of his mellifluous voice. He'd been adamant when she asked him tentatively about his life-style:

"Pottering about in the guise of a tramp suits me down to the ground," he'd said. "I spent most of my working life clad in a succession of ghastly suits, and I'm buggered if I'm going to look the part now. I owe the world no image – or anything else, come to that."

"I owe the world no image," Angela thought as she walked along - but it rang hollowly somehow, seemed merely grandiose, a figure of speech thrown away by an overly-articulate man.

To walk away from an image, though: that was quite something no matter how you broke it down. It epitomized freedom in her mind. Mike had, in his own way, also turned his back on a conventional image. There was a big difference, however: his instinct was to flatten any restriction; the professor apparently did not care sufficiently to resort to violence.

Mike would hate him, as he did all university- educated people – and the other man would field Mike's hatred with his powerful indifference. Angela was tempted to introduce them. Her husband was her performing dangerous animal, and she could gauge his reactions precisely.

On an impulse, she scrambled over the groyne and approached the man. She'd forgotten how tall he was, over six foot and sarsen-straight, despite his age. She realized that she did not know his name, felt like a schoolgirl in his presence. Swallowing, she spoke:

"I was wondering if you'd like to join me and my husband for a drink in the George Inn later."

To her relief, he smiled at her as if he'd been waiting for this moment a long time.

"Splendid idea, Mrs. Heneghan," he said. "I'd be delighted. I have, of course, seen your husband several times over the years but have not – that I can remember, at any rate – exchanged more than a terse nod with him. Men, you know: their communication can tend toward the Neanderthal.

"Tell you what: if it's a fine night – and I think it will be – shall we meet on the balcony outside, at nine? If it's cold or rainy, I'll be in the Lounge Bar from nine onwards. Good God, I'm doing it again: taking over, I mean. My wife always accused me of treating other people as if they were my students – and I daresay she was right. Put it down to incipient Alzheimer's disease, and too many days spent communing with the soft furnishings."

Angela was taken aback, though charmed too. The man put her in mind of her father. It was a comforting thought.

"He's amusing," she thought. "Not just sarcastic, scoring points, like…"

But the thought slithered away from her, a bloodless miscarriage.

"The balcony sounds fine," she said. "I'm not very good at arranging things — probably would have missed you altogether, gone to the wrong pub or something equally stupid."

The professor laughed and gently rotated his head, as if he were ironing out a source of discomfort. Angela felt emboldened by this very human touch.

"I must ask," she said, "Um. Oh hell! This is all round the houses, isn't it? Did you think it was strange of me to ask you, outright like that, when we barely know one another?"

A ready blush painted her cheeks and neck as the implication of what she had just said hit home.

"I didn't put that very well, did I? Sounded like some kind of improper suggestion."

"The spirit is willing, Mrs Heneghan, but the flesh is weak," he replied. "Still, a kind thought. Nothing strange in it either; in fact I was touched.

"I rarely find congenial people to talk to these days. A great deal of the conversation I overhear is pretty superficial: Mrs Jones' latest gynaecological trauma, the outrageous price of meat, that kind of thing. Most refreshing to get to the point without having to wade through the verbal equivalent of a full surgery's waiting room."

Angela laughed, relieved.

"Ah, I see you've met Mrs Jones as well," she said.

"Met her? I sometimes feel that I am in a long, and grotesquely-unhappy, polygamous marriage with her and her equally grisly sisters, Mesdames Evans, Thomas, Davies et al. The human vultures, I call them: they're forever waiting to swoop on the slightest morsel of emotional carrion."

The image appealed to Angela.

"I don't know your name," she said. "So sorry. I should have asked months ago!"

"Edwin Russell. I can live without the honorific these days – puts me in mind of some of the dreadful old bores I knew in the old days. See you this evening, then. I have to say, I am looking forward to it."

"You don't know what you're letting yourself in for," Angela thought – but, to her surprise, she felt exhilarated and amused rather than fearful. She had a sense of making things happen. Giving Edwin Russell a cheery wave, she clambered back into her own sand square.

"Home," she thought. "Put pies in oven, let dogs out, tidy house; feet tired, take bus!"

Laughing at her own note-form thoughts, she walked up over the sea wall to the bus stop opposite the Marzipan Factory.

"Time enough to be worried when I get home," she thought, as a little wave of fear crept up on her – and then, "Oh God, what have I done!"

**

Evening began as a smudge on the contours of the day. Miriam, who'd spent the afternoon in Mrs Roberts' class, told Flora about loud Rhodri, his twin Arianwen, and tiny, very young genius, James-surname-unknown.

Tom smelled the death of the sheep before he viewed its corpse.

And Heneghan, finding he had the house to himself, indulged in his favourite fantasy concerning a gym full of thirteen-year-old schoolgirls in navy-blue knickers.

***

Heneghan put on his checked blue-and-white cheesecloth shirt and buttoned it to the navel; over this he wore the imitation black leather jacket. He knew he looked good and he felt strong, assured.

He left the hat at home since he didn't hold with headgear in pubs. He wasn't keen on going in the lounge bar, come to that, but wanted to go along with Ange this once. Her determination had startled and rather pleased him.

He felt a simmering of angry lust towards her. The pliant row of navy-blue gym knickers rose up before him once more and he smiled with thin lips at his reflection in the mirror: broad chest, narrow face with hazel eyes and straight dark brown hair; muscular, sinewy body; long feet in the worn cowboy boots.

This doddering old professor didn't faze him – all brains and no balls; he knew the type and could handle the guy, no problem there.

The house smelled strongly of rabbit pie. Ange was a good cook, though his daughter's pursed mouth and fussy refusal to eat more than a mouthful had infuriated Heneghan. She was becoming a real stuck-up, opinionated little piece, was Rachel. She needed discipline; that was for sure.

Ange came into their bedroom, hair wet and tousled from the bath. As she bent over to peer in the mirror, Heneghan slapped her hard on the bottom. She jumped and then smiled at his reflected leer. She had a good idea how the evening would end, this being Mike's typical reaction to any male, even an aged professor.

They set off at eight forty-five. Rachel turned aside when Heneghan kissed her.

"Watch your step, girl," he snarled. "You're getting right up my nose today."

"Oh leave it, Dad," she cried. "You're good at threats but you don't mean what you say, not really. I don't like the smell of your aftershave, that's all."

"Ooh, la di da," sneered Heneghan. "Prefer a bit of sheep shit, would you?"

Angela moved firmly towards the front door. She always wanted to run away when Rachel and Mike started sniping at one another. Looking at her sons, she could see they felt the same way.

"We'd better go, Mike. James, bed at nine; you two, no later than ten. It's a school day tomorrow."

Though less clear, the day was still light. Heneghan unlocked the TR7, still brooding. He was very competitive about his cars. He'd got this model because Old Brewer up the road had one.

"Just be thankful Robin Brewer didn't opt for a Rolls," Angela told herself wryly.

"What's he like, then, this bloke?"

Heneghan was actually very keen to know, though his casual approach belied this.

"Late-sixties or early-seventies, I'd say, retired anyway: tall, has swept back white hair, dresses like a tramp, beautiful speaking voice – nice actually; doesn't give a damn, if you know what I mean. Bit different, I'll say that. English."

"Christ-all-bloody-mighty," said Heneghan.

"Wait till you meet him," Angela said and knew she sounded smug – so she was not entirely surprised when Mike slammed his foot on the brake, stopping the car, and turned on her.

"Let's get one thing clear," he hissed, "I'm doing you a favour and, if I don't like this bloke, I'm not fucking about in that pub till closing time, all right? I'll be down the Farmers Arms soon as I've had enough."

"Right," said Angela. "You never know, you might like him."

"I doubt it," Heneghan replied. "I've met his type before."

"You really do label people, don't you, Mike? Where do I fit into this scheme of things?"

"Come on, Ange, it's not like that. Don't be so daft."

The deepening dark seemed to rush at them as they drove towards Borth's main street. Heneghan fell silent and Angela, sensing discomfort or fury, did not question him.

There was a space down by Borth Station, which he took, and they walked the rest of the way. It wasn't far, a matter of yards. Angela shivered and hoped that Edwin's temperament and constitution would not force him out onto the balcony.

When they walked into the lounge bar, she felt unexpectedly nervous. This was not Mike's familiar territory. He'd be far happier perched on a stool in

37

the public bar, drinking with the village lads. She felt a surge of guilt.

Then she saw Edwin Russell. He was tucked away in a corner, with a glass of white wine in front of him. Angela was astounded. Tidied-up, he looked like an ageing Oscar Wilde in black suit, white shirt and maroon cravat. It suited him, as did the pipe he held curved in his left hand.

Angela knew she'd gone too far to turn back, whichever way it went. Mike was stiff beside her.

"Hello," said Angela, pleased and proud despite her fear.

"I'm Edwin," the old man said, concentrating on Heneghan. "What can I get you?"

"Mike Heneghan."

His voice sounded as if it had been squeezed through a narrow pipe. Angela winced for him, knowing what this cost.

"God, Mike," she thought, "Edwin's not against you, you know."

But, if he knew, he wasn't heeding.

"Pint of Best," Heneghan said.

The metaphorical gauntlet dropped into the silence.

"Right..."

Edwin turned to Angela.

"... and you?"

"It's not fair," she thought desperately, "why should I be the arbiter? What do I say?"

"Gin and tonic, please," she said.

They sat down and Edwin went off to the bar to order the drinks. He appeared to know everyone and was stopped several times for conversation. Eventually, he threaded his way back to them, sat down and, wine glass in hand, said, "Cheers dears, whores and queers!" before sitting down straight-faced.

Angela glanced at Mike. As slack-jawed as he ever got, shocked disgust vibrated through him. She feared she was going to laugh, and laugh loudly.

"Got that little gem from one of my students. Completely politically incorrect, of course, but damned funny for all that," Edwin said and laughed.

Angela joined in, relieved that she had a polite excuse for her imminent hysteria. If she laughed longer than was strictly necessary, no one gave any sign.

Edwin was taking his wine in contented sips; Heneghan all but biting chunks out of his pint glass. She gurgled into her gin.

Edwin started on a recent production of *The Trojan Women* he'd seen at Bradfield College, performed, as always, in the original Ancient Greek. Heneghan drank half his pint in one swig. Edwin moved on to the forthcoming merger between the Liberals and

SDP. Heneghan belched loudly and wiped his mouth on his sleeve.

When the older man started again, Angela wanted to ring a bell, and announce round three - but felt she'd better not, all things considered.

She needn't have worried, for, at this moment, the pregnant woman made her way into the bar and the place fell silent. She was beautiful, each part of her perfect and yet strangely separated from the rest. The curve of her pregnancy within the red dungarees hinted at the odd intimacy of Life-drawing nakedness. Angela could imagine, superimposed upon the scarlet canvas, a white foetus curled up.

The woman wore a shawl draped loosely over her head and shoulders. The fringes of it, luminescent in the bar's light, crossed over her breasts and then swung back over the red straps. Each line of her face appeared sharp, as if carved. There was intelligence in those features and a watchful knowingness.

With her were four Arab men, yet she was white-skinned. It seemed incongruous to the onlookers and they found themselves wondering which one was the father, the husband, the brother-in-law. There was evidently a connection of sorts since each of the men formed a protective amulet at one corner of the woman's auric square. They all had bare feet, which seemed to be strangely acceptable in this pub, and this part of the Principality.

The talk beat strongly once more, though the watchfulness remained.

"She will come and sit by us," Angela thought, and tensed herself for the excitement of that anticipated moment; but she was quite wrong. The woman sat down at a table opposite and waited for the men.

Heneghan was very quiet. Angela wondered if he found the huge belly a turn-on.

Edwin Russell found he was intensely aware of Heneghan. He seemed to be ebbing and flowing on the tide of the other man's mood, aware of the great white sharks underneath but sufficiently bloodless himself to avoid direct attack.

"He is an outsider and angry with it, a dangerous combination," Edwin thought to himself.

The younger man was, to Edwin, a hidden landscape of unhealed gashes, with the Harlequin soul of the clown-demon. A man for whom, 'Know Thyself' would not be allowed over the threshold; one who would resist change until his dying breath; Sir Agravain, with his hunched and misshapen spirit, tarnishing the glowing glory of the Round Table.

"That's what comes of too much dabbling in Middle English Romances," Edwin mentally chastised himself.

Still the four Arab men stood in silence at the bar and the woman, alone, cupped her chin in her right hand so that her face was in profile; the fingers of her left hand filled in the bass line of a complicated piano sonata.

The Heneghans and Edwin Russell had allowed her arrival to create a hiatus.

"Do you think she's beautiful?" Angela asked, unable to contain her fear at the range of possible answers any longer.

As if in response, four stools scraped at sand and splinters and the men sat down.

"Oh, yes," said Edwin. "She has the perfect face, with those cheekbones and the lines of her neck. She's aesthetically pleasing rather than sexy, though, isn't she?"

Angela gave bitter laugh. She felt caught on the raw by this woman.

"Looking like that, she doesn't need to be sexy, does she? Probably has to fight them off."

"Bitch," said Heneghan distinctly, though Angela wasn't sure whether he meant her, the woman or some unknown third person.

"Why do you say that?" Edwin asked, looking curiously at him.

It was all he said, but Heneghan glanced at him for the first time that evening – a blank look but still a link.

Edwin looked into the younger man's eyes. They were the grey-green of dirty pond-ice, and just as chilling.

He held Heneghan's glance. Something feral peeped out behind the wintry colour. This was a submerged man; an emotional grindylow ready to pull anyone who got too close into the dreadful mere; too busy building an emotional dam to count the cost.

Angela was frightened. She sensed the men fiddling with the dial on one another's air waves, trying to find a mutual station – and felt as if she had reverted to friendless-child-in-the-playground status.

A lifetime's sense of inferiority around other women – and the debilitating threat-pain this caused – rose up in her. The pregnant goddess, with her four attentive male guards, was a symbol of something far more complex.

"All she has to do," Angela thought, "is to flutter her lashes or show a hint of swelling breast – and Mike will be gathered up in her net, lost to me."

The connection between the two men crackled and hissed. Something was exchanged, at the subliminal level – and Angela knew she was excluded from it.

Heneghan finished his beer and stood up.

"Same again?" he said generally, looking at no one in particular.

The stone harshness had broken up. It was now small gravel fragments and not personal. He did not smile. Angela, relieved, did.

"Splendid," Edwin said.

"Mike – look at me, please," Angela cried inwardly.

Heneghan didn't. He addressed his remarks to the plant on the left.

"Oh God," she thought and drooped.

The plant was aggressively alive, nubile. It had hot-pink flowers and perched like an adolescent breast. Angela's foot itched with anger. She couldn't take her eyes off the shape and colour. It was Rachel, and Gwawr, and the woman opposite - and God alone knows who else.

Heneghan's bottom was neat in the distance, slotting exactly through the bar-liners. Angela's eyes were heavy. She knew Edwin was watching her and damned his intuition.

"Something about the lady over there seems to have upset you. Do I detect a hint of jealousy, of fear relating to Mike?" he asked gently.

"He's my man, isn't he?" she snapped, trying to find an effective barrier.

Edwin felt that he was a discreet man; he wasn't sufficiently involved to be anything else. He also knew that Angela was fighting her awareness of this as hard as she could. He respected this, and was saddened too. He longed suddenly for his second glass of wine.

The silence conjured dark shadows. Two students were playing darts. Angela picked at the corner of her beer mat. A million pieces of compressed fury emerged.

"Yes," she cried. "Of course you bloody well do. I feel absolutely raw with it all. That woman. The way he is."

Edwin, who felt he had got the measure of her, did not comment, though he felt a twinge of irritation at her need to make a scene out of nothing. He could only suppose her anger came from a long-dormant volcano finally erupting – and he, like ancient Herculaneum, was caught in the boiling lava as it gurgled down towards Pompeii.

Perhaps she saw something of this in his face; at any rate she smiled slightly cynically at him, as if she'd caught him out on a naughty thought.

"Jealousy and insecurity, the terrible twins spawned from passionate love," she said in a gentler voice. "But, then, what is love?"

"No idea," said Edwin, recognizing truth as he spoke it, "other than in the realm of literature. I suspect many writers create such rich and, frankly hyperbolic, literary devices because they don't want to admit to being as foxed and frustrated as the rest of us. Lofty metaphor and earthy simile can cover a deep pit of human failure and cruelty. Thank you," he added, in mild relief, as Heneghan, returning, handed him his drink.

Angela watched a lemon pip detach itself and float to the bottom of her gin. She imagined its subsequent inebriation.

Heneghan turned to Edwin.

"You were saying?"

He was looking at the other man calmly. Angela was astonished. She'd never known Mike to back down from one of his sullen silences, even with her.

She tried to recall the minutiae of the previous conversation, but found she could not. The image of two gladiators, battling it out in a Roman amphitheatre, had been more seductive than the words themselves.

"A fishing-related query," Edwin reminded Heneghan. "I daresay of a somewhat illegal nature. Do you have any contacts among the salmon fisherman up the River Dyfi way?"

Heneghan smiled at this and seemed to be thinking.

"Fancy a bit of stealth-fishing, do you? Yeah, I can get you set up, if that's what you want."

"Tell me more,' Edwin said. 'Even the most law-abiding person needs to break out occasionally."

"Under cover of darkness and all that?" Heneghan laughed.

"Something like that," Edwin admitted.

"A group of us get up around dawn some days, take the nets along the Machynlleth Road to that spot just off Eglwys Fach – or else down by the water wheel, whichever seems best at the time.

"Never met anyone else in either spot. The serious fishermen go elsewhere, or so the story goes. Avoid them myself; not my scene, to be honest. Sell the fish sometimes, depends. Gwilym's the contact. He knows everyone around here. You interested?"

Edwin nodded, smiled.

"It's great," Heneghan said. "Something about being up that early, pretty much alone by the water. Makes a change. Kids don't appreciate it, though. Take one look, 'Not bloody salmon again!' that kind of thing. Kids today don't know they're born. Plan to go Saturday week. Fancy coming along?"

"Yes," Edwin replied, "I'm tempted by the lure of fresh food. Excellent change from my usual widower-fare of rip open box and bung contents in oven..."

"Fancy her?" he added switching tacks so suddenly that Angela jumped.

The gravid woman. Of course.

Heneghan, male frequencies tuned, knew instantly.

"Nah," he said, "too old."

They left it at that. Instinct or complicity picked out the basics and dismissed the rest.

Angela, seeking further reassurance, felt the need to strike back against male complacency.

"My round," she announced, and thought, "Check mate!"

Women did not go up to the bar; it was as simple as that – though they were welcome to flash their charms behind it. It was the man's task, like fighting saber-toothed tigers, and too deeply-buried in prehistoric caves for conscious chauvinism. The difference between protection and control had become blurred during the intervening millennia.

Angela, who had always accepted this, felt a rush of rebellion. She would be the only woman at the bar. Good! It would make a clear point.

Heneghan snapped off the conversation's thread with a guillotining glance and abruptly-turned neck; Angela, taking this for tacit agreement, and not caring anyway, took her purse and left.

At the bar she was joined by two of the men. Close up, she could see that they were, in fact, of Egyptian origin. They did not appear to notice her, and were served before she was.

One of them turned round and called across the room, "Ice, Naomi?" in a voice so English that Angela was startled.

Naomi? Yes, that figured. She would have to possess a biblical name.

Naomi looked up on hearing her name. Her face was shining slightly from the heat in the small room. To Angela's frustration, she nodded her head but did not reply.

Angela wished she had the courage to speak to these people, to join them at their table, but she did not dare: going to the bar was adventure enough.

The evening felt inconclusive to her, as if she had started a story and had been unable to decide upon the ending – or, perhaps, had not felt she was allowed, as a woman, to make this kind of decision for herself. But then she was not really very clear what she had expected to happen. Atmosphere was her strength; plot was not. The evening seemed barbed with wiry inconsistencies.

She had envisaged minor characters, and events, fitting neatly into the scene she had written. They hadn't. She was not the protagonist-turned-playwright.

She walked back, drinks on a small tray, glancing at Naomi as she passed, but the other woman was unaware of her. She had a sense of fairy-tale-coincidence wasted.

Time slowed to first gear. Gin numbed her mouth. The men talked fishing in low, relaxed voices and, after fighting awhile with herself, she felt oddly soothed by it. By placing them in a parental role, she was able to relax and feel safe.

"I like the sound of your voices," she said at length.

Edwin smiled at her - and, taking her words on board, the men wrapped their conversation around her so that she felt blanketed and warm.

It was obvious to her that Mike was enjoying himself. He liked the role of teacher, particularly when his listener was an educated man. Mike was not an easy-going man, and sometimes insidious flattery was the only way to relax him.

Time was called and they left the pub.

"Saturday, then," said Heneghan.

It was not a question.

Edwin walked briskly down the street.

***

On the way back to the car, Heneghan took Angela's arm. She wanted to make something of this, sensed there was nothing to be made, walked on. The silence between them vibrated. Something had left with Edwin Russell. She sighed.

"What?" Heneghan said.

"When you said '*bitch*', did you mean me?"

"What if I did?"

He was defensive straightaway, though she was not aware of having attacked. His anger seemed only loosely connected to the moment.

"Oh, well..."

Her words tailed off.

"Go on, spit it out, woman."

"I can't with you snapping like that for no reason."

She felt sickened, the effort of words huge.

"Jesus."

Heneghan unlocked the car and turned to face her.

"Look, you got what you wanted, right? It wasn't as bad as I thought it'd be. Now, for Christ's sake, leave it, will you? Never mind what I said or didn't say or what you thought. I'm not interested."

"Why don't I hit him?" Angela thought as they drove along.

"Because he's stronger and he'd hit me back," she answered herself, "and that's totally acceptable, even commendable, in rural communities. Probably run CSE courses on dependent bashing at the local schools."

"You bloody man," she hissed silently to herself.

She knew, from past experience, that he would restart the conversation in a while as if nothing had happened, and would be genuinely baffled, upset even, if she remained angry when he was not.

"The old lecher," he said eventually, smiling to himself in the dark. "He wanted to get his leg over that pregnant mare. He told me so."

And, equanimity completely restored, he whistled cheerfully, while Angela fidgeted fretfully with the image of Edwin Russell astride that enormous abdomen.

"Like him?" Angela asked at length, wanting, with an urgency she found painful, to know.

"Yeah, he was all right."

Heneghan was laconic at first, fending off any definite commitment.

"Fair play, he had his wits about him, didn't patronize, not a bad guy."

"I was worried," she admitted, "that you would take a violent dislike to him, that you'd walk out or something."

Hands clammy with her own bravery, she waited. The silence - leavened by Heneghan's renewed good humour - rose beyond storm-cloud.

"Yeah, well, nothing you could do, Ange. What happens, happens. You can't make a forecast with people. I'm easier without words but, with him, that didn't matter, after a while. Maybe you don't see," he added calmly.

"Maybe I don't," she said sadly. "Words can be a bar."

"Um," said Heneghan, moving fast onto something else, "Wonder if I can trust him not to bugger about on Saturday. He might not be very sure-footed, could go slipping and sliding all over the place. Can't carry dead wood."

"I think he'll be all right," she said with sudden certainty, thinking of the old man's grace and confidence down on the beach. "He knows what he's doing. He wouldn't go unless he was sure of himself. He seems to have a strong affinity with the sea, did you notice?"

He paused and lit a cigarette.

Cors Fochno rustled and groaned on their left, a sinister presence Angela had never come to terms with.

"He didn't mention the sea, not to me," he said finally, in a voice that was almost aggrieved – as if he'd missed out in some mysterious way.

She was startled.

"Yes," she continued, as if there had been no break in the flow of her thoughts, "he said something very strange to me, soon after I met him the first time. For him, the sea represents the beginning and end of his personal life cycle - and one day, when the tide goes out, he will go with it.

"He wears a metallic wrist-band to that effect so that, when, or if, he's found, it will be clear this is a deliberate choice rather than accident or murder. It sounds fanciful, but the way he said it made perfect sense."

"That's as good a definition of inner power and control as any I can think of," she thought, but did not say. Words like *'power'* and *'control'* were locked up in tightly-conventional little boxes, for men like her husband to own and use, often against those who loved them.

The road was in complete darkness by now, the occasional winking animal eyes coming as a shock. Travelling at this time of night, one had to rely on instinct and familiarity. Heneghan took the corners mechanically, with confidence.

Angela thought about the strangeness of it all, living here and being English. It was direct, like abseiling down a vast rock-face, crunching abrasion and ecstatic descent both equally likely – and you were never sure whether it was painful or exhilarating, but certainly the glory of being up at that height could not be ignored.

She could not imagine living anywhere else. There was no easing off, little overt welcome. You stayed because you chose to, not because you were loved or wanted. It meant that you mined deep for the precious coal of friendship, and this made sense to her as a way of being.

There were no emotional overtures, except the ones you created – but, at the heart of everything, lay the overwhelming love of land. Being here was between you and your conscience. No one else could be held responsible. For Angela, who'd always relied heavily on the culpability of others, this was a first and, in its way, an absolute. She thought of the other English families who lived locally – Martha Redmond, Deborah Tremaine, Robin and Tracy Brewer, and those girls in Pritchard's Farm cottage – and wondered why they stayed, what they found in this uncompromisingly harsh land.

Heneghan had found the land itself, and its peculiar fruits.

The smell of honeysuckle was strong in the air. Set against local Cymraeg legend and geology - the forbidding crags and folds of Cader Idris; the dip where, according to legend, King Arthur's horse's hoof burned red-hot, leaving its mark on stone; the fierce red-haired tribes-people from Dinas Mawddwy - the sweetness of this little flower seemed fragile and forlorn, until one remembered that it was an opportunistic floral cuckoo, binding itself firmly to other plants' branches and refusing to let go. It was just another example of juxtaposition in this mystical place.

"Wonder if the kids are still up?" Heneghan said, breaking her train of thought. "They'd better bloody not be."

"Doubt it," she yawned. "You know what Rachel's like..."

"Yeah. Remind me to drop in on Gwilym tomorrow, will you?"

"Sure. Next Saturday?"

"That's right. See who else he can rustle up at short notice: Bryn maybe, or Owain, that lot."

Tired, very tired, Angela felt; right hand turn, deftly achieved; up the avenue of trees, slipping into the warm niche of home, ivied, familiar. They clung, wordlessly, at the bedroom's watch.

For Angela, it was like leaning against a tree trunk; Heneghan did not give an inch. Instead, he swung her round so that her feet left the ground for a second, and nudged the light switch with his elbow. The room was instantly, and profoundly, black. She did not move and tried to block any thoughts out of her head.

Heneghan pulled her jeans down in one single move. They were tight and his strength caused pain in her hip bones. She said nothing. The material bunched stiffly around her ankles; but she did not step out. She could hear him unzipping his trousers. Her knickers remained.

He pushed her though not viciously and, since the bed was inches behind her, she fell lightly onto the thick continental quilt, her restricted legs tight against the bed edge. He pushed her underwear out of the way and she could feel his stiff cock travelling slowly down over her pubic hair and stopping at her vagina. He was teasing her.

He thrust into her suddenly, making no sound. She could move very little, and his movements caused her right hip to crunch.

When it was over, and he had dribbled flaccidly out of her, she was aware of an ache in her spine, and the faint bubbles in her head from the gin.

While Heneghan moved around in the bathroom, she lay, in the same position, unwilling to move. She stared up at the ceiling, which gradually became clear, and felt damp and cold between the legs.

The hairs on Heneghan's chest glistened with sweat. He smiled, a thin rictus, and wiped himself carefully all over, enjoying his body.

They slept oceans apart. Angela was careful and neat in her self-assigned two feet of bed; Heneghan, revolving on his axis all night, was vocal in his sleep in a way he rarely was awake.

SATURDAY 13th

They set up their nets by the cold silent water. Calyxes of darkness were night-pollinated around them, swelled and grew.

The car was backed into a gorse hiding-place. Two men in thick clothing lurked behind the road bend, out of sight but able to see any car lights for miles. Bryn, the larger of the two, had a sheepdog whistle ready as a warning. One shrill of the familiar, *'That'll do,'* command and the others would, in a trice, dismantle the nets, drag the sanded footprints into oblivion and join the car in its safe niche. Turns, during the fishing hours, would be taken, each man assigned to guard-duty for thirty minutes.

Edwin enjoyed the wordless comradeship, the rhythm of smooth, certain moves across the dunes and into the dips at the river edge. There was no moon and a coven of hills, navy-blue crone hats nodding together, held a Sabbat across the estuary.

Owain winked at Edwin, glad of the older man's company. Gwilym lit a Woodbine and thought about the stallion.

Heneghan, his back to the nets, stood apart and was watched by two wild rabbits hovering by a clump of hardy seagrass tufts.

Night moved very slowly into morning, and paused at the in-between state.

Guards cleared the area they could barely see three times. The second time, early morning lovers, with nowhere else to go, kept the men in a cramp of irritation for over half an hour before finally roaring off.

Hours lightened the sky and, in the blushing silvery shiver of fish after fish, the men − though peripherally aware − let excitement carry them along into the fiery fuchsia-gold of six-thirty. They knew the risks, but that frisson of danger was their shared addiction. Their last glittering fish, roseate flesh dappled with purple and gold from the sun's rising, was huge, an ancient monster taken from the tales of Taliesin.

***

It was Saturday, Miriam's first day off since starting at Pwll-Coedwig Primary. She and Flora were going out for the day. It was something they had done a lot at the beginning of their relationship, getting into the car and driving for miles with complete spontaneity and a splendid contempt for time.

Now they were less relaxed and, accordingly, more watchful. They felt that their leisurely life was commented upon, and, in some cases, disapproved of.

Flora woke first, which was unusual. It was six o' clock and wet, but not raining.

Opening the window, she judged they were roughly half-way between two storms – and that the first one had been ferocious, but not conclusive. She spent some moments calculating how much time they had before the next one, and then got dressed.

Miriam woke irritable. One of the farm dogs had barked incessantly throughout the night and early morning, and she did not have Flora's ability to sleep through anything. The damp day matched her mood perfectly.

But, once dressed, she was drawn to the back room's window – and, as night's snake shed dark skin, and took on the bronzy-red scales of day, Cader Idris was caught briefly in this serpentine transformation, igniting Miriam's own inner flame.

Miriam drove fast, confidently, and enjoyed the glide of the Golf up the tarmac and past the woods dripping, as they were, in the glorious six-thirty light.

She headed for Machynlleth, thinking it would be fun to turn off suddenly, somewhere Flora had never been before. Bubbling with mischief, she signalled a left hand turning.

They were bumping down an uneven track, beneath the quick darts of early morning sky. Things were dappled, now light, now dark, in front of Flora's eyes. She feared that this turning, so close to home, would lead to an area they had visited before, and felt disappointed. The roadside flowers nodded, as if in agreement, their petals soft with sleep and rain.

Miriam parked a mile from the beach and, getting out, they crossed the dunes high up, unseen. Traversing the curve down to the estuary, they came across the men with shocking suddenness poised, as they were, directly above them. One moment the foreshore was empty; the next, four men stood stiffly by the water.

One of them was Heneghan. Flora could see the distinctive set of his shoulders, squared and somehow combative, even from here. His body language said, '*Fuck off,*' even when there was no need.

The men bent to their task, whatever it was – and the girls could not quite see, though they strained their eyes.

Something slithered, wriggled and leapt in the men's arms. Flora saw it only as glistening muscled movement, before it was riveted by flame-hued rays which, impartial, moved quickly on and furrowed the sand with colour. The rippling between the four pairs of hands represented, and indeed was, life, a fish, big too, almost magical in its intense fight to escape.

Flora could see that it took all their strength to subdue it and bring it to the waiting net. She heard their straining.

One of the men was fiery, gleaming copper-blonde in the early light. Hugely tall, he had the reddish-blond hair, braided with leather, of ancient Viking warriors, the ghost of a horned helmet on his head only a millennium or two distant: Gwilym, a man with the knowledge, and the secretive nature, to handle this situation. The sight of him stirred something in her.

They had the fish firmly in their grasp now. The mood lightened perceptibly, even from this distance.

Gwilym took a cigarette out of his jacket pocket and half turned to protect the match from the slow but effective sea breeze. Heneghan bent towards him. Flora could not hear what was said, but she guessed - rightly as it transpired - that he'd asked for a smoke.

Thus far, they had not looked up and seen the girls. It seemed that they were totally engrossed, alerted only by engine noises.

The two men were hooded in their enclave of tobacco. The wind pared inessentials like a whittling-knife. Ash flew.

"That's Gwilym," Miriam said, waking suddenly to the reality of the scene before them.

"It's cold," Flora snapped, suddenly irritable. "Let's go back to the car."

"Looks like they're packing up," Miriam commented, watching the scene below. "We could walk down by the beach. It's quicker from here and they aren't likely to see us, if we keep near the dunes."

Flora scowled.

"It doesn't matter if they do see us," she said belligerently. "We've got just as much right to be walking as they have."

Miriam knew, instinctively, that Flora was wrong – but she did not say so: better to let things be, and just hope there was no unpleasant confrontation.

The day was turning pale, drained at the edges of the light. As the girls descended the path leading to the beach, they saw that the fish and the nets were gone, and the four men were standing, quietly smoking, seemingly unaware that they had company.

Miriam stepped silently on to the slats of the dune causeway and slid forward. It did not seem to matter; the men were very relaxed – but the memory of the dead rabbit kept her in a state of wariness which Flora, in her anger, did not share.

It was with a sense of foreboding, and inner horror, that Miriam heard the other girl's feet clattering uncaringly behind her. Flora was banging her toes against the wood as she walked and it seemed that each blow echoed for miles.

The men had stiffened. They did not move but Miriam could see that they had instinctively huddled together for an instant before separating out again and turning, blank-faced, around.

Two of the men returned to their former easy stance and smiled at the girls; Gwilym winked; but, looking at Heneghan, Miriam stepped back in fear for, although the man had not moved an inch, he was tensed as if about to strike out at her, facial bones standing out with the tightness and anger in his expression. He did not say a word, offered no overt aggression, but Miriam knew no attack could have affected her more chillingly.

Now that they faced the men, Miriam felt she could not pass by without a greeting of some kind. She wanted them to say something instead of standing there in so forbidding a little knot.

She walked off the last wooden plank, wishing the men would go. Heneghan alone wheeled around suddenly and walked away very fast, fluidly – though his Rover remained, part-hidden, mute testimony to his eventual return.

Flora, joining Miriam on the sand, was unashamedly relieved to see the back of him.

For a moment they all stood there looking at one another and then the tension, which had wavered with Heneghan's departure, broke.

Gwilym wandered over. He was in no hurry. This could have happened now or in a week's time and it would all have been the same to him.

They'd passed him and smiled; heard of him and kept carefully-blank faces; knew he lived in a ramshackle cottage further down the road from Pritchard's Farm - but this was the first direct contact.

"Ullo," he said and grinned.

His smile was completely unselfconscious and, in its way, beguiling. He stamped his feet on the sand.

"Wish I was at 'ome. It's fuckin' cold out 'ere!"

Flora started to unwind her scarf to give it to Gwilym. Laughing he gestured it away. Flora blushed, smiled, swinging the loose ends to and fro. Miriam turned her head away. Flora sat down on the log barrier.

"Hello," Miriam began, with prim caution. "I'm Miriam and …"

"Christ, love, I know 'oo you are!" he said, with a laugh that took the sting out of his words. "You an' 'er both!"

"Um…" Miriam began.

"Fantastic," Flora said, and she began to laugh.

Gwilym turned and smiled at her. Miriam, more socially inhibited, wondered if he always swore so fluently.

He knocked ash into the palm of his hand, then shook it and flung it over the wet sand.

"What are you all doing down here?" asked Miriam, aware of a censorious note to her voice.

"Poachin'!" he said - and it could have been a smile beneath the long reddish-blonde moustache and the jumping Woodbine.

"Oh," Miriam was taken aback. She'd thought he'd at least cover his tracks. "Aren't you afraid we'll report you?"

"Not you, love," he said easily.

It was a smile now, a smile that began with the eyes, friendly and yet curiously impersonal.

"'t's funny..." Flora thought it out aloud. "We've lived down the road from you for ages and this is the first time we've spoken. Did you think we were unfriendly?"

This made Gwilym laugh.

"Nope," he said, and grinned at Flora. "I just thought you was stuck up!"

Miriam was uneasy. This unfamiliar man felt too close to her. He smelt strong, somehow meaty. His presence frightened her.

As if on cue, he farted.

"Sorry," he said. "You should 'ear me in bed, man."

He sat down on the log and talked mainly to Flora. She found she could not stop laughing.

"Yeah," he continued. "I frighten the dog some nights: bloody great explosions from the bed; dog dun't know where they've come from - thinks they're 'is own, you know? Leaps around like a mad thing, sniffing up 'is arse. E's a one-off, my dog."

"Catch anything?" Miriam said, desperate to change the subject.

"Oh, aye, you always do if you know where to look. My mate knows this area like the back of 'is 'and – times, tides, the lot, even oo's likely to be around at that hour – mostly the local pigs, ya know? E's a good bloke to 'ave around, is Bryn: the law turns a blind eye to 'im, more or less!"

"What exactly are you fishing for, though?"

Miriam wanted hard facts.

"Jus' salmon, love."

"Who're the others?"

Flora could hear the impatience in her friend's voice.

"My mate, Bryn, Mike 'Eneghan, two you can't see cause they're on guard – that's two brothers from the village, Owain and Rhys – an' a new bloke called Edwin Russell. Used to be a teacher, but we don't 'old that against 'im!"

"What about Mike Heneghan?" Flora asked. She found the 'Mike' both strange and unnecessary, but put it in for form's sake. Only the men around here referred to one another by their surnames – officially.

"Local shit," said Gwilym cheerfully. "Thinks 'e's God's gift to women. Show-off, too. Ace shot, my arse! Couldn't aim accurately if you killed it first and nailed it in place for 'im. E's a bag of wind, that man!"

"I saw that dead bunny," thought Miriam. "Rage is his aim..."

But she did not say it out loud: she wasn't sure enough of her ground, and sensed that Gwilym was a traditionalist for all his lawlessness.

"Better go," he said, walking away. "Gotta get to work at eight. Ta ra!"

The open space felt empty without him, though the ghost of his fart lingered in the still air.

Miriam was relieved. Flora, imagining Gwilym in bed, had quite different thoughts.

The four men were busy packing their discarded waterproofs into the Rover. Now back on the sand, Heneghan stood with arms folded, overseeing things. The others looked like his slaves from this distance.

"Bag of wind!" Flora thought of Gwilym's words as she watched Heneghan, then she giggled to herself: "Well, he's a fine one to talk, if this morning's performance is anything to go by."

Heneghan put the Rover into reverse and slashed past the girls. A lyre-snake skin pattern was carved in the sand from the violence of his exit. Flora shivered.

***

"Let's go," said Miriam.

"Where?" asked Flora.

"Aha," replied Miriam, enjoying the suspense she created. "Not telling you. It's a secret – I'll spoil it if I give anything away."

They got into the car. Flora felt a wave of happiness and excitement. She loved not knowing in this way. The lane was too narrow to turn in, so Miriam drove back to the beach and turned round there, registering, with a twinge of dismay, the spray of sandy particles clinging to the smooth sides of her car.

The tide had retreated even since they first arrived. It was, Flora thought, clever of the men to have known exactly when to come.

The roads, out of season, were quiet and empty of traffic at this time of day. They could bowl along fast without worrying, though the Eglwys Fach bend slowed them briefly to ten miles an hour while a tractor lumbered past on the opposite side.

Eventually, after miles of forest greenness and limited horizons, all touched with palest gold, the world opened out over the grey-stone wall - and became the boundless dun smoky line of sea and estuary and, faintly behind that, the white-tipped ridges of Cader Idris.

There wasn't as much as a bruise behind the drenching mists of the sky. Evidently, the second storm held its peace for the moment. The woods, verdant to their right, hung close.

They drove past the *'Croeso y Fachynlleth'* sign, round the town clock and out onto the Dolgellau Road.

Flora shut her eyes through the boredom of the next few miles. She didn't like to be reminded of council houses and dull grey buildings.

When she looked once more, they were caught between two wild places, the road merely a scratch in the mountainside. She chewed a Fruit Pastille, strawberry-flavoured, and sang *'I'm a Gnu'* at the top of her voice.

Miriam thought of the German shepherd dog she'd seen in the yard of one of the council houses, a beautiful animal, lord of its four square-feet of concrete – and all around it the hills where it should have roamed.

Flora kept her inner certainty until they gave Tywyn a miss – and then she admitted to Miriam that she had no idea where they were going. Miriam smiled affectionately at her, but still could not be prevailed upon to say anything.

They drove along the pastoral lowlands of Gwynedd and, though pretty, the scenery was too close to safety to appeal to Flora. She almost dozed at the strung-out whitewashed cottages, the orchards and sprawling farms.

Then the lane veered suddenly, sharply, to the left, a tricky bend requiring concentration – and, when they'd righted themselves, Flora saw that the teeth of the land had locked once more, and only jagged bicuspids of civilization existed from this point.

She felt a chilly prickling along her spine. This was a place of ancient mystery; it communicated clearly to her. Yet the lane rumbled along quietly enough and was, in fact, much like a thousand other lanes of its kind. The hills on either side had crunched and torn their way, over millions of years, through the soft green grass until they now stood, an almost uniform grey, forbidding access even to the sheep.

Gradually, as they drove, the land flattened out again though it lost none of its harshness. Flora felt uneasy, though she couldn't have said why. She bent her head to get the Fruit Pastilles out of the glove compartment and thus only sensed that they'd joined a wider track and were rattling, roaring up it.

"Bird Rock," Miriam said, quite clearly and dispassionately.

Flora looked up and saw it, across the fields to their right, a vast overhanging rock, shaped as a bird of prey about to pounce – wings taut by its side, beak turned to the left, rudimentary talons gripping the ledge below.

Any moment, she felt, the thing would descend, with a great grinding of stone, and pluck them from their car.

"Impressive, isn't it?" said Miriam, breaking into Flora's thoughts.

"Frightening," Flora said. "There's something evil about it."

"Yes, I know what you mean. It formed quite naturally during the Second Ice Age."

"Any legends associated with it?" Flora asked.

"I should imagine so," said Miriam, "not that I know any details. But, if there aren't, I daresay you can invent some!"

Flora blushed.

"It's true,' she thought to herself, 'my mind does run on like that."

"Is this the…"

"Shhh!" Miriam admonished. "You'll break the…"

"Spell?" queried Flora, not without a certain irony.

"Something like that," Miriam admitted. "In a moment we'll be almost directly underneath. They say it is bad luck to look up."

Flora didn't doubt it. But she did look up. From this close, she saw the vast ring of its eye, bored in the rock – a mesmeric, slightly imperfect circle out of which, for a millionth of a second, streamed a rainbow-coloured ray. It formed triangles in Flora's mind so that she felt as if she were falling.

They drove on, stopping at a village near Cregennan to buy food for lunch. The lake itself was a disappointment. They felt it should have been sinister; but the last of the year's tourists, with their wholly inappropriate bulges of fluorescent wild-terrain gear, took away its power.

"Perhaps," thought Flora, "with the winter behind it and no people, it might be worth a visit."

They came at last to their destination. Flora recognized the moment of arrival immediately from the slight shaking in Miriam's hands.

She turned off the ignition and sat for a moment breathing deeply, as if unwilling to begin the next stage.

They were in a lay-by, spruced and nestling in dark green pines; behind, the sound of water boomed its centuries-old echo. Opposite, the hills rose out of, and folded away from, the purpled tufts of the wild-land.

They got out of the car and walked back up the road to a wooden stile set back from sight. It was solid, well-constructed with the nails driven in firmly and the wood lying in pale unmarked joints.

Miriam put her foot lightly on the first plank and stepped over, pressing down the grass on the other side as her breathless weight re-asserted itself. Flora passed the bag of food to her and followed.

They walked single-file along a thin track veined with roots, high up, above water. The ground was damp, mossy; leaves were beginning to fall; pine resin cut cleanly through the early-autumn mistiness.

Gradually, through the trees, the water came into view. In places, it was the smooth green of polished Aventurine, which broke into chips of white crystal as the water met the bank-side roots; in other places, where natural deep pools formed, golden sunlight worried at the calm surface and paler green falls of sunny water tumbled into the depths.

The girls sat down on the bank above the water and pulled out their provisions - sandwiches, nectarines and a bottle of white wine, which Flora opened straightaway. They had forgotten glasses so sipped the wine directly from the bottle, giggling and wiping the rim ostentatiously each time.

Miriam nibbled like a little mouse, not sure of her hunger, determined to fit all the pieces of the day into place within her allotted time span. Flora, joyously ravenous, tore through her food, sending crumbs in all directions.

They said little. The sun, patchily warm, caught the wine bottle every second or third time it was raised. Green-gold prisms danced on a nearby tree trunk.

Flora threw her nectarine stone high in the air and then sent it, with all the strength of her flattened palm, spinning across the river to the other side where it landed, with a barely audible plop, in a nearby bunch of nettles. She began to laugh, wanting to repeat the trick, but Miriam was reluctant to part with her carefully-diminished piece of fruit.

Flora shook her lightly, holding onto her thin shoulders.

They walked on, descending slowly to the water's edge.

"Strange, meeting Heneghan like that," Miriam said.

"Umm…" Flora replied abstractedly. She did not want to talk. There was something strange in the water ahead.

"He seems to crop up in the most unexpected places," Miriam said, her voice quivering. "I feel he is a sort of malign spirit. Do you know what I mean? I don't think I've ever seen that man smile. Flora! You're not even listening."

There was unusual anger in her voice.

Flora, her mind on the dimly-perceived object ahead, jumped.

"What? Oh, I'm sorry. I was miles away. Heneghan?"

"Precisely."

Miriam's anger thinned to acid.

"Ah, we're back to him again, are we?" Flora replied. "He wouldn't even be remotely interesting if he weren't so brutal. He's probably just a boring little man, going through his boring little life. He wouldn't recognize the man we all love to hate."

"He's bad, Flora, nasty through and through."

"Oh, come on, Miriam! I think that's going a bit far. There's plenty more men like him, dotted around the country. There's something in the water over by that bush. Coming to investigate?"

Flora raced off, but inside she was shaken by Miriam's perception. For some reason, she found herself keeping her own counsel and guarding her fear. She sensed that they were all giving Heneghan power, and shuddered.

When Flora, heart in mouth, reached the water's edge, she found that the thing she'd seen was only the shadow of a bush. She felt clammy all over with relief.

It was hot, almost summer still - and removing her pullover, she sat down, fanning her face with it. The water looked inviting.

"Only a bush," she said, laughing, as Miriam joined her.

"Heneghan hates us. He thinks of us as the lesbians. You can see it in his face."

Miriam looked at Flora as she said this. Their eyes met.

"Are we? Lesbians, I mean?"

Flora was heavy with this thought.

"I don't know," said Miriam. "Does it matter?"

"Yes," said Flora. "I want us to be indefinable. I don't want to be pinned out on the dissecting board by a man like Heneghan."

"Probably don't allow lesbians in this part of Wales," Miriam said. "Probably gets you defrocked or thrown out of chapel!"

"Suits me," Flora laughed. "I haven't stepped foot inside a religious building since I was twelve, and see no reason to re-enter one now. Changing the subject completely, I reckon we should do something totally outrageous! Be ourselves. Sod the rest of humanity."

"Oh yes?" Miriam gave a long, consciously-ironic, glance around the countryside. "Like what? I mean, there's not exactly overmuch scope around here, if you get my drift. Complete absence of audience too."

"Hilarious," said Flora. "Sarcasm really is the lowest form of wit."

"Well honestly," retorted Miriam. "You get these loopy ideas miles from anywhere, with just a few sheep for company. You can't pose in a vacuum. Look at the Bloomsbury Group."

Flora laughed, and then squeaked with delight.

"I know..." Flora giggled and leaned her head back until her thick blonde plait touched the grass behind. "We could nick a sheep, bundle it into the car and drive off with it."

"Brilliant," said Miriam, "And how do you propose getting the sheep to come with us, eh? Go up to it, say, 'Nice sheep! Fancy a ride?' and have it follow you about like a dog? I can assure you, a sheep peering out of our back window is going to cause some comment from passing motorists. No..."

She poked Flora in the stomach as the other girl opened her mouth to interrupt.

"My idea is far simpler. We find a secluded pool, strip off and dive right in."

"Oh God," said Flora. "You're serious, aren't you?"

"Of course," Miriam laughed. "It'd be very bracing."

"I don't think I want to be braced, thank you."

"I dare you," said Miriam, looking at Flora wickedly out of the corner of one eye.

"No," said Flora resolutely.

"Coward," jeered Miriam.

"Yes, and proud of it," said Flora. "I meant outrageous, not suicidal."

"Well, I'm going in," said Miriam.

"Fine," replied Flora. "Just remember that I don't know you if you get arrested for indecent exposure."

Miriam ran off, jumping over the stones so quickly that her feet hardly seemed to touch the ground. Her thin, excited voice drifted back to Flora as she lay there, and she could see flashes of the bright strawberry-blonde hair every now and then.

"Flora!"

"What?"

"Come here. I've found the perfect paddling pool."

She sounded like a playful child. Flora grinned and slowly followed in the direction of Miriam's voice – and stopped, astounded.

It was perfect. Despite her cynicism about the whole idea, Flora was enchanted by the plashing pond Miriam had stumbled upon.

A natural hippocrepiform of rock surrounded three sides of the basin; trees bent low into the water;

steep slopes on either side hid the whole scene from passers-by.

The pool was deep and round, with the long branch of a tree lying so low one could use it to lower oneself gently into the cold water. There was no wind. The air was clammy. Patches of sunlight, large and regular as lily pads, sat placidly on top.

Miriam stripped. Her body looked white, almost green, in the strange watery light. She had come out of herself for this moment and was sparklingly alive. Flora watched her with an odd tenderness.

Miriam crossed to the tree and, holding it with one hand, stretched out her left leg in a single beautifully-fluid movement so that she stood, for a few seconds, poised like a ballerina. She rotated her ankle slowly and an arm followed the leg out and up. She seemed completely unworried and unhurried through this. Her buttocks tensed with each leg movement, so that they were lifted perhaps an inch high than usual and their shape redefined.

Then she plunged, with shocking suddenness, into the middle of the pool and emerged, gasping and shaking her now-dark-red hair, over by where Flora was standing. She smiled and flicked her feet under the water to stay afloat.

The water was so clear Flora could see the entire length of Miriam's body, distorted whenever she moved, in it.

Miriam swam off, away from the branch. Flora was intrigued, tempted. She put her index finger into the water and it was cold, but bearable.

She took off her clothes and waded into the shallows, shivering and trying to summon up the courage to leap suddenly under.

Miriam, warm and carefree, laughed and raised her arm in greeting.

"Come on," she called. "It's fine once you're in. Really lovely actually."

Flora sat down with a gasp. Her breasts ached with the shock of the cold. Then she began, slowly, to swim towards Miriam. Her hair was warm with sun. She loved the way the water slipped over each part of her body; it was a hugely sensual feeling. She moved and felt the way her bottom cleaved the water, streams of it sliding between her buttocks and labia, chill-thrilling her.

She felt aroused by the directness of it all; by the way her warm body transmuted the element she moved in so that it became, in a very real sense, an extension of her flesh.

Flora and Miriam reached the branch at the same time. They laughed at this coincidence and then each one stretched up a hand and grasped the wood, testing its flexibility and strength. It bent to their hands, dancing supply in the water without snapping.

At first they hung there, smiling and bouncing up and down slowly. Then they grew adventurous.

Miriam, more agile, used her hands to hoist herself up until she was hanging over the branch, her naked belly scratched by the abrasive bark. Her hands and arms shot splinters of wood over Flora, and a fine cascade of them dropped into the water.

She then positioned herself so that her back touched the tree; her legs hovered straight up for a moment, hands gripping with all their strength, and then she disappeared into the water, head-first. Her eyes, when she surfaced, were huge with delight. She laughed and pulled herself up onto the branch once more.

The air was cool by this time, and getting colder all the time. Flora left the water to Miriam and dressed quickly, her skin gritty with pool debris. Even her scalp felt rough.

It was good to watch Miriam, though the other girl's dexterity frightened her. She shivered at the imagined cold, but Miriam seemed not to notice it. Not a single tremor broke the pattern of her limbs. She seemed to bend time, and command weather, to accommodate her own needs.

A dog barked somewhere close. Flora jumped and peered round. She could see a golden tail wagging briefly in the bushes nearby.

Miriam, higher up than Flora, saw the two hikers approaching along the path first. They were a middle-aged couple in stout walking boots and bulky Guernsey sweaters.

Flora thought Miriam looked unearthly, like a mermaid, sitting with her hair streaming out all around her, her eyes the green of large lily leaves.

She felt the intrusion keenly. The walkers were calling to their dog, taking turns in the perfect harmony of some long partnerships. The dog sulked, wanting to prolong its moment of freedom. Flora wanted to throw something at it. The couple drew level with her. She tensed.

"Afternoon," called the man.

"Lovely day, isn't it?" added the woman smiling.

It came out smooth as sea-glass, part of an intimate routine, Flora felt, perfected over the years.

"Yes, glorious," she said with relief.

Either they hadn't seen the naked girl on the tree or they were too well-mannered to comment. She suspected the latter.

The couple walked on and the dog, after a few furtive snuffles in the undergrowth, followed them. It was a fat golden Labrador, oddly at variance with the trimly-athletic couple.

When Flora turned round, Miriam had vanished. Once the latter returned, she was dressed and disappointing. Her lips were purple with cold, but she looked triumphant. Flora took Miriam's thin right hand for a moment and studied it. The finger tips looked bruised from the cold water, and the hand itself was cool to the touch.

"God, Miriam, I think you've overdone it this time. You feel like a slice of death."

"I feel fine," Miriam said firmly, then turned and smiled warmly at Flora. "Don't you think that was fun? I thought it was incredibly exciting and dangerous, if you know what I mean? I almost wanted people to see me. Funny that, the perversity, I mean."

"Exhibitionist," said Flora fondly.

"Yup," said Miriam, swishing nettles with a stick she'd picked up. Leaf fragments flew through the air, releasing their scent as they went.

Flora relented.

"It was a beautiful feeling swimming without clothes – very free and strange."

"I'm glad you liked it," said Miriam. "There's nothing worse than a fantasy which goes flat on the other person. Do you know what went through my mind?"

"No," said Flora, though she could guess.

Miriam gave a secretive smile.

"I thought..."

"Did you..."

Flora breathed along with the unspoken thought, keeping it hidden.

"Well, yes..."

"Hmm..." said Flora. "Home?"

"Yes," said Miriam. "It'll take a while."

A dried cataract, molded like toffee, lay underneath an old stone bridge. Miriam imagined biting a chunk off it.

"Do you know?" she said. "I used to dream of finding a place like this. Strange, isn't it, the way things turn out: meeting you and being here and us getting to know so many interesting characters."

"Yes," said Flora. "I wouldn't be anywhere else. There's something about this area. It's addictive and I don't really understand why since there's nothing much to do here, no social life to speak of. Perhaps that's the secret: you have to create your own lifestyle as you go along and that makes it more intense."

"Exactly," said Miriam.

They walked on.

"Miriam?"

"Um?"

"I don't remember this flat grassy bit."

Neither, looking at it, did Miriam, but she wasn't going to say so. Getting lost, she felt, was a serious business, certainly not to be undertaken just for the hell of it.

They had climbed high above the river and were now on top of the slope. The trees formed a clipped tonsure around the bald scalp of hilltop. Peering down, Miriam could see three possible paths – and no red car.

"We're lost," she announced.

"Ah!" said Flora. "And for my next trick, I will…"

"Don't be facetious," snapped Miriam. "I tell you we're lost and it's serious. Anything could happen out in this God-forsaken hole…"

"You loved it a moment ago," said Flora.

"I still do in principle," said Miriam. "You're not helping, by the way."

"Zombies and vampires come irresistibly to mind," Flora said, pushing the needle in a bit deeper. "I'm sure I've seen that sheep somewhere before."

"It's probably been following us," said Miriam in her coldest voice. "Local SAS exercise, no doubt."

 The sheep chewed grass with its fellows.

"It doesn't look like a sheep," Flora continued. "Do you think it speaks Russian?"

"Do you?"

"No," said Flora.

"Shut up, then, and get a move on, or we'll be caught in the dark."

"All right, all right! I think you're being a bit uncool about this whole business – car can't be that far away."

"Find it, then," said Miriam and sat down.

A huge bird darkened the sky briefly and was gone.

"Buzzard," said Flora.

"I don't care if it's the Ancient Mariner's albatross," Miriam retorted snidely.

Rough stone walls leaned over the hill edge; barbed wire kept the trees back; the crossing was harsh. They looked at their fragile skirts. There seemed little compulsion to move.

"Ladies first," said Flora.

Neither of them moved – until the second dog of their day barked, that is, and then they both upped and ran, discovering whole new areas of athletic prowess in the process.

Miriam, slightly in the lead, soared nimbly over the barbed wire fence; while Flora, with the sheep dog's fangs closing on her hem, suddenly discovered how pleasant it was to roam about the woods half-naked.

The dog trotted back to its baffled owner proudly carrying a brightly-coloured strip of cheesecloth. Maldwyn Prydderch Jones scratched his bristly head in confusion, took the material from the animal and rounded up his small flock of sheep, mind firmly on other matters.

The girls, crouched in the neck of the woods, behind a log, watched in terror and did not dare move until Maldwyn Prydderch had made his agonizingly slow way over the brow of the hill, trailing his dirty sheep behind him.

"Oh my God," said Flora at length, inspecting the damage.

"Move," screeched Miriam, crunching her way through the layers of fir cones.

The wood sloped. They ran. There was wild garlic, lots of it, somewhere close, but they did not dare investigate lest Maldwyn P. caught up with them. Trees cast their spikes in flight, and the girls crackled over them until they reached the bottom, and the delicate light took over.

They struck off to the left, away from the pond, retracing their steps. The sky moved with them, changing its colours around slowly, so that a smooth transition took place, fire shades melting into rose and lilac.

The quality of sound had changed, becoming softer as the evening wore on, as if everything were packed with cotton wool. The water swirled; deep-throated birds replaced the earlier shrill chatterers. Their world was a bud, closing in for the night. The girls seemed to walk faster in the darkening sky, and reached the car with no problem.

They went back the way they'd come. Strangely, it was not a boring journey since the points of emphasis had changed, and places sun-lined that morning were now obscured by shade.

The illusion of extreme speed in darkness persisted, and Flora was frightened by the rushing corners. A few times, she felt sure they'd never stop, or slow down, and then she wanted most of all to scream to dispel her sense of helplessness.

Objects passed by on the side of the road jolted Flora into an awareness of the familiarity of this area: the red Renault always parked just at the bottom of the big house's driveway; the old lorries, one a startling bright purple, which lay on their sides in the yard by the estuary; the small miner's cottage, set back from the road; and between all this, the miles and miles of silent coast road with the dunes and trees just waiting, it seemed, for an opportunity to climb over.

Smoke, from the chimneys, perched above Pwll-Coedwig. The lights in the Farmers Arms pub were bright; the Saturday night crowd had spilled out onto the garden benches, and Flora could see one or two familiar faces.

Once home, Flora let the cat out. The animal disappeared into the undergrowth, curiously modest about her bodily functions. Flora felt at peace in the garden. There were no intrusive streetlights or screaming cars; you could think without interruption.

Bed time. They slept, deeply, in a pitch-black silence dented only by intermittent smoky sheep coughs. The rain busied itself; railway tracks bubbled under the late night train.

FRIDAY 19th - SATURDAY 20th

The effects of imminent full moon were felt in all corners of Pwll-Coedwig. Dogs howled. Sheep skittered crazily. Villagers tossed and turned in beds suddenly turned hostile. Bloodied dreamscapes terrorized the vulnerable.

Rachel, in her Impulse-soaked room, felt clammy with the scent of salmon: the pink flesh seemed to lie luminously in her body, spreading and glowing. She took it despite nausea, knowing she could not evade punishment of some kind.

Down the road, an old man died, so quietly that the ripples preparing to spread out seemed grossly inappropriate. By his cooling side, his wife slept.

***

Eleri Morgan woke early and hurried out of bed lest another half hour of sleep stole over her. If she did not deal with the furnace now, the whole morning would be cold. Richard had done it yesterday and the day before; it was her turn now.

She put the kettle on and stood for a second, flexing her fingers under a stream of hot water, before turning to the enormous brass structure which dominated the room. It resembled a huge Easter Island Moai statue, alien and powerful.

Eleri opened the small door and carefully placed the daily libation of coal and paper inside. Five matches, puny against the great gulps of wind coming down the sinuous neck, joined the coal. The sixth one crawled across the paper and stopped.

Steam from the kettle filled the room. She tried two matches together and, miraculously, the thing took off. Tiny red flames waved underneath the coal, pocking its sides with colour. She was pleased; the warmth was satisfying. Smoke was already being swallowed, passed to the attic above. She shut the door and adjusted the dials on the side.

It was wet. Through the net curtains, she could see the rocks opposite, dark and shiny with rain. She made the tea and took a cup next door to Richard.

He was dead - cold and stiffening. She had an eerie sense of it straightaway, as if something had gone out of the room.

"Richard will know what to do," she thought and then, realising what she'd said, began to shake so violently that jets of tea shot over the bed and burned her legs.

She did not touch him. His white face seemed eyeless, like a mask used in Greek Tragedy, the gaping mouth testament to centuries of sorrow.

The room was freezing, though patches on Eleri's legs itched and blistered from the tea. There was a roaring in the house, in Eleri, as if a giant dragon were taking her ever-further from reality.

Through the inner cyclone, and paradoxical silence, she picked up the phone and dialled the Wyn Jones' number. Dr Wyn Jones answered, professional immediately.

"This is Eleri Morgan. My husband has died. He's dead in the bed."

In the dreamlike state of trying to explain exactly what she meant, she heard Wyn Jones say he'd be right over, heard him ask hesitantly if she'd like his wife to come round as well, and caught the echo of her own surprisingly firm, "No."

This done, she turned her back on Richard and waited, aware only of the fluid trembling of her hips and legs.

***

Tom ran through the fields, dark hair sleeked flat against his skull, happy to be out in the rain. Today had been good so far. Iestyn trusted him, had actually said so and, as a token of this trust, had asked him for the first time ever to round up the sheep and bring them towards the front gate.

The sheep were widely scattered, seemed oblivious of the boy and his dog. He tried to remember all the things Iestyn had told him when they'd done this job together: "Keep calm, don't panic them and don't chase them – leave that to the dog."

He stopped running and looked around wondering, now he was in charge, where to begin.

As he glanced towards the fence boundaries, he saw Dr Wyn Jones's Renault 4 shooting by at a great rate. Tom was surprised because it was unusual to see anyone this early on a Saturday morning; he wondered vaguely what was going on.

The dog, sleek with rain, stood pointing her right fore-paw. He gave the command and watched as the animal leapt forward, belly to the ground. She was well-trained, this one, obedient to every command. She swept behind each block of sheep, keeping well away - then dropped gracefully to the ground, her ears alert for the next move.

The quivering in her body, obvious even at this distance, showed her impatience; but she didn't move a single muscle until activated by the next blast of the whistle.

Then she slunk forward, the feathery tufts of her belly brushing the grass. The sheep moved, unhurriedly, pausing frequently for food. Still the intent dog inched forwards, shooting out and chivvying back any errant ewes.

Tom was impressed by the dog's skill, her controlled movements and her athletic ability as she glided over the gate. She was fierce, wary of affection, yet her pleasure in this work was apparent to the boy.

The sheep waited, with their habitual docility, by the gate while he untied the string. The dog, never relaxing for a second, patrolled the outer perimeter of the ovine semi-circle, worrying the trotters of would-be-deserters.

This bit was the most difficult, Tom knew, and he felt clammy with nervous tension when he saw Iestyn watching from a distance. Some sheep would attempt to sneak back into the field; they always did - and the whole operation demanded split-second timing, combined with complete concentration.

"Now," he thought to himself, as the gate swung open.

The sheep surged out, knocking into one another in their desire for freedom. He felt the beginnings of panic as five of them set off at a brisk pace back up the field.

The dog circled with such speed that he saw only a flash of black. Iestyn said nothing. Tom moved, driving the main flock away from the gate, round the corner and into the yard. Behind him, Iestyn secured the enclosure. They grinned at one another, and the man winked.

"Good, Tom," he said. "We'll have a break."

They climbed into the front of the Land-rover, Iestyn throwing some of the sacks into the back to make room. Lad, the old dog, who had been asleep, gave a short bark of displeasure as one landed on top of him. They could hear him moving slowly about, trying to get comfortable again.

"He's deaf and nearly blind, that one, but I've never met a dog like him with the cattle," said Iestyn, and there was admiration in his voice.

Tom, who'd often thought the dog ought to be put down, felt ashamed.

"He can't hear the whistle, though, can he, so how can he obey commands?"

"He knows – knows what he's doing, does Lad, never misses a trick; he's often in there before I've even thought."

Iestyn unscrewed the Thermos and steam misted the windows, obscuring the view. The rain was heavy outside. Tom bounced impatiently; he didn't like to sit still for long.

"Two sugars, is it?"

Iestyn was in a teasing mood. His usually taciturn face was twisted humorously at the edges. Tom felt a rush of liking for him.

"Aye!" he said.

Iestyn laughed openly.

"You're learning."

"Mum'd skin me if she heard: It's always *'yes'* and *'no'* for her."

"Aye, well, that's your mam," said Iestyn, handing the cup to Tom. "She's got her reasons, I daresay; doesn't do to upset, does it?"

The tea was sweet and piping hot. Tom took a Mars bar out of his pocket and broke off half for Iestyn.

"Saw Wyn Jones this morning," he said at length.

"Oh, aye?"

"He was in that bloody stupid car of his, driving along fast."

"Language, boy, language!"

"I wondered, that's all," Tom admitted.

"Well, whatever it is, you'll soon know, small village like this," Iestyn said.

The boy put his cup down.

"Time to get going," said Iestyn. "Got to check all those sheep are marked with our number."

Tom didn't mind: he preferred being outside in the rain to the warm Land-rover; there was more space and a greater sense of freedom.

***

Heneghan drove into the forecourt of Pwll-Coedwig's garage. No one seemed to be about. He parked over the bell cable so that an unbroken burst of shrillness filled the air.

He did not like waiting; spots of anger burned in his mind as the noise continued. Where the fuck were they all?

Idris Parry shuffled out, apologetic in his red service jacket. Heneghan neither liked nor disliked Idris, though the older man's ingratiating manner annoyed him. He liked crispness and clarity, not this soggy wittering, fumbling a hundred words into one business transaction.

"Morning, Mr Heneghan, sorry, sorry, we're a bit tied up inside. Terrible weather, isn't it? I heard on the forecast that we're in for high winds — they'll have the sand bags in town today, isn't it? What can I be doing for you, then?"

"Fill her up," Heneghan said, turning away from the eager verbal flood.

He tapped his foot, loudly, obviously. Idris, easily flustered, knocked the pump, spilling petrol on the asphalt.

Gethin, the old man's nephew, came out, his usual cheer missing.

"Another great talker," thought Heneghan in disgust, as Gethin craned in through the open window. "Impossible to get anything done round here."

"Dreadful about Mr Morgan, isn't it?" said Gethin.

"Never thought he'd go so sudden, like," added Idris. "Him such a strong man and all; don't know what his wife's going to do."

Heneghan was shocked into fury.

"What," he snapped, "are you talking about?"

"Oh, don't you know then?"

Gethin was obviously surprised that the word, in a place this size, hadn't reached Heneghan.

"He died sometime last night. Mrs Rees across the road heard Dr Wyn Jones arriving early this morning, wondered what was happening, said the doctor called on her and asked her to sit in with Mrs Morgan.

"Funny woman that, you know: Elin Rees says she never made a sound of grief, no tears, no nothing – just ever so polite, like she was at a tea party, not her own husband dying: 'Tea, Mrs. Rees?' 'Sorry the house is so disorganized, Mrs. Rees,' and all in that posh voice of hers!"

"Now then, Gethin..." The old man was plainly troubled by this criticism of a bereaved neighbour, however unpopular. "She's probably in a state of shock."

Heneghan cursed the simplicity of these people.

Idris handed him back the ignition keys.

Heneghan thought of Richard Morgan, the powerful aura the man had had. A man he'd liked, an easy man to be with. Then into his mind came a clear picture of Eleri with her wiry dark hair and painter's smock. All those pictures painted, Richard standing by silent and comforting.

"How much?"

"Ten pound, *diolch yn fawr*."

Heneghan both wanted, and didn't want, to stay and tease out the strands of gossip. Old Idris, nervous in his presence, sensed this.

"Are you wanting me to check your tyres, oil pressure?" he asked, wiping his hands on a filthy rag.

"No, I've things to do."

"Right you are. Give my regards to Mrs Heneghan, now, won't you? We don't see much of her these days."

Heneghan reversed the car and was gone.

"Funny man," Idris said to Gethin.

"You're too soft, Uncle Idris," Ross replied with an unusual streak of malice. "He's a nasty one. Doesn't care for anyone but himself."

***

Having driven out, Heneghan decided not to go home straightaway. The thought of the gossips leaning out of their windows and clucking at Eleri's house froze him inside.

With no definite sense of where he was going, he turned into a narrow track and drove up, and up still further, towards the hills.

The rain had eased off and the hills appeared to tumble, through wan sunlight, into the valley below. The skyline was clear, almost white. A darkness of pine trees moved ahead, in the dimmest corner of Heneghan's vision: seeing them, he knew where he was and where he was going.

The road down to the lake undulated like the back of a paradise-tree snake. There were more pot-holes than road, and he soon gave up trying to avoid them.

The trees dropped their needles with a gentle consistency, so that nothing was ever seen falling but the air was always sweet with the smell. Layers of coarse bank jutted out over the water's edge. An old stone hut, deserted now, lay to the right and, beyond, he could see the quiet space of the lake.

He got out of the car. Rain, surprised by the door's violent slam, fell flatly on his head. He was hemmed in by trees. Pieces of timber lay all around him. He objected paying for coal; a few of these big logs would see them through the first grips of winter.

"Later," he thought, "by night: bring Tom and a torch; it'll be a lark!"

He could very easily have slipped a few logs into the car then, but scorned such simplicity. He loved high risk; in fact, the bigger the risk, the more worthwhile the venture.

The thing about this lake, he had noticed before, was that you never quite knew how it was going to be. In winter, it was usually iced right over, held aloft by tiny glistening webs which creaked upon touching one another; now, after the hot dry summer, the water level was low and the revealed patches of marsh were cracked despite today's rain. The going should be fairly easy, with luck.

He started at the highest point, from habit, and strode off down the narrow track at a cracking pace. Trees, mirrored by water, drowned on the far side. Purple cropped grass bounced underfoot; leaves curled out of the trees; but he noticed none of this preoccupied, as he was, by a series of inner pictures which rapidly diminished in size as he walked.

Soon his way was unfettered by thought. His purposeful gait, hands clenched aggressively by his sides, allowed only flickers of sensation.

He walked rather more slowly, making it last, reluctant to drive back to the village.

At the half way point, he paused. Something was different, not as it should be. The physical certainty struck just ahead of sense, and then he had it: the rotting wooden plank, which served as a rough bridge across the stream, was gone.

The water was sluggish, mud-coloured. No bridge was needed but Heneghan, who liked order and consistency, began scouring around for an alternative way over the minute ravine.

The trees, pushed unnaturally high by slate, rose up and then fell away somewhere out of sight.

The stream continued, echoed below him as he peered backwards into the dark and dripping forest. He would have to go down until he reached the tapered end of the water's course, then he could leap across in one easy bound.

The place he walked into was damp and strange-smelling. Somewhere close was a large cave of water; he could hear the gurgles as they rose to his right.

The smell of decay was strong in here; damp moss clumps, brilliantly green, squelched under his feet;

a thin smear of light moved cloudily, like a mirage, somewhere in front.

Only watery echoes broke the silence. Twigs, which lay in profusion on the ground, were water-logged.

He rushed down, putting a hand up to grab the sinewy trunks of passing trees as they flew up to meet him. He felt out of control, as if one false move could send him tumbling down the track into oblivion.

Ahead, the shimmering was brighter, more intense. A large body of water was casting bright green shadows erratically; they bounced off rocks and tangled with the trees. He felt dizzy and moved his head aside to the width of piney darkness on the left.

He could see a path, wide, scattered with pale grey flint stones, logs of all sizes piled haphazardly around. He jumped, powerfully, his boots sending out showers of stone from the bank as he landed.

The path sloped down towards a gate and, beyond, he could see the sweep of a virtually-uninhabited valley.

The bitten green of sheep slopes was broken by three deep, glistening pools, irregular in shape. One backed onto the chimney-topped remains of a grey-stone house. Another house, small and white-washed, lay quietly beneath the woods, hidden from sight by the fields.

Between the house and the pools was a gash, a grotesque laceration in the earth, as if the two sides of the stone quarry had fought, and clawed violently away from one another. He could see a deep pit, yards long and a good six feet across at the bottom. Bits of rusted metal and old machines sprawled across the rocks, jutting out into the sun at strange angles.

He walked to the gate. There were no notices, seemed no reason not to wander around, have a look and get the feel of the place. The gate was the heavy *'lift up and push to'* variety, comparatively rare in this land of bale string and snapping thumb-trap springs. The pool to his left as he walked was wispy with weed at the edges.

It came to him, as he walked on, that this would be the perfect place to live: no people, few cars and miles of Forestry Commission with all its enticing secrets.

He picked up a stone and sent it spinning above the dusty path towards the split in the ground. It twisted in mid-air, with a grace that left him unmoved, and fell into the depths.

113

He waited. A fox barked in the wood and was answered by a working sheepdog, dotted from this distance in one of the distorted fields. The stone landed with a metallic clank several seconds later. He felt the impact in his body.

"Rachel would hate it here," he thought, and smiled.

He imagined the girl picking her way down the path in her ridiculous high-heeled shoes – and was unaware of clenching his fists.

***

Rachel slammed the front door behind her. Now the weather was getting colder, the old wood tended to stick unless you used real strength. Her job in the library in town was over for this weekend: no more dusty books, no more vile-tasting sticky labels.

She hated it, loathed the rude Welsh speakers who refused to ask for books in English. She needed the money, though, and it got her out of the house, with its cloyingly-earthy smells and the uncertainties that crept from wall to wall even when Dad was not home.

"Mum!"

She untied the scarf that held her long dark hair in place. She liked to be neat, and well-dressed, at all times, though she often wondered what for: there was no social life worth speaking of around here and the only boys were either unspeakable louts like Tom, or too young to be worth the effort. She shuddered and kicked the dried slow-worms of mud, flung carelessly from Tom's boots, under the doormat.

"He's got no right to bring the farmyard and all its muck into this house," she thought savagely. "How can I bring friends home to this revolting place?"

There was no sign of her mother; no sign of any of them come to that. She was aware of guilty relief. The house was hers for a while, a rare enough pleasure that she intended to make the most of.

She went up to her bedroom and was relieved to find that last night's liberal spraying of scent had finally done its job. The clothes she was wearing went straight into the linen basket. She felt soiled by them. They reminded her of the job.

She ran a bath, pouring in copious amounts of expensive bath oil. The water was boiling hot and she let it reach the three-quarter mark before reluctantly adding cold, then turning the taps off and stepping in.

Foam, displaced by her body, rose up behind her and dripped onto her hair. She loved the intense heat, the soft water surrounding her limbs. She shampooed her hair and then disappeared beneath the water, rubbing her scalp to clear all the dirt out. Then she floated, feeling completely at peace, until the water began to chill and her finger pads shrivelled up.

The front door echoed shut below. Submerged as she was, Rachel heard it only as a vague watery sound. There was no further clue as to who had arrived. She did not much care: she felt safe, protected in this womb of liquid warmth.

She got out and wrapped a huge white towel around her, then sat, on the edge of the bath, shivering. The hairs on her arm stood to attention, tiny soldiers awaiting attack from an unknown source.

"Ange!"

The voice came suddenly, and sharply, from downstairs. Rachel jumped in shock and her backside banged painfully against the porcelain.

Oh, God, it was Dad, the very last person she wanted to see.

"Where the bloody hell are you all?"

His voice had gone harsh, the way it always did when immediate service was not forthcoming.

"I'm up here, Dad!" Rachel called, aware of the tremor in her voice.

"Having a bath as usual, I suppose?"

The sarcasm came up clearly to Rachel; she could imagine the sneer on his face.

"You'd better not have used all the hot water, or there'll be trouble."

Rachel could hear her father stamping about downstairs. He was in one of his moods. She could tell from the way he was throwing things around down there. She hoped he did not want a bath right now. There'd be a scene if he did, since the tank took at least an hour to reheat.

All the pleasure and relaxation had gone for Rachel: she rushed the towel over her body, angered by the pools of water which clung to her back and under her breasts.

A spray of powder, badly-aimed, whitened the floor; she rubbed it frantically with the bath mat and succeeded only in making things worse. The floor was now smeared and messy. He'd have a fit.

Rachel dressed with care, knowing she'd have to face him eventually.

"A nice evening, father and daughter communicating," she thought bitterly; but she remembered with sadness a far-away time when she had climbed onto his lap and nuzzled into the thick material of his sweaters. His reception of this had been obscured by time, but Rachel could clearly recall the feeling of warmth and safety.

"All I get now is anger and sarcasm," she thought.

She considered staying in her room, but knew he'd create an even worse scene if she did. It wasn't worth the hassle, to Rachel's way of thinking.

The stairs creaked; she wished there were a hundred more of them. The living room door was half open and Rachel could see her father's legs stretched out from the deep chair in which he sat. His jeans were heavy with mud.

She held the door frame and peered round. He gave no sign of noticing her, did not even look up. She walked in and went to the mantelpiece, fiddling so that she didn't have to meet his eyes.

She was aware of a shaming embarrassment and unease: she had no idea what to say to him, and he was clearly disinclined to help.

Still he sat and Rachel did not dare look at him. She sat down, on the chair furthest away from his, and lowered her eyes to the carpet.

"Well?" he barked.

She panicked. Well what? What did he want? How could she answer something so vague? The warning note in his voice forced a flutter of words out of her.

"I was busy all day, Dad. Melanie and I didn't have a moment free - we were on the go all the time. One woman complained that we'd sent her the wrong book, but I had it written down on a card; she threatened to report me to Mr. Peters. I got two..."

"Not that!"

Heneghan's barely-restrained growl stilled Rachel mid-word.

Silence held her crouched in terror for a while.

"The bath, girl: Christ, you're so thick."

"I..."

"Look, I've been out all day while you've been queening it in that library of yours, right?"

"I'm, I'm sorry, Dad, I ..."

"And I want a bath. But can I have one? No. Because my daughter is too vain and selfish to think of anyone but herself."

Rachel could feel tears starting. She bit her lip hard.

"I didn't think..." she mumbled, completely at a loss.

"You never bloody do," he snarled.

He got up so suddenly that Rachel was taken by surprise. She cowered at the back of the chair. Heneghan's body was like elastic, sprung over her.

She could see his right hand. There was dirt under the rough nails. He reached out and punched her left shoulder into his powerful grasp, dragging her up from the chair into a lop-sided standing position.

His left fist curled under her clean hair and he smashed her head down hard on the padded arm of the chair before releasing her arm and, teeth locked tight, striding from the room.

Rachel shook with terror and pain. There was nowhere she could go. If she attempted to get to her bedroom, he'd get her again, she was sure of it. Staying here was out of the question.

"Mum, Mum, where are you?" Rachel cried out in her mind; but, even as the little-girl longing for comfort re-surfaced, she knew she could never tell her mum. They had a policy of non-communication where Dad was concerned.

She had seen from his eyes that it had felt good to lash out at her; no apology would be forthcoming. She began to cry quietly.

Heneghan was surprised to find he was aroused when he reached the bathroom.

WEDNESDAY 24th

Gwilym shut the back door on his mother's smiling face and walked up the lane towards home. Nipper followed him, whining and trembling in delight. He supposed he ought to give his condolences to Mrs Morgan, now Mam had told him.

Gwilym didn't know her very well; but they were neighbours, fair play, and it seemed rude to ignore her. Husband died sudden, Mam had said, over the weekend.

He opened his own front door and decided to go down to the Morgan place later. Putting the radio on loud enough to be heard from the garden, he went out to the log horse. It was an ancient wooden thing, with saw cuts all over it. He liked the feel of the wood under his left arm as he sawed away at the huge planks.

Logs for the fire dropped off the end and fell at his feet. Nipper chased the sawdust. Gwilym cut enough, and then a bit more. He thought of the girls down the road, wondered if they had need of wood, decided to find out. He hefted several of the larger logs into a sack and set off.

The blonde one, Flora, opened the door.

"Oh. Hello, Gwilym. Come in, won't you?"

"No, love, can't stop. I wondered if you and your friend could use some logs - plenty more where this lot came from."

He smiled at Flora, and was amused to see her blush.

"Oh ho," he thought.

"That's nice. Thank you," she said. "Hang on; I'll get Miriam."

Gwilym, waiting, hummed to himself.

It was the other girl this time, the red-head.

"Can a whole log go into the fire?" she asked when she saw the size of them.

He laughed.

"No, you 'ave to get the blaze going fierce first, like - and then, if you add one of these, it'll burn for hours, all night if you want."

"Did you enjoy the salmon?" asked Miriam, reminded of other things by his presence.

"Tell you what, love, why don't you and 'er come round later and you can find out. A few tatties, some 'erbs and a bottle of 'ome-made wine - yeah?"

"Yes, please. That would be lovely."

123

Miriam looked him in the eye for the first time, and liked what she saw.

"Right you are, then," Gwilym said and smiled.

He waved and was gone.

***

While a host of black-clad visitors walked uneasily through Eleri's open front door, Gwilym, banking his sense of guilt for the moment, scrubbed potatoes in a precise square of sun.

"Bung 'em in a pan," he thought, and did so. "Salt!"

With his thick fingers, he splayed salt all over the pan, cooker and floor; some ended up as a thin dust over the potatoes. He followed his instincts in cooking as in everything else. Behind him, the rows of powerful, assorted wines bubbled away. He liked the thought of introducing the two girls to such potent brews, things he'd made himself and could take a simple pride in.

The mushroom season had begun once more. Gwilym knew exactly where to go to find the most tender, tasty specimens. Many mornings, he rose early and wandered through the grass and unbroken silken cobwebs, picking mushrooms as he went, with a surprising gentleness for one so tall and fierce-looking. His life pleased him: the swell of soft, careless days spent building, foraging, occasionally standing beside the local vet watching his trade, inhaling the smells of animals and antiseptic. Any communication between the earth and his body gave him immense satisfaction: acts where fingers touched soil or dung, where feet were rooted to the peat or stone; in these, Gwilym was lord of his element: he did not doubt.

All the trappings of civilization - bed, clothes, furniture - were managed with a rough simplicity which left him just outside the realms of the truly untidy. He lived by his wits, and the guts of the land surrounding him.

None of this broke into thought as he cast a rough broom over the surface of the floor. He was not a thinking man, though he had a deep and enduring perception. The linoleum crunched with dirt. Simple: clear it out of the way. Yet he would spend hours lovingly polishing a strip of leather for a horse harness, not stopping until the thing gleamed in the light of the fire.

The spontaneity of his gesture to the girls was entirely in keeping: he saw no barriers to friendship. In a sense his friendliness bordered on disinterest. He did not cultivate Miriam and Flora for personal gain; he'd simply extended his hand, in the form of baked salmon, because he wanted to. If he'd known the delight he'd caused, he'd have been amused - and surprised.

***

When all was prepared, a sense of neighbourly concern drew him towards the Morgan house. He did not wonder; he simply went. The curtains were drawn, but the place was surrounded by cars of all sorts and sizes.

He knocked and waited. A young woman opened the door; she had neat blonde hair and eyes red from weeping.

"Yes?"

Her voice, carefully blank, seethed with a thousand questions.

"I've come to see Mrs Morgan. Tell 'er it's Gwilym from Knoll Cottage; she'll know."

Outrage chased curiosity across the woman's face.

"You know she's ..?"

Her voice died away. Gwilym grinned.

"Yeah."

She tottered off. Eleri appeared. To Gwilym, she looked much as usual.

"Mind if I come in?" he asked.

Eleri said nothing, simply opened the door wider and retreated down the hall, with Gwilym behind her.

Birdlike women perched on the edges of all available chairs, sipping tea out of refined bone-china cups; they murmured discreetly, evidently feeling that their ladylike presence was ample solace for the widow.

As one, they turned and glared, through insincere smiles, at Gwilym. Maybe it was his casual attire that grated; or the long braids, and leather band encircling his brow; perhaps the rough reddish beard, 'tache and vivid blue eyes were felt to be an affront – his vast presence a reminder of Viking invasion, and making a mockery of their conventional response. He took them as they were and remained standing. Eleri hovered.

"Sorry about your 'usband, Mrs Morgan," he said, looking at her. "He was a good bloke. I liked 'im."

The indrawn breath of the assorted ladies caused a clattering castanet of dentures against fragile cups.

Gwilym's words touched Eleri: she felt the warmth and honesty and was nearly overwhelmed. The day of honeyed lamenters had left her unmoved; they might as well have been cardboard cut-outs - but this man put her in mind of Richard and the mainly silent outdoor life they had led. She nodded, unable to trust herself to words.

"That's it, Mrs M."

He prepared to leave.

"Won't stay - reckon you've got enough on your 'ands!"

He turned and smiled at the roomful of ladies; one or two of them grimaced back.

At the door, Eleri touched his arm briefly in thanks.

"Bye, love," he said gently as she shut the door.

A stutter of whispers reached Eleri as she walked:

"Well, really! I know Gwilym's one of our own, but must he be so coarse and scruffy? Bit of black would've shown respect."

"I know. The nerve of it, coming here dressed like a hippie. Needs a haircut!"

"Don't know what his mother's thinking of, letting him go out looking like that."

"Oh, Eleri *bach*, tidy cup of tea, this."

Eleri forced herself to smile and, in playing the part, to forget the much-needed breath of fresh air blown in by Gwilym's visit.

The wings of evening quivered and touched end to end. The worthy village wives took their leave with relief, pecking at the air near Eleri's still face with pursed lips, moving in twos and threes.

Eleri sat by Richard's open coffin, in a room cold as dying love, and gazed down at the radiantly-white waxwork body of her husband.

***

Gwilym built up the fire and turned the heat on under the saucepan full of potatoes. Through the kitchen window, he could see the girls walking along the road from Pritchard's Farm.

The basics suited him very well: no frills, no pretension. The potatoes began to hiss and jump in their steam. There was a knock on the door.

"Come in an' sit down," he called. "There's a couple of 'alf-way decent chairs."

The girls seemed shy, and huddled in front of the fire, using the chattering of their teeth, and the hoarse roar of flames, as the perfect excuse not to talk.

Delicious smells roamed around the room. Gwilym squatted between the two girls. His jacket had risen up, revealing a small area of weathered flesh. Flora, thawing into curiosity, began to look around. Her eyes lit on the line of huge bottles

"Gwilym?"

"Yes, love?"

"What's in those bottles of yours?"

"Wine. Made it back in the spring: blackberry, elderberry and a secret recipe I'm not tellin'!"

"Oh, go on, please."

"Take a good look at it, love - that's right, the one on the far left. See? Now then, what's that remind you of? Sort of clear liquid; bend your nose - not too much, mind; it's pretty powerful stuff, that!"

Flora sniffed obediently. It was familiar, but she couldn't think what on earth it was.

"Hey, Gwilym, can I have a taste? I'm sure that would clarify matters!"

She turned huge, unintentionally appealing, brown eyes on him. His smile softened and he patted her affectionately on the bottom. Miriam stiffened.

"Grab three glasses, will ya? Over there, see?"

He pulled the cork and the smell, overpowering at close range, wafted into the farthest reaches of the room. He poured for himself first, to check, and gulped appreciatively.

"Ah! That's the stuff: best ... no, mustn't say. 'Ere."

A glass for Flora and one for Miriam.

Miriam was uncertain.

"Carrot," said Flora triumphantly. "That wasn't hard! Right, next one!"

"Carrot?" mocked Gwilym in feigned horror. "Christ, why do I bother?"

"Well, OK, turnip then."

Miriam sipped. It was raw but not unpleasant. She was aware of Gwilym looking at her intently.

"What d'ya think then, Miriam? D'you agree with your ignorant friend?"

"My name," thought Miriam, flustered and pleased.

"I'm not sure," she began. "No, it's more like ... um ... a meadow in summer."

Flora burst out laughing.

"Oh, that's so funny, so quaint. Miriam, honestly."

"She's close, though, closer'n you were, Flo!"

"OK," said Flora. "Another quick slosh. Maybe I'll get it right this time."

The evening slowed down. Flora bounced up and down by the bottle, laughing, her cheeks bright with excitement and drink. Miriam felt weighted in her chair. Each movement of Gwilym's hand seemed to take an aeon: she was intrigued by the grace of it all. He teased and told outrageous stories, in which the august figure of the local Drug Squad played a major role.

Miriam found herself counting stars outside the window. She resurfaced half way through a story. Flora, her hands demurely in her lap, drank in every word - and her fourth glass of the wine.

"....so I planted 'em, see, and they grew like fuckin' weeds; well, that's what they are really, isn't it? Come the day it was all ready and I 'ad 'ell of a shock. Warm day, right, and I'd just cut the buggers into small pieces for the wine, when there's this almighty bang on the door. Dog went mad. I was out with the lilac air freshener all over the bloody place - smelt like a brothel for weeks.

"Outside there's this pig; 'e starts on about this robbery in town, all these drugs nicked from a chemists. Inside info, 'e said: someone'd suggested they might be buried in my garden. I told 'im to dig it up, then I says, 'Doubt if you'll find much but dog crap and bones!' Fuckin' right: that's all 'e found! Didn't stick around long after that."

"Blimey. You *do* live, don't you?"

Flora was admiring.

"Oh aye, I'm into life, me."

Gwilym crossed to the stove and began to prepare the food, carving the salmon into large, uneven slabs, and dropping a vast pile of potatoes onto each plate.

Flora found she was starving. Miriam couldn't imagine anything penetrating the sawdust in her mouth.

Two packs of cards lay on the table, one blue-backed and the other red.

"Grub!" Gwilym called, and sat down, pouring a copious stream of tomato ketchup all over his food.

When they had finished, the last pieces of pink flesh scraped from the plate, a heavy silence hung over them. Gwilym did not mind: many of the best parts of his life were spent in silence; but, for Miriam, it was torment. She felt agitated and self-conscious.

Inhaling from the thick joint he had just rolled, Gwilym began to shuffle the cards, his hands quick in the smoky, fish-scented air: blue, red, blue, red - a blur of colour transfixed the girls until, missing the stroke, Gwilym broke rhythm. Cardboard showered down upon them all. A Joker, jeering brightly from above, landed in the saucepan of potatoes at a jaunty angle.

A dense ooze of syrupy slowness sweetened them, and they waded through languid seconds of muffled wordlessness.

133

Brisk fart-barks from the dog's bottom, and his subsequent crazed chasing of the odorous 'culprit,' cut through the dope-haze. A giggle, escaping Flora's throat, ignited hysterical laughter in them all as, outside, the full moon bisected the darkness and Nipper responded to its pull with a mighty, earth-shattering howl.

"Let's go for a spin," Gwilym said. "Mountain road be'ind Talybont's great when the moon's full..."

"Only," he added. "One of you'll 'ave to drive: stoned as fuck, me!"

***

And so it was that they piled into the Golf, Flora – with Nipper on her lap – in the back; Gwilym next to Miriam in front.

A mood of crazed joy, of moon-ecstasy, had caught them all – and, as they crept past the hunched arboreal beasts of night lining the potholed dip, and accelerated along the familiar Machynlleth to Aberystwyth road, fizzy bubbles of mirth escaped the thin glass of restraint.

Along the main road they drove, and then left into Talybont, the two lion pubs – one white, the other black – now closed for the night.

Up, and up still further, they wended their way, Miriam's hands tension-tight upon the steering wheel as sparse street-lamps gave way to vertiginous climbs through biblical-blackness: tracks, bordered by hulking saurian trees roaring out their threat - and hillsides, so misleadingly velvet and fiendishly unfenced at night that, one turn too abrupt to right or left would mean a crashing, cracking and crunching cascade of noise and pain and death, that last delivered through the ripping torment of boulders in deep-set valleys.

Sheep hollowed out their throats in misty coughs far below – and the birds of night, sable wings etched with pearls of moonlight, swooped and cawed, cawed and swooped.

The dam hit them suddenly, a magnificent and wild square of liquid moonstone frothing and fretting between land and the vast mouth of a stone bridge.

The devil was in them all now. Lunar promptings had triggered the huntress, the savage, the blood-letting. Only Miriam, fingers blenched from fear, wavered briefly and craved the normality of four stone walls.

They drove into position, the tongue of ancient-stone-newly-hacked sticking out, a covert menacing taunt, in front; the pillars – hewn in this silver-gilt world, from the blood of sacrifice and to appease the terrible gods of yore – standing, silent guardians of a far deadlier religion, harkening back to another time and place.

Moon-virus, contagious as plague, rampaged through veins as Miriam started the car and swept, stone rumbling underneath, onto the nubs and buds of the long tongue-bridge.

Suddenly, before them, a rabbit zigzagged in neon light, seeking safety in the bone-bareness of stone and ghostly light, Nipper's growl both warning and glee.

"Get it in the 'eadlights!" Gwilym called. "Stun it!"

Miriam, hand translucent in the maddening rays, flipped the switch to full beam – and saw the creature, interrogated by light, trembling in a glowing cone.

Nipper, up on hind-legs, screamed into the night and worried the back of the seat in his urgent need to be out and after his prey.

"Stop!" Gwilym bellowed. "Nipper, stay! *Gorwedd i lawr!*"

Through the creaking of stiff door-metal Gwilym climbed – and, patched by mist's wandering hands, bent down and grabbed at the dazzled animal; then, in a sudden move, swung arm up and smashed the grey form down upon the side of the bridge, once, twice, thrice for certainty. Blood dripped, spotting the man's hand in patchy red.

Nipper, deprived of his kill, growled with rage and lunged at the car's full freight of shadows.

"Yes!" cried Flora. "Oh, yes!"

Excitement, and a strange sense of triumph, bound them and blended separate bloodstreams into something wider and deeper than the individual. The mores of twentieth century life – and their attendant robes of hypocrisy – existed far below and mainly as memory.

Gwilym, rabbit held by the ears, folded himself back into the passenger seat.

"Make that into rabbit stew," he announced. "Tastes great with a bit of wine and some carrots and onions."

And so they drove home through the seductive moon and the spirited darkness, the thrumming of passion a plangent note in the air.

PART TWO: OCTOBER 1980

Vulnerable rails of the Pwll-Coedwig psyche juddered and shuddered under the jolting train of Richard Morgan's death. Metal sheared off. Windows ran with rain and tears, smudging the landscape. Grating signals sidelined the already-lost. The mountains, stony palisade around sea and marsh and homesteads, trapped the roaring rage. Grief and fear ran through nightmares unchecked.

Heneghan, waking from dreams he could not admit to, savaged the tender inside of his mouth with fury-sharpened molars. A confusion of barbed-wire lay coiled at the bottom of his mind, catching the lightest foray with a sharp rip. The urge to punch Rachel – at times so strong that only sitting on his hands prevented action – never abated: her very presence was enough to provoke fury's most deadly fire.

Angela's ill-thought-out platitudes – which did little more than paint Eleri, that superlative artist, with the colours convention demanded – drove a wedge of steel, which Heneghan had no wish to remove, between them.

FRIDAY 3rd

The day of Richard Morgan's funeral dawned grey, and shrouded as the corpse. Eleri, fastening the final button on her floor-length black dress, watched impassively as the undertakers screwed the coffin lid into place, shutting Richard's jaundiced withering out of sight for good.

Tears, for the moment, stemmed, she still woke, in a spasm of terror, from dreams in which her husband's fingernails, grown grotesquely after death, screeched and scratched their way through the lid and, tough keratin horrors, scrabbled towards her.

Catrin, their only child and her father's little princess, had arrived the night before, cushion-cosy in quilted body-warmer, a pretty blue-eyed blonde who might just as well have been a changeling as far as Eleri was concerned, so little did mother and daughter truly have in common.

Catrin's hysteria, hiccupping wails and screams had left Eleri both disgusted and unnerved. The younger woman's futile attempts to bring her mother in line with polite society had been met with a stubbornness that bordered on hostility, and brought back sharp reminders of battles from years gone by.

Middle ground was conspicuous by its absence. The man who had linked them lay in ruched silk, rotting quietly from the inside, discrete cotton stoppers preventing leakage.

Catrin saw Eleri as spiky, dark, a changeling. As a child, her mother had been a source of profound embarrassment, and she had longed for a parent who bandaged up cuts and made scones, rather than the one she had got, with her odd shyness, lack of friends and weird paintings.

But this was her duty. Dadi would have insisted upon the proprieties had he been in a position to do so. No doubt Mother would just have dug a hole in the ground and bunged him in, given half a chance – and then muttered incantations over the rawness in the soil.

So it was that the daughter, aided discreetly by her husband, had organised the funeral; so it was that resentment, placed upon the Aga of a lifetime's rage, grew ever-hotter; so it was that, while the mother, oblivious, cleaned paint-brushes with Turpentine, the adult child made lists and phone-calls and sandwiches and seethed in silence.

***

The sky above Pwll-Coedwig, primrose-cool in a sudden slant of secretive sunlight, shunted clouds along and hovered above the sloping field, dotted with old grave -stones, that held a hundred or more years' worth of locals at questionable peace.

Arrows of light penetrated the stained-glass Magi in the local church and a brief splash of colour fell upon the coffin.

Meirion, the grave-digger, red-spotted kerchief knotted around sunburned neck, paused in his labours to fling sweat from muddied forehead and, looking down, to hear the slow and plaintive bells ringing out the death.

Hole now long and wide enough, green cloth in position, Meirion rested upon his spade and watched as the long sea-serpent of mourning undulated its way along the roadways of these tiny villages. The biddies, he noted with a certain scathe, were out in force today: nothing like a good funeral.

Dai Eglwys, local vicar, led the procession, the widow and her daughter just behind him. Up they all came, local parishioners, a surging sea of weeping darkness rolling up the early-autumnal lanes and into the field. Men, stiff in Sunday-best suits, stood by their wives.

Mourners huddled like a crab shell without its claws, as Dai Eglwys dressed up the deceased in fine word-weeds once more, before consigning his crated meat to the worms far below the spade-cut incision.

Heneghan, unfamiliar in black suit and tie and too late to join the crowd, hid behind thorn-sharpened hedges and lowered his hat as Dai muttered, *"ydy,"* to Meirion and, with a creaking of ropes, the coffin was winched down into its final resting place.

"Come, Mother."

Catrin's querulous voice rose in the still air and took off like a flight of crows. Pillowed in velvety ebony, she ripped her remaining parent from the charmed circle of dreams, and hustled them both gate-wards.

* * *

No one passing noticed the figure lurking to the left of the gate, nor heard the crash of head against bark and the fierce triplet of swearwords which were ground out from between tight-gritted teeth.

Incandescent, Heneghan wrenched the constricting garrote of material from his throat – and, capering, almost gibbering, like a demonic imp of old, scorched his way back home. The rhythmic swish-click of wheels on rails, furnace of coal shovelled in to fire the machine, jerked him along – but the minute vents were not enough to allow steam to escape and the internal combustion hurtled on to certain disaster.

Back in the house, he paced, smoked, emptied the packet and gnawed finger-nails. Only the peaty strangeness of single malt whisky helped, though even its burn could not prevent a crash.

Glass after glass filled and swallowed, thought reduced to peripheral black dots – an annoyance and nothing more – Heneghan, taut with a loss he did not understand, bounded up from the armchair in which he had festered, brooding, much of the afternoon and early evening and, slamming the empty glass down, lunged for the kitchen door.

Angela, who could feel the imminent storm of him from miles away, cringed and kept herself very still, out of sight, out of danger.

He snarled his way into the room, the breath of the Scottish Isles skirling around him.

"Off out to the Farmers for a pint."

Barely civil, it was more growl than speech.

"Might be best not to drive, Mike,' Angela said. 'You may be over the limit."

"Bollocks, woman, I know what I'm doing. You questioning my driving or something?"

Angela, looking into the omen of black clouds, feared that no approach could work this evening.

"What if you damaged the car? That could be expensive."

"Fuck's sake," he muttered. "Bloody moaning females. All right, have it your own way, you stupid cow."

With a look that warned of reprisals at some later point, Heneghan pushed past Angela and, banging the front door hard, left the house.

***

Autumn's earliest Crone, busy daubing faint colour on the leaves and drying them with their eventual fall's death-fire, barely paused in her labours as the personification of wiry tempest swept past.

Caradoc Pritchard, perched atop his tractor and warbling a chapel hymn, waved at Heneghan and was ignored.

Plumes of smoke, from the open-hearth fire in the Farmers Arms snug, rose warm and reassuring from ancient chimneys and hung, suspended in gentle October air, for brief seconds before being dispersed around the little streets and grey-stone houses of Pwll-Coedwig.

The three old men, sitting on their usual bench, pipes fugging out treacly tobacco, nodded and called out the scattered syncopated syllables of, "*Nos da!*"

Inside, Heneghan ordered a pint, with a whisky chaser, and then stood, immovable as granite, daring comment and conversation from the regulars.

The stream of cosy farming talk, conducted predominantly in Welsh, flowed by in a tide of damp, rippling sibilance. Time ticked on.

Putting a pound note in the slot machine, and drawing out a packet of twenty Benson and Hedges, Heneghan retreated to a dark nook near the back wall and, sitting, lurked, second pint half way down already, attendant whisky shot a distant memory.

The door cracked ajar, letting in late evening sun and a crowd of the younger village men, Gwilym in the thick of their cheerful banter.

Gwilym, thronged by various friends, saw Heneghan straight away, and felt a passing surprise: antisocial bugger, he was, rarely bothered to come in here; certainly not to sit there, almost hidden, glasses piling up in front of him.

The older man, now Gwilym peered more closely, looked rough as all hell and the atmosphere coming off him, pungent as slurry, was not inviting: black suit too, and white shirt; must've been to Richard Morgan's funeral - though Gwilym, who'd popped in to pay his respects, hadn't seen hide nor hair of him.

145

But, he was a mate – of sorts – and a near neighbour, and the code had firm words to say about this sort of meeting: at the very least, offer a handshake, a drink and a few words.

He raised his right hand in greeting and, calling, "All right, Mike? What 'ya havin'?" walked over.

Heneghan looked up, eyes a patchwork of broken veins and glittering spite.

"Gwil," he acknowledged. "Yeah, whisky. Cheers, mate."

Drinks bought, passing-temptation to leave the miserable sod to himself and rejoin the others having been faced and overcome, Gwilym drew up a stool opposite Heneghan and sat down.

"You been to Richard Morgan's funeral?" Gwilym asked. "Shame, eh? Feel sorry for Mrs Morgan, I do..."

A look he could not interpret rushed across the other man's face. Close up, Gwilym could see that the guy's lower jaw was dark with stubble and, from the smell of him, he'd been drinking for hours.

"Yes," Henegan barked. "Fucking typical: only friend I had in this Godforsaken inbred hole and he ups and dies. Heard the gossiping bitches pulling Eleri apart, have you?"

Gwilym thought back to the plump hens settled upon the widow's soft furnishings, clucking and squawking away, and gave an involuntary grin at the memory.

"Yeah! All in need of a good goin'-over by the cockerel, you ask me!"

"Evil, narrow-minded witches, that's all they are," Heneghan hissed.

"Hey, steady on, Mike," Gwilym said, "bit of a generalization, eh? They mean well, most of 'em, just don't know 'ow to deal with other people's grief. Think of Eleri as a snob, see, that's the problem. Janet and that lot don't know 'ow to get friendly with her, think she's lookin' down on 'em all the time..."

"Get real, Gwil. When Richard was alive, none of them gave her the time of day; now, they're all over her like a load of ravens. You just wait: there'll be rumours flying around before the week's out."

"Mebbe," Gwilym replied.

"My round," Heneghan said abruptly. "Got to go to the Gents first. Pint of Best?"

He was up and weaving through the crowd within seconds, trademark hat jammed low on his forehead, habitual scowl cemented on face.

"Fuck knows 'ow much 'e's 'ad already," Gwilym thought. "But you'd never guess lookin' at 'im. 'E don't just 'old his drink; 'e controls it.'"

He took a drag on the ever-present Woodbine, balanced it on the lip of the over-full ashtray and blew smoke from the side of his mouth, all the time thinking about the Morgans.

Eleri had been in the same class as Janet Davies, Helydd Jones, his own mam, Blodwyn, and the rest of that gang. They'd all trooped off to Pwll-Coedwig Primary, with their little lunch boxes, and gloves attached to string, forty and more years gone, just like Gwilym and his brother had two decades later.

What'd Mam said? Yes, Janet and Helydd had been two blonde, pretty, popular girls, almost like-enough to be twins (cousins or similar, wasn't it?), who were always at the two power ends of the skipping games, choosing who jumped in and who was left out.

Eleri, the outsider, for all that she was born in the broken-down old stone barn just down the track, always passed by or tripped up or laughed at – because she didn't fit; something in her was away with the fairies, when they all giggled about boys and teased and did each other's hair and traded secrets.

Mam had felt sorry for her, felt guilty to this day, but had been too scared to lose out on her place in the gang – and so had turned from the legs thrust out to trip; the bruising *'collisions'*; the break times when Eleri had walked, all alone, round and round, trying to belong and failing.

Maybe Heneghan had a point.

Emrys Bont Goch wandered over, sat down, talked farming, offered Gwilym a week's laboring work during the Harvest, packed his pipe bowl-full of foul-smelling baccy and, lighting it the old-fashioned way (no lighters for Emrys, *dim diolch*!), blew silage-strong wafts across the table.

"Who was you with then, boy?" Emrys asked. "I seen another bloke sitting here. He getting a round in?"

"Aye!" said Gwilym. "Slow tonight. What they doin'? Cuttin' the hops? Brewin' the stuff from scratch?"

He looked up. There was no sign of Heneghan at the bar. A slight unease stole over him.

"Keep my place, will ya, Emrys? I'll just go an' 'elp carry the drinks."

Squeezing through the usual mid-week suspects, he made his way to the narrow passageway which led past the toilets to the back door. Heneghan was just the sort of rude bastard who would decide to bugger off without saying a word – but, just in case, Gwilym pushed open the door marked *'Dynion'* and started to go in.

He saw the blood first – and then Heneghan, spark-out on the tiled floor, pale as hell and breathing in a harsh snorting way that Gwilym didn't like the sound of at all.

Wedging the door open with his speedily-removed left shoe, he ran back into the bar, grabbed Bryn and a few of the stronger lads and, telling Gwawr-behind-the-bar to phone 999 for an ambulance pronto, dashed back into the confined space of the Gents.

***

Angela waited until Heneghan had gone and then, shaking with nervous tension, picked up the phone and dialled Edwin's number before fear stopped her. She half-hoped he'd be out and, when the phone rang and rang at the other end, she exhaled with relief. Then she heard his voice.

"Hello? Edwin? Angela Heneghan here. I'd like to talk to you. Can you meet me in the George Inn later...oh good...When? Yes, that's fine...Yes, Mike's out... He's left both cars...Yes, I'll drive up...Right, see you soon. Bye."

Angela supposed she ought to check on her children, make sure they were all right to be left: Rachel got a bit funny sometimes.

She poked her head round the boys' room first: they were listening to Radio One, and James was making a model of a plane. He was absorbed. Tom grinned when he saw her and turned the radio down. Angela was touched by his thoughtfulness.

"Hiya, Mum," said James. "What's for supper?"

"Typical," she thought, "absolutely typical."

"Well, James," she said. "You three can have a rummage in the fridge: there's plenty of cold salmon left and some salad. Your father's out and I'm off to the George in about half an hour. I'll leave a phone number for you, just in case."

"Mum, honestly," said Tom. "You do fuss. What do you think's going to happen to us? We're old enough to look after ourselves for a couple of hours. James won't burn the house down or anything."

"Nevertheless," Angela said, catching echoes of her own mother. "I'd feel happier to know we can be in contact - okay?"

"Sure," Tom said amiably, then he grinned. "Hey, Mum, you going out with a fancy man or something?"

Angela winced. This joke was a bit close to the bone.

"Naturally," she said. "Don't wait up for us."

She ruffled her younger son's dark hair. He squirmed in irritation. His older brother winked.

"Bye, boys."

Tom saluted. He was so easy, that one, she thought: not as bright as his younger siblings, but enthusiastic and even tempered - unlike her volatile sullen daughter.

Rachel's door was firmly closed. It usually was. She liked her privacy. Angela knocked, remembering how she'd hated being burst in upon when she was a teenager.

Rachel opened the door. She was crying. Angela didn't feel able to cope with this now.

"Why do I have to be a mother all the time?" she thought.

"I'm going out for a while, Rachel. See you later."

The girl just nodded and closed the door in her mother's face.

"Charming," Angela thought. "Little bitch. I'll talk to her tomorrow."

Despite her anger, the child's face worried her. Angela felt a stab of guilt at her wish not to get involved. Rachel was becoming increasingly uncommunicative, which struck her as strange because the girl had been the most spontaneous and loving of her children when very small. James had always been an enigma. Tom, who had been placid right from the start, would involve himself for hours in his own quiet little games, singing to himself as he played. Rachel had been much more restless and openly playful: rushing up to her mother and chattering away, needing to touch people in order to corner herself in this big adult world.

Angela loved small children, had adored her three when they were tiny - had spent hours crouched on the floor playing with them. She acknowledged that she did not like teenage girls very much, and wished that Rachel would hurry through this singularly-charmless phase.

Angela found it difficult to allow herself pleasure. A large part of her believed that the needs of her family came first. The business of phoning Edwin and arranging to go out had not been easy. Now, in the face of Rachel's obvious misery, she felt tempted to stay at home.

When she asked herself what she wanted to do, she realised, with a jolt, that her own wishes seemed both formless and irrelevant. She felt distressingly un-liberated: fancy wishing to please in these days of Feminism.

She sat down on the bed, knowing that time was passing, and felt her vague unease turning into panic. She became convinced she was deserting her family and, acknowledging how difficult it was for her to slip out of the role of wife and mother, she felt trapped and miserable.

Angela was no longer clear why she had contacted Edwin. What did she want from him, from this evening? She felt a need for comfort and reassurance - and it distressed her that, despite her recognition of life's essential loneliness, she still needed to be validated by the attention of men.

The house was completely silent. Evidently, Tom had not turned his radio up after she left. This galvanized her as nothing else would have done: the idea of the lad waiting for her to go before he allowed the blasts of sound to fill the house upset her. She had no wish to inhibit her children.

She twitched her social self into place. It wasn't easy. The image she sought eluded her despite the deceptively firm mascara and lipstick strokes. She was nervous, lightly running from point to point and catching fragments of herself in the many mirrors: pallid nasal bridge, the white-gold cross, blue eyes, an upturned velvet hem, mid-brown hair just touching her shoulders.

Angela rarely considered herself in more than lightning glances. Twirling, she chuckled. The rustling material, and flashes of flesh, mirrored her laugh and sudden satisfaction. She met the moment with a mist of perfume and hurried on.

***

Angela drove down the Borth road, pushing her unwelcome expectations against the steering wheel in a way which made the car jerk from side to side.

Bulrushes bent sluggishly towards the cracked surface of the drainage ditch; fat frogs croaked out the steam of the long hot day. The sun, succulent and earthy as a vast red watermelon, hung above the sea, downy with gold flecks.

As Angela watched, the sun began to set, a pale echo treading its line over the sea's surface. She expected to hear the briny water sizzle. Soft rosy light scooped the sand from groyne-to-groyne, fading into lilac at the far end. The whole town shone.

She parked the car, glad of Mike's absence. He was the ultimate back-seat driver, particularly where women were concerned; it was yet another facet of his lack of trust.

Guided by instinct, Angela went round to the side of the pub and climbed the stone steps to the balcony. Below her, light still tumbled and danced on the sand.

Edwin sat at the furthest of the tables. He smiled warmly and pointed to the glass of rose wine he'd got for her. Angela was touched: she'd wanted to be spoiled, looked after and his correct reading of this delighted her. She sat by his side and for a while they shared a silence as soothing as the scene below. The awful urgency of Angela's impulse had peeled away, leaving simple pleasure in Edwin's company.

"Where's Mike tonight?" Edwin asked.

"Oh, him..."

Flustered despite her wish to talk about Mike, she experienced a strong hostility, and fear, now the point had actually arrived. She felt that he stole all the attention even when he was absent.

"He's gone off to the local pub in a temper."

Angela laughed in a dismal attempt at levity. She wanted to rage about her husband, but wasn't sure whose side Edwin was on.

"He gets like that," she added lamely.

Edwin smiled.

"We're all at sixes-and-sevens at the moment," she said. "Mike's in a mood; my daughter won't speak to me and spends half her time crying; my younger son writes strange stories which make no sense to me. Sometimes I think that Thomas is the only sane member of the family. I just wanted to be out of it for a stretch - that's why I phoned you. It was easier when Mike was here, wasn't it?"

"Only because you took a back seat," Edwin said. "You hardly said a word all evening. I don't know your husband. He doesn't reveal himself to me. Granted, we talk but it's about things that don't matter intrinsically, things of safety where you follow a certain understood male code. The things we said were in no way a threat to you or your presence that evening. It's good to flex that particular verbal muscle but, if that's all there were, life would be grim indeed."

"It is anyway," Angela said flatly.

"At the moment, yes," said Edwin. "I think you're too sensitive to his moods."

"He's my husband," said Angela.

"Yes, but not your twin. You don't have to be miserable just because he is."

"I feel I can't help him," she admitted. "I had this strange dream about him a while back. It seemed as if

157

all his non-communication, and inner rage, was transmuted into a huge and menacing black sludgy shadow. This thing clung to him like a grossly-exaggerated second skin. He fell, from a height, and it burst and ate away at him - and, even in the dream, I was helpless to do anything.

"That's what's so hard to face: that you can love someone and yet be powerless to help them when something goes wrong. I've tried to talk to him but he simply doesn't want to know. His great criticism of me is that I'm too introspective and emotional. If I am - and I'm not denying it - then he goes to the opposite extreme."

Angela touched the sticky stem of her glass and licked the sweet wine off her fingers. The dream had lightened.

"Maybe all I want is to talk," she said.

"Nothing wrong with that," said Edwin gently.

"No," said Angela sadly. "It's just that I bottle myself up, and the thoughts become so dug in to the soil of withdrawal that I'm no longer sure what I've said and what is left to silence. You're a good listener, Edwin. You seem to understand what's going on with me..."

She paused and the unspoken, "unlike my husband," hung between them, a reminder of the power the man had over her.

Edwin was a man who had seen loneliness, Angela thought, and yet he was in no way diminished by the experience. If anything, he had been mysteriously buttressed. He had an inner strength, though it was very different from Mike's. He must have been an inspiring lecturer.

She wondered how old he was. Dare she ask? She found herself laughing at this thought.

He looked at her, a smile beginning on one side of his mouth. It was an inquiring look.

"I wonder about you," she said. "You seem so content with your life, as if you've come to terms with things."

Edwin leaned forward.

"I am content, Angela," he said. "I can't say that's always been the case, however. Coming here just after the death of Celia, my wife, was very hard at first. I was lucky: I met a lovely woman, three years later – and, although the relationship didn't last long, she saw me through the worst of the bad times.

"I think age does dull things to a certain extent: I feel just as full of life and intellectual curiosity as ever; but I find it harder, as the years go by, to feel passionate about people. That being said, I do retain immensely strong feelings - love, almost- for this area."

"It is a dramatic place to live, isn't it?" Angela agreed. "On the surface it's just like any other beach resort - and yet, when you first enter the town, the whole place is hemmed-in with hulking hills. It's as if there's something far older, and more sinister, lurking behind the sweet rock and sugar dentures."

Edwin laughed at this unexpected touch.

"There's drama - sometimes comedic; more often a variation of tragedy – inherent in being a foreigner in an oppressed land, knowing that you are the hated tyrant or, at best, an outsider to be put up with. I've lived here for twenty years and I'm still The Englishman, *y Saesneg*; I always will be, I suspect. These are good people, but the land doesn't give easily."

"There is a distance," she admitted. "I am always Mrs Heneghan, never Angela, let alone Angie, to the women. Sometimes I miss the easy intimacy, and resent them for taking out on me things done hundreds of years ago, by people I probably would have hated just as much as they do. They're very insular here."

"They feel constantly threatened by insidious pressure from outside," Edwin said. "Welshmen and women have their own language and a culture which makes our heterogeneous collection of arts seem arid, superficial and messy in comparison. I can see their point. We want them to exchange something tight and powerful for our flabby ways. It's more than simply taking a bit of land here and there; it cuts right down to the roots of who they are. Compared to them, we have no culture to speak of, and little positive national spirit."

The steps clattered behind them.

"Oh no," Angela whispered. "Late-blooming grockles. Bound to be."

A familiar figure, tall and auburn-haired, joined them. It was Gwilym. He looked worried, which was sufficiently unusual for Angela to feel a surge of unease.

"Ah, Gwilym," said Edwin. "Didn't know you frequented this place."

"I don't," Gwilym said curtly.

Then he sat down next to Angela.

"Mike's 'ad an accident, love. 'E collapsed and is on 'is way to 'ospital. You better come with me and I'll drive you in."

She did not cry or make any sound. Instead, she found herself looking at Gwilym's honest face as if attempting to draw a denial of the truth from his eyes. No such revelation was forthcoming. Gwilym, usually at ease in his world, was looking distinctly uncomfortable.

For a moment, the scene froze into a tableau of static horror. The shock waves seemed almost palpable entities in the air.

Edwin moved then, draping Angela's coat over her shoulders. He took her arm and led her to the car, with Gwilym close behind.

Nothing had been said, but Gwilym knew that the older man was coming along too - and he was relieved. He felt confused and irritated, and didn't like either emotion.

It had all seemed perfectly normal at first. Blokes did pass out from time to time from too much booze - God knows he'd done it himself on several memorable occasions. But, as he and the other men had crowded into that tiny dim place trying to bring Heneghan round, watching helplessly as the blood flowed onto the tiled floor - despite wadded-up toilet paper pressed to the scalp - he'd realised that this was out of his experience, an ambulance job.

He hadn't liked bringing the outside world into the pub, but he'd seen that it was necessary. The flashing blue light had seemed an intrusion, a faintly sinister portent of a world Gwilym did not want to know about. It had diminished him in some strange way, so that he'd felt useless and in the way.

He shuddered, inwardly, knowing that he had no words to make the truth any less blunt for Heneghan's missus.

Angela got in next to Gwilym. Edwin, a vaguely soothing presence in the back, said nothing.

"I want to know what happened," she said in a voice so reedy that Gwilym thought it was an echo in his head for a moment.

"He went to the gents, took 'is time, so I went to check 'e 'adn't scarpered, like, and reckon 'e must've slipped – flat out on the floor, 'e was, bleedin' like a stuck pig. Oops, sorry, love, that just slipped out. Couldn't do nothin', no room for starters, called the ambulance in the end."

"I don't understand,' said Angela. 'Why would Mike fall? He's so sure footed."

Gwilym felt pity for her. Surely she must have seen the state her husband was in even before he went out.

"He was dead drunk, love, didn't know what he was doin', I reckon."

"They always take head injuries seriously, Angela," Edwin added from the back. "The scalp bleeds profusely, though that doesn't necessarily mean anything; but any bang can disguise more serious problems inside."

"Yeah," said Gwilym. "They don't want to take no chances, see. Don't you worry too much, love: 'e's a strong bloke, your 'usband. 'E'll be all right – 'ave 'ell of 'eadache for a while!"

"We'll stay with you," said Edwin, "and we're not leaving till we know what's happening. Right, Gwilym?"

"Right, *gwas*."

The lights of Aberystwyth shone ahead of them as the car swept down the steep Penglais Hill. Gwilym drove into Bronglais hospital's car-park. The whole place looked forbidding.

Once in Casualty, Gwilym took charge by the simple expedient of grabbing a young nurse and rattling off a stream of less-than-perfect Welsh at her.

Despite herself, Angela smiled: even in this situation, Gwilym had made an impression.

"Might as well sit down," he said, doing exactly that.

They perched on a hard bench.

"What was that all about?" Angela asked.

"No point in goin' direct to Matron, the old witch; I've 'ad bust-ups with 'er before. That little nurse says they've taken 'im off to a ward somewhere. She's gone to find out where 'e is. Dunno whether we'll be able to see 'im, though, so don't get your 'opes up, love."

The place was quiet. Apart from them, the only person in sight was an old man holding his roughly-bandaged left hand and staring at the wall.

"All right, man?" said Gwilym, friendly as ever. "What you done then?"

The old man smiled tremulously. He appeared glad of the opportunity to talk. It seemed that one of his dogs had turned bad and, before his son had managed to shoot it, had savaged his hand. Since his injury was not life threatening, he'd been waiting here for two hours.

"You've hit a quiet spot," he said. "They've been tied up with a nasty car accident: woman went through the windscreen. Her face was all mangled."

Angela felt sick. Thank God they hadn't arrived half an hour earlier. The nurse came back, accompanied by a doctor. He stopped by Angela and sat down.

"Ah, Mrs Heneghan. Dr Jarvis. I saw your husband when he came in. He's had a skull x-ray, and there's no serious damage - just a fairly deep cut. He hasn't regained consciousness, however, so we'll keep him in for twenty-four hours or so, to be on the safe side."

"Can I see him?" Angela asked.

"I don't see why not," said the doctor. "Just you, though. I'm afraid these gentlemen will have to stay here."

Gwilym was unashamedly relieved. He took out a Woodbine from his pocket, lit it and inhaled with obvious pleasure.

The corridor seemed a mile long to Angela; her legs felt wobbly, stomach hollow. The doctor asked basic details about Mike, and she gave them. She wanted to run away, but the scream of the ambulance siren suggested worse horrors behind.

"In here," said the doctor and opened the door for her. She was in a small room with four beds, two of them occupied. Mike was in the bed nearest the window. Angela walked over, gritting teeth to stop her face from shaking.

He lay there, quite still, black stubble stark against the soft pallor of the face. He looked dead, apart from the dark hairs in his nostrils which quivered slightly from a faint drawing-in of life. There was no wound to be seen; a thick bandage obscured that. To her, this man was a stranger: she did not like to see him thus felled; it took away his choice to bend naturally.

She had no desire to touch him; he was as distant as a corpse. He would recover - Angela knew that now - but she feared the memory of this moment would always stand beside her, a shadow he would be nervously aware of. He did not look childlike or soft; even unconscious, he was undoubtedly Mike. In some strange way, his stubbornness and strength was fighting through it all. Though his face was relaxed, an inner watchfulness was at work. She half expected him to rise up at any moment and stare her down with cold greyish-green eyes, but he did not move. She made her way to the door and rejoined the doctor in his room.

He smiled kindly at her.

"Not as bad as you were expecting?"

"No. It's a big relief."

Dr Jarvis nodded.

"These things often look a lot worse than they are. He's been lucky, though – must have a hard head! Now I suggest you go home and get some rest. You look tired, if you don't mind my saying."

When Angela returned to the outpatients' area of Casualty, the old man with the injured hand was still there. He smiled at her as she passed.

Edwin and Gwilym immediately popped up like a pair of well-rehearsed corks. They looked vaguely guilty, as if caught mid-doze. Angela's relief turned to a state close to tears. She was glad to be out of that room, pleased to have the two men there.

"He 'asn't snuffed it, then?" said Gwilym, blunt with relief.

"No, no," she said. "You were right. It would take more than that. Oh God..."

She didn't know whether to laugh or cry.

Edwin eyed her with concern and said nothing.

Gwilym took control.

"Right then, 'ome. *Nos da, gwas.*"

He waved cheerfully at the old man and walked out.

Edwin shrugged at Angela and winked.

"Incorrigible," he said.

They left. Gwilym's down-to-earth approach had calmed Angela more than kindness would have done. She felt great liking for this young man, always known but never close.

In the car, she felt awkward, wanting to thank them but not knowing how. The silence blew up like a balloon she wanted to burst. She often felt at odds with her own emotions in this way, trying to create the perfect line of speech.

It all felt overwhelming to her then: her frustrated wish to say something, the relief and other dark, unresolved things she could not put a name to. She cried a bit, quietly to herself, not wanting to attract attention; but when Edwin's hand alighted on her arm, she felt soothed.

The house came into sight. There were no lights on. She imagined the children curled up in sleep, knowing nothing. She wanted someone else to tell them, so that this flight from direct responsibility could last a bit longer.

The front room was untidy. Instinctively, Angela began to clear things away, to disguise the noise of the disappearing car and her own loneliness.

The whisky glass was exactly where Mike had left it, sticky now and rimmed with tiny insects. She couldn't bring herself to touch it, though she carried the near-empty bottle away to the kitchen and thrust it to the back of a cupboard.

His sardonic imprint, a slight rearrangement of the contours of the chair, remained.

MONDAY 6th

In the field, mist wandered vaguely, whitening the air. Trees shivered and shook off a thin robe of darkness which fell and drained into the soil.

Gwilym climbed over the gate and made his way to where the stallion stood. The animal was completely still, emerging as an increasingly bright reality the closer the man got. Dampened, the stallion's coat was the colour of a fresh conker.

Gwilym had no fear of Rameses, and horse gave back this trust in equal measure, allowing the man to approach with a freedom denied to others. Rameses didn't move, even when Gwilym fixed the halter on him; he accepted the confidence in the man's hands, pushing affectionately at his arm.

Gwilym leapt onto the stallion's back. He could do this with ease, preferring the warmth of the horse to a saddle. Rameses was powerful, and Gwilym could feel the energy trembling beneath him as he nudged the left flank and moved the horse off for a quick canter round the field.

It was great having the wind in his hair, the trees flashing past - the total freedom of it all. This pleasure was as instinctive to him as most others, since he had ridden before he could walk.

At the other end, he jumped off and, opening the gate, led the stallion up the lane. He believed in giving Rameses a bit of exercise before he served one of the mares, thought it gave the stallion a good work-out, got him pumped up for action..

Iestyn was sweeping the yard when Gwilym arrived, helping his dad since the older man had injured his back in a fall back in August. Caradoc, frustrated by his stiffness and pain, stood to one side.

There was no sign of Tom, who usually went wherever Iestyn went, and, for a moment, Gwilym was surprised - till he remembered Heneghan and the events of two nights ago.

In a swift darkening, he wondered if Heneghan had come round. He didn't like this complication to his life, though he recalled Heneghan's strange behaviour, and Angela's misery, with a sympathy no less sincere for being detached.

"*Su mae!*" called Iestyn.

Gwilym waved back in response. Caradoc rubbed his back and grinned at the younger man.

"I'll go get the mare," Iestyn added.

"Hope she's a bit more co-operative this time!" Caradoc added.

Gwilym laughed out loud at the memory: the rearing mare, just like a terrified virgin, and the look of indignant surprise written all over the stallion as his prize lashed out at him yet again.

Old Pritchard had been trying to get a foal out of the mare for years, but the animal resisted with the firm conviction of a chapel-going spinster.

"Frigid," had been Gwilym's parting shot the last time.

He just hoped it didn't come on to rain in the middle of the act. Halter loosely wound round his hand, he lit a Woodbine and stood, enjoying the silence and the smell of horses.

The quiet tapping noise startled him, until he looked up and saw Flora's head framed in the upstairs window.

She waved and mimed, "What's going on?"

Gwilym was just getting into the mood of this mimed conversation - gesturing a stallion erection so gigantic the mare would have died of fright - when Iestyn returned.

"Ready?" asked Iestyn, as if nothing had happened.

The mare looked remarkably calm, almost bored; she always did at this stage. The stallion's interest was growing in a manner which had Flora rushing next door to grab Miriam.

When Gwilym looked again, he saw two fascinated faces in the window. Having seen it all many times before, he found their interest highly amusing.

Iestyn held the mare and the two men stood facing one another for a moment. Iestyn was tense. The stallion reared forward, his front hooves landing on the mare's back. The mare's body rippled with a convulsion so strong it knocked the stallion off, and then she lunged back striking the concrete with a crash of sparks.

Iestyn steadied her and held the halter fractionally tighter. The mare's eyes were wide, terrified; sweat dulled her coat.

The stallion was ready again, arching through the yard onto the mare. Gwilym held him with no apparent effort. The mare, trembling, held her ground, the halter tight against her neck. The stallion drove on into her and, though she tried to twist round and kick her way out, Iestyn was now completely in control. His face was grim from the pressure.

"Thank Christ I don't 'ave this trouble with women," Gwilym muttered.

The stallion's hooves hit the ground once more. The released mare went wild, throwing herself into the air in a vast 'S' shape. Iestyn lengthened the halter rope and stood back. He didn't have Gwilym's natural affinity with horses but this, fortunately, was routine.

As Iestyn had predicted, the mare calmed down the moment she felt that no one was fighting her anymore. She landed with surprising grace for so large an animal and snuffled at Iestyn's pocket for sugar.

Both men laughed: couldn't trust the mare as far as you could throw her but, Duw, she was a beautiful animal and they could quite see why Caradoc was so anxious for a foal. Time would tell, but Gwilym had a feeling they'd been successful this time.

The stallion stood, huge and motionless as a latter-day dinosaur.

"Come on, then, lad," said Gwilym. "Ta ra, Iestyn, Caradoc. Let us know if she don't 'old to that one!"

Iestyn watched Gwilym with a gnawing of envy, as the younger man, brother in all but blood, sauntered back down the lane. Their relationship had always been careful, as if they were finding ways round one another, though there was genuine warmth and affection beneath it all.

Iestyn was aware that his more analytical mind occasionally cut lines through the simple farming life he led. The animals sensed it. He knew that he had to work long and hard for his effectiveness as a farmer to be sure: each task was a deliberate working through with the mind and an attempt to still his inner fastidiousness.

His strength lay in physical bulk and muscular determination. Over the years, he had used this to cover his instinctive fear of horses, though it had been hard.

Gwilym was the son his parents should have had. It was sad for both: Iestyn, whose body wasn't in it, would eventually have Pritchard's Farm and its miles of good land, while Gwilym would get nothing - and, though Iestyn's parents never said a word, he often feared their thoughts ran parallel to his.

He was always glad to have Tom working for him: the boy's obvious admiration did a lot to heal the sense of hurt he never admitted to.

He jumped aboard the tractor, soothed by the metal. He felt happier with machines.

"Good God! Have you ever seen anything like it?" Flora said to Miriam.

***

The day tightened and, in spasms, gave out dull heat. Heneghan woke, instantly alert. The period of unconsciousness, and two days of heavy sleep, might never have been. He remembered nothing of the accident, though he could trace through Richard Morgan's funeral with absolute clarity.

The ache in his head made some things clear. He was in hospital; that much was obvious - and it was mid-morning, dull and muggy. The sheets seemed unnaturally stiff and restricting. Heneghan felt angry:

he loathed not being able to leap out into the day on his own terms.

From the window, he could see an ascending grey monotony of houses and not a single blade of grass in sight. Lorries thundered by. The bloke in the opposite bed looked like he was on his last legs.

As Heneghan watched, the man began to moan and scrabble about, as if attempting to dislodge the many tubes entering his body. Heneghan pressed the bell next to his bed: if the guy was going to croak, he didn't want to watch it.

A nurse came in straightaway. The man had pulled a tube out of his arm and blood dripped onto the sheet. The nurse pulled a screen round the patient. A doctor rushed in, followed by another nurse.

Heneghan's interest in the proceedings, never acute, waned. The second nurse smiled at him and came over.

"And how are we today, Mr Heneghan?"

"Can't speak for him over there, but my head hurts like buggery!"

He was delighted to see a slow blush spread unbecomingly over the nurse's face.

"I see," she said coldly.

Her smile had disappeared.

"Since you lot are obviously busy waiting for the Grim Reaper to call, and I'm not on his list, when the hell can I get out of here? Two bloody awful days is more than enough!" Heneghan snarled.

He disliked the feeling of being in pyjamas at this hour. The nurse looked at him. He had flustered her; her bedside manner was strained. She was middle-aged, plain - and Heneghan's contempt was coming over very clearly.

"I'll ask your doctor," she said finally.

"You do that," said Heneghan.

"Nurse!" yelled the doctor from behind the screen. "If you could tear yourself away from Mr Heneghan's undoubted charms, we need your assistance here."

Heneghan smiled thinly to himself. He appreciated other men's sarcastic humour, though he squashed any evidence of such a trait in women.

The screens were pulled away and the man, now still and tidy, lay quietly in his bed, the first nurse by his side. The doctor came over to Heneghan. While a nurse was removing the drip and changing Heneghan's dressing, the doctor stood with folded arms looking down at him.

Heneghan began to feel defensive and edgy; he didn't like being stared at. He tensed his muscles and the nurse, taken by surprise, pulled the needle out harder than she'd meant to.

"Watch what you're damn well doing, you stupid cow!" yelled Heneghan as pain shot through his head in waves. "Christ!"

The nurse finished her task and rushed off. Dr Jarvis broke the silence.

"You can go home today," he said. "This afternoon probably."

"Right," said Heneghan. "I don't remember a thing. What happened?"

"A combination of too much alcohol and a bang on the head," said the doctor. "You were found in a collapsed state in the pub. We kept you in because you didn't regain consciousness for a while. The x-rays show there's nothing seriously amiss. There won't even be much of a scar. You're very lucky, you know!"

"Yeah," said Heneghan. "So you say."

"I'll call your wife - and check you over later, just to be certain that all is well," said the doctor.

He could see that Heneghan had something on his mind. The man was not concentrating fully.

179

"Anything wrong?" he asked.

"Living dead over there," Heneghan said.

"Mr Hughes?" The doctor was surprised. "What about him?"

"He looks like he's on his way out," said Heneghan

The doctor resisted the urge to laugh.

"That's our concern, not yours," he said mildly.

Heneghan felt as if he were being patronised.

"It is my concern if the bastard snuffs it while you lot are elsewhere," he snapped.

The doctor felt a fleeting sympathy. Beneath the anger, the man was evidently afraid. He kept his voice light, sensing the hostility.

"Mr Hughes is simply recovering from an operation, Mr Heneghan - a fairly minor operation. In any case, should there be a problem, we are monitoring him carefully."

If Heneghan was relieved, he did not show it. Here, the doctor suspected, was a man who disliked losing face.

He turned to go on his rounds, relieved that Heneghan's stay was not going to be extended beyond today.

***

The phone rang just as Angela was hanging out the washing. When she'd phoned earlier, they'd been guarded, saying only that Heneghan had finally emerged from two days of heavy, almost comatose, sleeping. Now she was to fetch him some time this afternoon.

Her earlier mood of cautious relief had given way to unease. She realised she was frightened of seeing him. She never drove with him in the car if she could help it; the very thought made her stomach seize up in fear.

She thought back to the horror of Saturday morning: she had woken early and had searched the stillness of the house, trying to find the right way to approach the children. In the event, their sudden appearance in the kitchen had rather forced the issue.

She had blurted the whole thing out before she could think of a way of making it easier for them. James' tearful reaction had surprised and irritated her. In the heat of the moment she had yelled, "For God's sake, pull yourself together! He's not dead."

This had resulted in Rachel, always fiercely protective of her little brother, screaming back at her mother. The ensuing row had caused Tom to withdraw into himself: he hated scenes.

Once Rachel and James had stormed off, Angela had poured herself a generous slug of whisky. It was then that Tom's continued presence in the room had hit her. She sensed shock and concern behind his carefully bland face.

"Why are you drinking, Mum?" he'd asked.

"Because I'm in a bloody state!" she'd heard herself shout.

"Ah well," she thought now, two days later, as the sheets, heavier than usual, billowed and flapped in her face, "I defy things to get much worse."

She had a sinking feeling, however, that, given her family, further disaster was highly probable. She felt they were in a rut together. Tension seemed to be the only link. She tried to remember if it had ever been easier than this, and was unable to do so.

***

Tom had his father's ability to block all unpleasantness from the mind. On Saturday, he'd turned away from the reek of whisky and his mother's white angry face, leaving only her familiar warmth and the sky, like mud, pressing in against the window. He found that he could detach himself from any scene by concentrating hard on an object some distance away.

Now, he looked longingly at the farm down the road. He hated missing even a day and was always secretly afraid that some other local boy would take his place. His mum had just driven off – to fetch Dad - and he was, to all intents and purposes, in charge of the house.

He began to clean his boots, for something to do, welcoming the physical nature of the job. Water, from the leaky tap, sprayed in all directions; spindly lines, like blood, ran down the rubber, melting the mud humps.

Tom attacked with the nail brush, scrubbing until his hands tingled and dark grainy water filled the sink.

And, all the time, he was fixing in his mind the image of Heneghan's leg, muscled and certain, and the gun lying beside it.

All his admiration for his father rose up at the thought and he whistled happily, banishing pain and hospitals.

***

Heneghan decided to leave the black stubble, despite being offered a razor: it was his assertion of identity, of virility and independence, a sure sign that the hospital had not smoothed away all his edges.

They'd brought him his clothes an hour ago. The black suit, which someone had pressed in the interim, and the white shirt, starched and smelling faintly of antiseptic, felt stiff and alien to touch. He felt, as he put them on, as if he were performing the lead role in his own death drama: as if Richard Morgan's funeral had been but a rehearsal for the real thing.

His eyes alone kept the illusion at bay: their ferocity burned through the general pallor, though Heneghan did not see this.

He sat on the bed, a stiff figure, unapproachable. The nurses skirted him nervously, unwilling to have the simple time of day minced up and spat out.

He waited for an end to all this.

***

Angela knocked on the door of the doctor's office: he'd asked her to check with him first. He smiled at her, pleased that he could give her good news, relieved that she had appeared so promptly to take the man home.

There he was: pale, plaster on his forehead, a strange smile. She did not put her arms around him; she felt his remoteness even from here and sensed she was going to have to get to know him all over again. His unshaven lower face aroused her. Her lower belly felt heavy with lust.

"Mike," she said.

184

"Let's get the hell out of here," he said. "I can't stick this place a moment longer."

"Yes. Yes, of course."

She caught the false brightness in her voice before his scathing tongue responded to the existence of something so loathsome.

They walked to the car. Heneghan did not falter once even when pain, reactivated by movement, caused dizziness. Angela felt there was much to say, and nowhere safe to say it.

He looked strange in the passenger seat, lounging with his feet on the dashboard, relaxed yet watchful. Angela was not deceived for one moment by the studied ease of that gently-swinging foot. She started the car and felt his body checking every move she made, though he said nothing.

The beauty of the hills took her over, as it usually did, simplifying matters. The traffic was patchy, the detritus of the holiday season ebbing. She wished it would rain.

"How do you feel now?" she asked.

"Not bad," Heneghan said.

He smiled.

"Headache. Strange to think that I've lost part of my life. Wonder if I'll ever remember what happened?"

"Hmmm," said Angela.

"What about you?" he asked.

"Edwin and Gwilym came with me," she said. "They were very kind. I don't know what I'd have done without them."

"I'm glad you weren't alone," was all he said.

She knew he was pleased to see her, in his own way, and she was relieved.

The miles opened up without threat.

Heneghan shivered through his muscles, settling them back. He felt physically in control once more. This was his land, his place: the rough heather on the hills, red and gold now, and the sea somewhere off to the left - it was all familiar and, in its wild stretches, allowed for limitless freedom. He experienced a formless sense of well-being.

Angela sensed much of this. His body told its own story.

"There'll be another storm, I reckon," he said.

"God, I hope so."

She laughed.

They smiled at one another.

Outside the house, Heneghan stood for a while, looking around. He felt he'd been away longer than three nights. Below, he could see the tiny limping figure of Caradoc Pritchard, working as hard as ever despite the accident - and he felt reassured that everything carried on in its usual way.

He went inside.

***

The afternoon darkened suddenly, and lights went out in houses all over Pwll-Coedwig. The village children, fractious and quarrelsome, broke into a vicious fight around the village green: stones were thrown and hair pulled, the screams oddly muffled by the heavy air. Flimsy nasal membranes broke without the aid of a punch, and mothers sighed at the bright drops of blood on stone kitchen floors.

Eleri sat in her kitchen, stretching the morning to its evening limits. Even in her nightdress, she felt too hot and was aware of the sweat running freely down her back.

Catrin was in her room, reading, tired out from the long drive yesterday. It felt strange having her in the house. Eleri felt as if she were creeping everywhere, keeping a part of herself - the bright centre which was not widowed sorrow - back.

Catrin would not want to know; Eleri knew that instinctively. Her daughter's expectations were the heavier for being unvoiced. She wanted Catrin out of the house. She felt stiff with other people's concern, entangled in convention's tight net.

"Mother!"

"Oh, God," thought Eleri. "Here we go…"

Catrin stood in the doorway, plumply-immaculate, an expensive soft furnishing. The look on her face equated the unfamiliar with derangement. Eleri could have laughed but did not: it was ludicrous, and sad at the same time, to think that this child of hers had emerged from the womb already curled, wanting no truck with hard edges. Eleri felt more spiked and angular than ever.

"I couldn't be bothered to get dressed," she said, appeasement on her mind.

"You should have come to me for company," Catrin said angrily. "I wouldn't have minded. After all, that's what I'm here for. You can't just let yourself go like this, Mother. How can you be comfortable in that lot?"

"I'm perfectly all right, Catrin. It's very warm, isn't it? I think we'll have thunder later."

Catrin sighed and sat down opposite Eleri. Her eyes were red from yesterday's weeping. Richard had been central to her life. Their pride in one another had always irritated Eleri: little blonde Catrin and her attentive Dadi. Even now, Eleri felt the sting of that childish need in the grown daughter to have a mother of her own choice.

"Perhaps it is time to get dressed," Eleri said, wanting Catrin to laugh, but no humorous response was forthcoming. "I think I'll sort out your father's stuff. Do you want to help?"

"You know the answer to that, Mother," Catrin said quietly.

As an uneasy truce, it was curiously painless - at least for Eleri.

She dressed carelessly. Her awareness of her body belonged to a far-off time. Now she clothed herself for comfort alone: brown cords, thick baggy sweaters in black or brown, suede boots. She supposed it was strange to have such long, untamed hair at her age, but it suited her way of being and, besides, when naked she took pleasure in the feel of it against her skin.

Catrin's curls were tamed and sleek: no hint of the social outcast there. These things became important to Eleri, an obsession she was unwilling to give up. It seemed vital to accentuate the differences between them.

They sat stiffly in the elegant sitting room, drawing the heavy curtains to shut out the looming threat of storm.

***

The sky thinned, vibrating like an animal-skin drum as pent-up atmospheric tension curdled clouds into metallic monsters. The bulging burlap of rain, cadaver-grey, loomed overhead.

Angela, placing food on the table to celebrate Heneghan's home-coming, felt the imminence of violent weather as a ringing in her ears and a sense of control slipping. The children were edgy, fussy. Heneghan, back at the head of table and family, waxed grim and taciturn and subtly combative. Windows rattled in warning.

The scraping of cutlery on plates grated in the sullen silence.

The sudden shocking glare, a neon knife of almost physical intrusion, was, in its way, a relief: lightning, fiercely and frenziedly close, bolted down in silvery tangles and illuminated the orchard in weird, blinding striations. Thunder, primal as the creaking of tectonic plates, followed - and then came the rain, an onslaught of sweeping and swiping viciousness; an insidious enemy swooshing in the giant footsteps of the booming and blundering light-and-sound gods to wreak havoc of a very different kind.

Tom cheered and clapped. Rushing to the window, he danced with excitement – and relief. The breaking of tension's thin skin above dwarfed the familial variety below.

Emboldened and heartened by the wild lunacy of nature, and her son's optimism, Angela went in search of the special pudding treat: fresh peaches, glistening in shades of sunrise upon five gold-rimmed plates. Clotted cream ready, she was about to go back when she heard Rachel's voice, raised, obstinate and red rag to Heneghan's ever-present bull.

'I don't like mushrooms, Dad. I've told you before. I'm not eating them...'

The crash of a knife upon the table and subsequent rattling of plates was, in its way, even more frightening than an outburst or a slap. The sense of boundless and unpredictable temper froze Angela where she stood. The unspoken had such ominous presence and weight in this world of external chaos and internal fear.

Even Tom's initial excitement over the storm had dwindled to the occasional apologetic half phrase.

Angela's wish, as she walked into the room, was to hide the peaches under her sweater, pretend they were not there, but the children knew and their faces told her that this was not possible. Her hands trembled as she lowered each plate into the heavy silence.

James's eyes asked permission to be pleased and Angela found she could not acknowledge the look. She cut her own fruit into quarters, putting off the moment of tasting. The sound of teeth working so mindlessly was beginning to irritate her.

High winds cornered the rain at each window bay. The family shivered in their cold room.

Heneghan's second peach stone was rotten: it split easily in half with a tap from his knife.

"Have mine," Angela said and pushed her plate over in his direction.

He glared at her until her eyes dropped.

"How generous," he spat. "Christ, some fucking homecoming this is. I had more fun in the hospital. What the hell's wrong with you all?"

"Nothing," Rachel mumbled.

Angela winced. Did the girl never learn when to keep her mouth shut?

"I said 'nothing'," Rachel's voice was louder this time. "We're all right. It's you...you that's..."

"That's what?" Heneghan said, his voice ominously quiet. "Eh, girl? You'd better have a good answer because I'm sick of your snide remarks."

"I don't know. If I knew I'd be able to do something about it, wouldn't I?"

"Christ all-bloody-mighty! You need a damn good hiding, you do. Is that the sort of thing they encourage in that school of yours?"

"We never get anywhere," Rachel said at length. "All these arguments and nothing is ever settled. I mean, what's the point in it all? Why do we bother? It seems so stupid."

Heneghan looked at her. His eyes were strange.

"What do you want - a gold star every time you're rude? You can't have it all your own way."

"I just want an ordinary family life without all this tension," Rachel said sadly.

Heneghan looked thoughtful. He hadn't barked straight back at the girl, Angela noticed with relief. He popped a quarter of the rejected peach into his mouth without thinking.

Angela had a sense of the futility of it all. She felt sympathy for Rachel, but could not see a way back into the situation without causing an almighty row.

The rain, settling, was depressingly steady. Angela wanted it either to bite hard or slacken off. Her awareness of working an analogy to suit her own needs saddened her. At times like this, she wished they were not all so careful with one another.

As lightning stitched another bright seam across the darkness, the door-knocker crashed, slipped and then crashed again. The unexpected noise startled them all and Angela rushed to the door, instinctively wishing to protect the caller from Heneghan's hostility.

Gwilym stood outside, hair flattened against his skull. He grinned and shook himself like a dog, a merry-go-round of braids sending water everywhere.

"Gwilym, hello. Good God, come in; you're soaking wet."

"Aye, love, it's pissin' down out there. Is 'imself back? Thought I'd drop in and see if 'e's still in the land of the livin'!"

Gwilym's vitality did not stop short at the lounge doorway. He bounded in, leaving damp prints over the hall carpet. Heneghan looked up and the two men's eyes met. Heneghan smiled.

Gwilym sat down with his customary energy. Things groaned in his presence. He lit a cigarette, offering the packet to Heneghan.

"How are you, then, man?"

Heneghan fingered the plaster on his head and winked. Gwilym brought back his sense of adventure, allowed him to view his accident as something more than a sordid drunken fall.

"You called the ambulance."

Gwilym sensed the hostility. Heneghan wasn't a man who relished being seen when down.

"Sright! Makes a change, mate; s'usually me carted off in the statistic-mobile with the blue flashin' lights!"

"Yeah, well..."

"It's a pity," Gwilym said. "There's this rodeo Saturday, out Tregaron way. I was gonna ask if you wanted to come along, ride in it mebbe."

Heneghan perked up at this.

"What are we now? Monday. Right, five days. Reckon I'll still come along; wouldn't mind seeing you fall off."

Angela brought coffee in and put a mug on the arm of Gwilym's chair.

"Great, love. Ta."

His blue eyes, twinkling up at her, were fond and knowing. She was glad to see guarded enthusiasm return to Heneghan's face.

Rachel and James slipped out bored, Angela suspected, by this talk of horses.

"Why don't you bring Tom, then? He can ride if 'e wants; they've got a section for under-twenties. I reckon you'd like it, Tom. What 'ya say, Mike?"

Heneghan looked at Tom. The boy was keen.

"Why not? I can pick up the pieces."

Angela wasn't so sure. The thought of her eldest being injured terrified her.

"What happens, Gwilym? I mean, is it safe?"

"Pretty much so, love: there's not far to fall and it's all done on good, soft grass-land. You get bounced about a bit, but nothin' bad. Any'ow, they don't give the real wild ones to younger people, not in my experience. You get 'oisted on, see, by this bar thing, then they let go and the 'orse goes rushin' off around the arena with you clingin' on like 'ell! They time it, see, and the winner of each section is the bloke that stays on longest. I've been goin' for years and I've never seen no serious accidents."

For Angela, that was good enough. She trusted Gwilym. He was completely reliable where it mattered.

"O.K, then, that's settled. You drive us, will you, Mike? I can't drive long distances except in an emergency: little misunderstandin' with a police car Saturday night. I was doin' 105 on the 'ome stretch and this pig was lyin' in a layby waitin' for me..."

Angela laughed, knowing Gwilym's famed lawlessness: he seemed to jump from one risk to the next, shrugging calmly if caught.

"I might just surprise you all," Heneghan said.

They looked at him but he would say no more.

Gwilym shivered.

"God, man, cold as a witch's tit in 'ere!"

"Yeah, well you know how it is," Heneghan said sardonically. "Convalescing man - can't do much and all that!"

"Bollocks!" Gwilym laughed long and loud. "Come on, Tom. Let's get some warmth into this morgue. Don't mind if I borrow ya boy do ya, Mike?"

"Go ahead! Keep him if you want."

"Typical Gwilym," Angela thought. "Only he could carry on like that without causing offence."

Gwilym and Tom rushed along the passage connecting kitchen to out-house. Rain seeped in through cracks in the wall; the passage smelled of mold, cobwebs and damp logs.

Gwilym stripped off his jacket and flung it over a hook.

"Got a lamp, Tom?"

"Yeah, hang on."

Tom took the lamp down. It was old, made of fine glass, beautiful.

"Nice! Where d'ya get it?"

"It belonged to my Great-grandad. Dad likes it a lot."

Tom pumped it up and then lit the little wick inside. It flickered and then flared, throwing long shadows on the walls. The rosy light was comforting, took the edge off the cold.

Gwilym heaved the wood horse into position and, with Tom's help, lifted a log onto the cross beams. Their shadows – one tall, the other much shorter - undulated beneath the swaying lamp. They took one end of the saw each. Sawdust buzzed, fell to the floor, flew up and into their eyes. Gwilym dropped the cut logs into a waiting basket.

"Right, Tom, where d'you keep the coal around 'ere? And newspapers - got any of those?"

Tom went off to find newspapers while Gwilym dipped the scuttle into the coal hole, then hefted the heavy receptacle along the passageway and into the living room.

The table, when they returned, was cleared. Heneghan and Angela sat in armchairs. The recent tension was gone.

Gwilym swept out the grate, and built a pyramid of small sticks, paper and coal. Tom put the log basket down by his side. Heneghan smiled.

"D'ya want the back boiler, Mike?"

"Might as well, Gwil. Saves on electricity a bit."

Gwilym twisted the dial so that the drawing heat would feed into the family's water system. Smoke ruined his efforts, pouring into the room.

"Shit! Must be somethin' up there. Get us a broom, Tom, quick!"

Handle first, Gwilym rammed the broom up the chimney. Soot fell, quenching the delicate flames. He felt the resistance just before the rook fell down into the grate.

Angela screamed.

The thing wasn't dead. It began to hop unsteadily around the room, one wing hanging, its feathers charred and burnt flesh showing through.

"Ugh! God! Get it out, Gwilym. I can't stand those things. It's coming towards me."

Attracted by the noise, the creature lurched in Angela's direction. She went white.

"Don't move," Heneghan said.

Gwilym flexed the broom and slid it slowly in the bird's direction.

"Get a shovel!" he hissed at Tom. "An' for Christ's sake shut the door after you; we don't want this thing wanderin' all over the 'ouse."

A strange noise was coming from the rook's scorched throat. Angela was close to tears, horror and pity so finely linked she couldn't sort them out. She wanted it dead or out, but not here, so terrifyingly close. The noise came again. Its eyes were dusky. Shit fell on the carpet behind it.

"Why doesn't it die?" Angela cried.

"Shh," Heneghan whispered.

Tom crept back in with the shovel and handed it to Gwilym.

"Right! Get ready to open that door quick when I say – an' then run to the front entrance. It'll try an' get off the shovel."

The rook swayed, a pitiful crackling sound in its ruined body.

Heneghan stood up silently and eased the door handle into his palm, waiting for the signal. Angela shut her eyes.

Gwilym slid the shovel along the carpet, stopping every now and then, watching the rook. It moved to the side. Gwilym changed tack. The shovel scraped on carpet pile and was suddenly lifted: the dying bird, caught off balance, had fallen into the centre of it.

Gwilym straightened up carefully and made for the door. Rain swirled outside. The rook tried to get up; the shovel swung dangerously. The bird was fading.

Gwilym shut the door behind him, not wanting Angela to see; then he put the rook down and, before it could re-orientate itself, smashed it over the head with the shovel. He knew its chances of survival out here, with a broken wing, were nil. The battered shape lay at his feet; he tossed it over the hedge and wiped the shovel in the wet grass.

Inside again, he rebuilt the fire and stepped slowly aside so that the warmth circulated.

They fell to discussing Eleri Morgan, and the weird new girl who'd suddenly turned up in the village one day. Gwilym, who knew more about this than he was willing to let on, just smiled.

If Angela, always more observant than her husband, noticed, she gave no sign; but Gwilym, for all his direct ways, saw a thing or two and, to him, she looked as if her bones had been sucked out, she was that relieved. He supposed it was getting rid of the bird for her. Women were funny like that.

When Heneghan turned on the television for the news, Gwilym left and made his way to the pub.

Angela got into bed first and lay watching, as Heneghan stripped carelessly in front of her. Even after three night, he looked thinner, frailer, the dark body hair standing out against his skin. His cock lay still. Angela had hoped otherwise but, seeing the way things were, she couldn't be bothered to do anything about it. He looked too tired for that anyway, she told herself, as she turned on her side and closed her eyes.

***

Heneghan slept immediately and then dreamed - which was unusual.

In his dream, he was back in the graveyard up on the hill. It was a dull, heavy day. He was aware of being both buried and visible at one and the same time. He shared the consciousness of Richard Morgan, though there was no panic or distress in this. He could see himself beneath the earth, with the wreaths wilting above and the birds calling in the trees; at the same time he stood, still in the black suit, behind a tree, watching and waiting.

The sense of anticipation was strong. The tree was winter-thin; time had passed speedily on from the dancing leaves. The grass was damp.

Eleri was on the sky line, far above him, on the back of a stallion. The horse was monstrously tall in the dream. It felt like coming up beneath a vast oil tanker outside Southampton Docks.

Even though Heneghan was standing, he felt as if he looked up forever to gauge the height of the horse - and somewhere, above that, was Eleri. She was wraithlike, possibly naked.

Heneghan was dream-jolted into a two a.m wakening. The room heaved with the aftermath of sleep. It had not been a nightmare as such, yet he felt disturbed – and, as he lay there, he puzzled over the slip in his memory's clarity: was she naked or not? For some reason, it mattered.

***

Gwilym hadn't believed Kate would be in the pub again, but there she was. He had to mentally kick himself as they walked up the silent road together later. She was small, sexy; he didn't know where she came from originally and he didn't much care. She'd moved in, that was the main thing, and he could see things brightening up around her.

The rain coughed a few times and stopped. Eleri felt the mountains behind her as she walked in the clear air. She had a sense she could go anywhere, do anything. In the darkness, she felt powerful and unafraid.

TUESDAY 7th

Heneghan sat in Eleri's front room. There had been no trace of the woman in his dream. She'd seemed friendly enough, though slightly vague and distracted, with the flour from some half-made recipe standing out against her dark skin.

She'd gone back into the kitchen immediately, leaving Heneghan in the wide velvet chair. He could hear the noise of her indifference and it stirred something in him. He placed a careful boot tip on his knee, watching the dust collect in the furrows of his cords. He wondered if Eleri had forgotten about him and, in a way, hoped she had, since it gave him the excuse simply to be here with nothing expected of him. He relaxed.

The identity of this latest visitor had hardly registered with Eleri: she'd switched instinctively to the standard procedure she'd adopted since Richard's death. She had no objection to people cluttering up the house and drinking tea as long as they made no emotional demands. She'd seen no reason to abandon her plans: visitors, she'd learned, could be entertained and kept at bay using a negligible part of her mind and energy.

Eleri waited by the oven door for her cake to rise, glad of the heat despite the warm and sunny day. She had no sense of time and only remembered the guest when the water she'd boiled for tea felt cool to the touch. It was then that the strangeness of this visit struck Eleri; normally, she'd have been besieged by now.

There was no sound. Heneghan wasn't doing anything; he simply sat in his chair, apparently uninterested in her possessions. It was refreshing to Eleri after the irritating predictability of people trying to read her character from her ornaments.

"Oh, you're still here, then?" she said, rather at a loss: usually, condolence-callers did all the talking for her.

Heneghan didn't reply; he just smiled at her.

She gave him his tea and he drank it, communicating pleasure through his eyes, disinclined to talk. Eleri waited, interested in spite of herself. She couldn't believe that he'd called for no reason, and that he wasn't eventually going to launch into the usual condolence speech. Maybe she ought to say it for him, get it over with, and then they could talk about something more interesting.

Accordingly, she looked full at Heneghan; something about him made honesty easy. She told him why she thought he'd called and precisely why she found this both painful and meaningless.

He listened, saying nothing, nodding from time to time.

Eleri faltered eventually, and realised she had nothing more to say. She'd said it, and the important had become unimportant in the process. She suspected this was true in many areas of her life, she said, looking up at Heneghan from her crouched position on the floor; then she mocked herself, imagining how she must appear in his eyes, curled like an aged child on the carpet.

Heneghan laughed at this and said that her imagination had nothing to do with him and if she wanted to torture herself on his behalf he wouldn't stop her. She found his laugh very open and bounding coming from such a tight mouth. She told him this too.

That was when he told her about the dream. Eleri picked fluff off the carpet and listened, unable to look at him now he was talking.

Heneghan glanced at her from time to time and saw that she was, indeed, like a child, with her long hair and strange eager face. He found calling her *'Eleri'* caused no effort of will, felt oddly comfortable with her.

Relating the dream made no more sense of it, but Heneghan found that he liked talking to Eleri; he liked her interest. Most of all he liked her lack of fear and he found himself telling her things he normally kept to himself.

In the end, Eleri set him making tea with her in the kitchen while she iced the cake. She felt happy with him perched silently on the stool, as she mixed butter icing in a Pyrex bowl. She felt a strong connection with him.

"Even the people die tidily around here," she said, not for one moment expecting him to know what she meant.

"No," he said. "You're wrong. It's not as tidy as you think, not with the slopes and hills as graveyards, and Cader Idris keeping watch."

"You mean things being wild and comfortable at the same time?" she asked.

"Yeah. You don't have to let it get you down," he added - rather cryptically, Eleri felt.

Time flew. Eleri had always sneered at this expression before and even now, with the seeds of understanding in her, she laughed at the thought of a fob watch with wings: incongruous, to put it mildly.

"Inc-what?" Heneghan queried, teasing her. His eyes were very bright.

She asked him to call again, as he shrugged back into the blue quilted body-warmer.

She watched him go, watched the roll of each foot and realised that the dream had moved her, both personally and as a painter. She got a soft pencil and her sketch book, wondering how close her interpretation would be to his vision. Eleri knew that she was assuming she'd see him again - and the thought gave her pleasure.

She began to draw, the hill emerging as a female shape enclosing the two men, who became one. The tree, perched on her abdomen shape, looked out of place, so she rubbed it out and started again, enjoying the sense of working with symbols.

Pale light flooded the page, giving her depth to work from. Casting her memory back to the funeral, she knew that was exactly the shade of colour she wished to incorporate into the final painting. She used pastels to mix it and experimented until she had a patch of pale lemon in one corner which pleased her.

Then she sketched Heneghan's face, softened as she'd seen it. Richard was mistier, less absolute. In the end, she cast literal representation aside and began on a male figure with two dead heads - one clearly Richard and the other Heneghan, with his wound unbound. Excitement flew through her fingers.

The finished painting was always both enriched and curiously undermined by the process. She knew, from past experience, that the place she reached in the end would simply be the culmination of each electrical moment; it would be the moment at which she recognised she'd exhausted the creative flow - and turned to something else.

As she worked, Eleri saw that Heneghan was gaining precedence over the two-headed death figure. He glowed even in the preliminary sketches.

She realised early on that the horse was the one thing she could dispense with. She didn't doubt its importance to Heneghan, but she had no sense of her own presence in a work involving the two men. She concentrated on Heneghan's face, using her pencil to express all he'd said: it was vitally important to her.

***

Kate had drifted here on the tide of rumour. This was an area where plentiful drugs could be had. They'd all said it, back in Oxford. Now there was Gwilym and an unknown village full of strange people.

It was a beautiful morning, warm and bright. Gwilym had risen early for work, leaving Kate shivering between flowered sheets. She'd heard him whistling cheerfully downstairs, and had wondered if he'd want her here when he got back. He'd said nothing and she hadn't dared broach the subject.

She'd gone down in the end, tightly wrapped in the quilt - unable, despite the nights on the beach, to get warm. Gwilym, in his blue working overalls, had been cooking a bacon sandwich for lunch, pouring thick sweet tea into a battered Thermos flask, flicking through The Sun. Seeing him like that had been a shock to her: he'd seemed so alien, rough and ready. He'd kissed her warmly and grinned.

The house, which had buzzed with his energy, now seemed flat to Kate. She didn't want to go into the village: she felt too shy, certain that she'd be stared at and whispered about. Then there were the tales Gwilym had told about the local people.

She was astounded that so rural a place could contain such violence and nastiness. She'd assumed they'd all be hard-working farming types, not particularly bright but kind and slow moving; instead she'd heard stories of wife beating, eccentric old women and lesbian activity. God, what the hell had she got herself into?

211

Those first two nights on the beach in Aberystwyth, she'd wondered whether she'd done the right thing coming here. Her mother's voice had panicked for her; a decent bed and a bath had seemed overwhelmingly important; she'd almost given up and gone home.

Then she'd met the boys from the university, and the constant strumming of Stefan's guitar - in the flat she'd shared with him and Martin on South Road - had reassured her, that and the initial handful of tentatively picked magic mushrooms on the first sunny evening. She'd even written a stoned poem the second day and Stefan had set it to music, twirling her hair as he created, humming and twirling.

That was when Gwilym had turned up. Known to them all – though not a student, and several years older - he moved in and out as the mood took him.

That night they'd all gathered on South beach, with a bonfire, and sung all Stefan's songs through, with him crying for Germany and Cornelia, whom he'd left behind.

Gwilym was the first person Kate had met who could roll a joint one handed; she'd watched, impressed, while he winked up at her. Then he'd gone, as abruptly as he'd arrived, leaving her to the sudden cold of the beach.

Martin had taken her, on the motorbike, to Gwilym's local the next day. A fast, exhilarating ride, a hundred and ten along the straight bits. Her ears had ached from the pressure.

Gwilym had arrived late, with two women, and Kate's heart had sunk, even when it became apparent that the two women were more wrapped up in each other than him. He'd joked with them all, completely at ease, funny, uncouth Gwilym, taller than everyone else and looking as if he had just stepped off a Viking warship. Kate had been fascinated and aroused.

Now, alone in a house she wasn't sure of, with farm sounds all around, she felt isolated and afraid. Her fear was that she would be found out and told to leave, though Gwilym had not worried.

"He's obviously done this before," Kate told herself dully.

Her greatest terror was that one of the villagers would call for some reason. Having heard about them, Kate didn't think she could cope. She huddled beneath the quilt, hoping she couldn't be seen from the window, alert to every sound.

When the gate opened, she had worked herself into such a state that she nearly screamed out loud. She tried to identify the stranger from Gwilym's descriptions: a man with two reddish-coloured dogs, knocking on the door; a man with a hat pulled down low, and no face visible because he searched the ground instead of the sky.

It was that Irish guy, she was sure of it, the wife beater, the one they all steered clear of. Kate froze, certain he could see her.

It didn't occur to her, since she hardly knew the man, that Gwilym was famous for his entertaining exaggerations. The stranger looked evil and that was enough for Kate. She fled upstairs and hid in the bedroom, ignoring the rapping on the door.

Heneghan, his head full of Eleri, wouldn't have cared if he had seen Kate.

***

When Gwilym returned, he found Kate still in bed. He was slightly surprised, but not angry: women had these funny moods, he knew from previous experience; perhaps it was her time of the month. He began to pull off his overalls, glad to be home.

"Get up now, and get us some tea, will ya, love? I'm starved!"

He could see she was a bit knocked aback by that; her face crinkled up. He smiled. Slowly she emerged. Gwilym watched with pleasure. He hadn't realised she was naked beneath the quilt; the sight of her tits peeping out did things to him.

He came over and grabbed her from behind, seeing the goose-pimples on her tanned flesh. Her back was warm against him. She began to respond, arching her body up and outwards against his, one nipple erect. His finger reached for the other one. The round weight of her breasts still amazed him. She was perfect, a very sexy lady.

"You stayin'?" he asked at length.

"I'm staying!"

"Great!" he said.

She laughed, delight filling her. He meant it. She made dinner, chops with loads of gravy, the way he loved it. She was aware of the sex flush all over her body. Gwilym, looking up from his food, saw it too and touched her hot face gently.

"I saw that Irish bloke today - you know, the one with the funny name?"

"Heneghan? Oh, aye?"

"He even looks unpleasant, don't you think?"

Gwilym laughed.

"HIm? Oh, 'e's got a bad reputation all right. Don't reckon 'e's been any nearer to Ireland than Manchester, meself- but 'oo knows, eh?"

"Is it true that he hits his wife, though?"

Kate was worried.

"Who knows, love? Most men give their missus a belt round the ear'ole from time to time, don't they? Don't mean nothin' normally. Like trainin' a dog, eh?"

Horrified, Kate stared at him.

"You are joking, I assume?" she snapped. "No one I know would put up with that kind of treatment."

"Sorry, Kate, me and my big mouth! Only teasin'! No, there's some blokes get a bit free with their fists after a night on the tiles, like, but that's not the way my mam and da brought me up..."

Kate felt her hunched shoulders drop a couple of inches.

"He knocked on the door," she confessed. "Sorry, I probably should have found out what he wanted..."

Gwilym laughed.

"Not dressed like that, you shouldn't! Not havin' 'im gettin' an eyeful of my girl. Na, don't worry: 'e probably wanted to talk rodeo."

Kate gawped at him. Rodeo? Here? Weird!

"I haven't drifted into the nineteenth century American Wild West by mistake, have I? You did say rodeo?"

"S'right, love! Fancy comin' along? Heneghan and 'is boy'll be there. You can get up close and personal if you want – but not too much!"

Kate smiled.

"They do say you should try everything except Morris dancing and incest, so – yes, count me in."

***

THURSDAY 9th

The urge to share the finished picture with Heneghan came upon Eleri suddenly. She was aware of a strange kinship – a wordless pulsating cord – with this man. It frightened the fastidious centre of her soul, but she yearned for its continuation at the same time.

Inability to cope with - let alone operate successfully in - day-to-day chattiness had long been her downfall. Incessant talk contaminated the inner realms. She would hide, pretend not to be in, rather than risk that feeling of insidious assault by the loquacious.

Catrin, a gaudy social dragonfly hovering above the deep ponds, had, without a doubt, suffered as a result of her mother's inability to be, as she put it, *'normal'* – and, in a shriek of frustrated rage, had once turned to Eleri and said, with sneering fury, "Has it ever occurred to you that you might be autistic? It'd explain a lot!"

Eleri had no doubts on that score, and was privately certain that she occupied one rung or another on the ASD ladder – but then *'normal'* did not appeal and never had.

Phones frightened her: the tinny sound; the domination of word-confident over shy and inarticulate; the angry misery of listening for over an hour to another's tedious story, all froth and no substance; the dulling sense of being lectured to – all meant an avoidance that was probably pathological.

And yet, she phoned Heneghan's number with barely a qualm, the probably tongue-trapped awkwardness between them oddly comforting.

As she said to him, "We humans rain words down because we have forgotten how to read one another…"

She covered the painting upon the easel with a soft cloth, paced and twitched.

Saying something is good is not the same as understanding it. Value judgments tend to be cerebral, and not from the cave where the crude pigments of creativity are mixed together and fired. So thought Eleri as she stood back and imagined Heneghan's reception of his naked self.

Bare-headed he stood before her, the black stitches on his forehead standing out lividly against still-pale flesh. He seemed tentative almost, a bruise of confusion marking that which could not be spoken.

So, she ushered him in, sat him down – and only then removed the cloth from the stark image on the easel.

Heneghan faced himself.

He whistled, a low and involuntary sound.

"Fucking hell, Eleri, that's just how I felt waking from the dream. How on earth…?"

"Sometimes…"

"…did you…?"

Their startled words clashed – but, signal strong, they tuned in.

"...I can just read people..."

"...know...yes, me too..."

She smiled at him, a touching relief in her face.

"It was so vivid - I mean the way you said it. It's the first thing I've wanted to do for months, feels like a release..."

Heneghan discouraged photographs of himself; seeing his face in miniature form was shocking, unexpected. He sat down on the sagging sofa, momentarily speechless. Eleri crouched by the easel, looking up at it.

"The thing is," she said, "I need to build your face up; it wasn't clear to me. I was working and reworking it until I realised there was something central I couldn't get at; something forgotten, I suppose. It's hard to explain..."

"And here I am, Eleri..."

"Yes..."

She was nervous, he could see that - and yet, there was a sort of light about her, the way there had been last time. Silence bound them for a long moment.

Heneghan stretched his arms out along the back of the sofa. Eleri began sorting through her pencils, a professional noting her medium. He was intrigued by her certainty.

"It doesn't matter so much for drawing," she explained, "but I like things to be just so: it helps the mood."

She asked him to move to a chair at the other end of the room.

"Don't pose," she laughed, seeing his instinctive rigidity. "Have a cigarette if you want; don't concentrate on what I'm doing. The more relaxed you are, the easier it is for me."

Heneghan lit a cigarette and tried to concentrate on not concentrating. It was difficult. He could see Eleri out of the corner of his eye and he felt she was all around him, the wild hair brushed out, a pencil held lightly in her left hand. He couldn't see the strokes she made, but he felt them in a dermal nervousness. He wanted to take cover behind his hand, but Eleri's slight frown stopped him. Curiously, Heneghan didn't mind. He liked her quiet assurance. Her commands were precise, minimal: she had him push aside the lock of hair obscuring the last of the stitches; she wanted his lips closed; he was to look slightly to the left.

After a while, it became pleasant, soothing; Heneghan sagged in the chair. She told him she needed more tension in his face; that the bones sank even with such a small bodily movement. Interest jerked him up. She was delighted; her hand worked faster, line after line. He was left in the sphere of the imagination.

"Do you want to look?" she said a while later. "It needs more work, but..."

She busied herself with the easel, as if ashamed of what she'd done.

His face confronted him.

"It's great, Eleri."

The light in her broke through.

***

Her mother-in-law's letter lay, like an unexploded bomb, on the kitchen table. Angela smiled wryly: apt imagery, given that this branch of the family lived alongside the simmering violence that was Northern Ireland.

Shaking, she slipped a knife under the flap at the back – and drew out the fragile airmail pages.

'1st October '80

My dear Angela,

Do forgive me for writing to you like this, secretly, and not including Michael, but Rory and I are very worried about him and have been since the visit he made over the summer, when you and the children were with your parents.

Has he said anything? Do you have any idea why he hasn't answered any of my letters? We had words, it is true - I'm sure Michael told you about that - but his father and I thought it was all settled before he came back over in August. He didn't tell us much.

I'd love to know what the children are doing. Thomas must be such a big boy now. Is he doing exams? I wonder, should we ring? You'll know what to do for the best, Angela; you've always been like a daughter to us.

With love to you all,

Mairead.'

Angela read the letter for the fourth time and still could not shift the shock of that first careless skim: it explained Mike's lengthy midsummer *'business'* trip; but why, she wondered, had he felt it necessary to pretend she was elsewhere?

She couldn't recall any recent communication between Mike and his parents, not since the awful quarrel at Kevin's wedding. She thought of the older woman's pain and confusion and felt worse than ever, for not realizing and unintentionally depriving Mairead and Rory of three of their grandchildren.

She knew Mike had hated it when they had moved back to Antrim after all those years in Carlisle. He'd taken it as a personal insult to have relatives living so close to Belfast and the Troubles.

"Bloody Irish mentality!" he'd said, scornfully, when Rory wrote to tell him. His shame and anger had created an undertone of tension in all family-related communications.

Angela wondered what to do. She felt guilty, as if she'd been carrying on a secret correspondence with her mother-in-law for months. However secretive Mike was, she felt her own deviousness keenly. She dreaded confronting him with her knowledge.

She thought about Mairead and Rory - and Niamh, Kevin and Padraig, Mike's siblings. Mike was different, but then he always had been. He was sharp as thorns, yet not as easily defined as the others.

She thought of him as a fencing sabre, wide when flat but slimmed to near-invisibility when viewed side-on. The other Heneghans were maces: they hit broad on and were consistent from every angle. Not for the first time, she wondered what it had been like for him growing up in that busy household. He said little about his childhood. Angela was left to supply her own fantasies.

Mairead was proud of all her children, and the many waifs she'd fostered. On visits, she loved to take out the old photo albums and show Angela. Mike rarely appeared. Mairead had explained that this was because he was the best photographer, had the steadiest hand. Angela, who'd seen the same thing repeated in his adult years, suspected a pathological dislike of any pictorial attempt to nail him down.

Mairead remained unashamedly and warmly Irish, and Angela wondered if Mike had felt in some way excluded by her vast maternal benevolence. For Mairead, with her brood of real and foster charges, *'the children'* had taken precedence over any individual child.

Angela knew she needed to respond, but it was difficult to get started. In her wish not to hurt, sheet after sheet was discarded as too formal and stilted. In the end she gave up and said it all straight regardless:

'9th October 1980

Dearest Mairead,

Your letter was a painful shock to me; I can't pretend otherwise. I've found it very difficult to respond. None of what you said was known to me. I had no idea Mike was in Ireland; I was most certainly not at my parents' house. I cannot think why Mike had to say that; it makes it sound as if we were unwilling to visit you and, Mairead, you must know by now that this is untrue.

The 'words' you had? That's news to me as well. Mike said nothing - but then, that will make sense to you in view of how little I was supposed to know about all this. Again, I cannot understand why he should keep something so important from me, especially if, as you suggest, it has somehow affected his mood since.

He causes me great concern too; you're not alone there. He's not very communicative at the best of times, but recently it has got much more obvious. I honestly had no idea that you had ever written.

My worry is that I could make things a lot worse by mentioning any of this to him: I fear he would think it was a conspiracy against him.

I wish I could reassure you, but that presupposes a level of knowledge I don't even have myself. All I can say is that I'll do what I can to sort things out this end. I think it best not to phone - for the moment at least. I'm afraid he'd take it the wrong way.

What I would like to say, is this: please don't stop writing to Mike. I'm sure he appreciates it at some level, even if he cannot admit to it or respond in kind.

Thomas is in his fourth year at school. We hope he'll get enough CSEs to get into Agricultural College.

The children often ask about you and Rory and wonder when we will visit again.

Love to you both,

Angela.'

She read it through several times, regretted every word, but couldn't bring herself to change as much as a full stop.

She looked up. It was nearly dark. Had it really taken that long? She wondered where Mike was. It occurred to her suddenly that she hadn't seen him for hours. She imagined him wandering, uncertain of his bearings, and felt fear.

***

Heneghan sat in the forested area above the Pritchard place, near where Pritchard's donkey was tethered, and laughed aloud. The laugh went its own way and gurgled back at him when he least expected it. Silver sun patches, lithe as eels, swam over the boulders.

He could see Old Pritchard, far below, braced against the field's slope, baling the hay - to the cattle's intense curiosity. Wind ripped deftness from the old man's hands; his curse snaked up through the shorn ground.

He looked up and, seeing Heneghan, waved.

Heneghan had walked through heedlessness and the map's inch of miles until his energy had abated and he sat for warmth and sun alone. His contentment had a face: his own, for the first time in his life.

Eleri's hand had found things he backed away from; seeing them, and recognising the courage of her gesture, he felt free to be with her. He wondered how old she was, whether she'd been happy with Richard, what she thought about.

Her honesty had been a mirror for him to look into; it hadn't reflected her. He could see this now, with uncounted hours separating them. She was strangely hidden. He felt she'd eluded him.

The old man bobbed up and down behind a hedge of black faces. The facial crags beneath his hat jutted even from this distance. He was a hard man, Heneghan knew: hard right through in a way that he envied.

The man turned, without fear, from the cattle, and limped back to the house, the orange bale-string belt vivid against the hills and fields.

The touch of envy passed. With new insight, Heneghan thought of the painting Eleri would do of Old Pritchard. The way the old man had blended in with his surroundings had given Heneghan a clue, but he was battling with unfamiliar thoughts and he could only latch onto confused images of grey land and light and paintings.

The paintings were concrete and therefore slid more easily into his mind. He'd been in Pritchard's house several times, but had never previously made the link between the man and his wall prints. He saw them as an extension of the man's character: indifferent landscapes, and the chapel-fearing Welsh dame with the devil cunningly hidden in her shawl.

He never knew afterwards how long he sat there; but it was dark and the pins-and-needles had long since given way to numbness before he moved on, back to his house.

***

SATURDAY 11th

Saturday morning, Gwyneth Pritchard watched her husband take bacon rind and chop bones to Lad, the old dog in the yard. He didn't know she could see him; had he known, the uncharacteristic pat on the dog's head would have been modified, and there would have been no pink tongue snaking out to lick the man's hand. Gwyneth knew how soft he was underneath, but she respected his decision to keep it well hidden.

"There's daft you are, *cariad*," she said to herself and dodged behind the curtain lest the sight of her gave him cause for shame.

Six in the morning struck.

***

It was cold. Heneghan pulled on two thick sweaters and the body warmer for extra protection. He buzzed with the frustrated energy, needed to get out of the house. Hunger approached in a wave and passed by.

Penning a few lines for Angela, he left the house.

He lit a cigarette and drove towards the first faint stirrings of sun. The road was deserted and he drove fast, enjoying the silence.

He felt wide-awake and full of anticipation. It was hours before he had to meet Gwilym, and pick up Tom. Breakfast in town, away from the family, appealed.

***

Angela read Heneghan's note with a sinking feeling.

'Just nipped into town to do some business. Back later. Don't wait in.

Mike.'

His bold signature held her as ever. She'd never got over the surprise occasioned by his handwriting and, particularly, that big Italic *'Mike'* – always written in black ink.

During the good times, it gave depth to their intimacy, and an unspoken erotic charge. She wasn't sure what it signified now. She wondered what he was up to and, in a spasm of distrust, imagined him driving to catch the Liverpool - Belfast ferry. She felt she would put nothing past him these days: he could be anywhere, and she wouldn't know a thing.

"You devious bastard," she said out loud, glad the children were still in bed.

She thought of all the agony she'd gone through writing to his mother and sending the letter, knowing she wouldn't hear a thing for at least a week, probably more, and thought, "Christ, is he worth it?"

She wondered why she was protecting him.

If she hadn't been alone and distraught, Angela would have suspected that she was over-reacting; but, with the events of the past two months, she was no longer able to be rational. He was out, gone again, and could be away for hours, days even, while she waited here, trying to fit her life into that dreaded mold of loneliness. She reached for the phone, and dialled Mairead and Rory's number.

***

Heneghan felt on top of the world. He'd escaped the family for a few hours and it had been incredibly easy. He wanted to celebrate: The Cabin, which he normally avoided - feeling it to be too pretentious for his taste - now seemed the perfect venue.

A triangle of the Irish Sea, silky-grey, peeped between the buildings as he walked. The wind was apologetic for this time of year.

He strode fast, having no wish to get Eleri out of his thoughts. Figures scuttled past. They seemed ant-sized to him: he felt he could squash their tiny bodies, and total lack of significance, underfoot.

Walking into the café, he saw a few familiar faces. He nodded and was nodded to in return. A sprinkling of lecturers sipped orange or rose tea and discussed poetry in languid voices. The café's owner shifted up and down the counter like the margin-setter of a typewriter.

Heneghan ordered a coffee, focusing his eyes on the large number of students as he waited. Their posing in Army greatcoats and collarless shirts irritated him, and he felt relieved that his formal education had stopped after O' levels.

"Bunch of wankers," he said to himself. "Never done an honest day's work in their pampered lives!"

Heneghan slid lower in his seat. The blend of public school arrogance, sense of entitlement and endless posing got his goat. Tea, in a variety of flavours, dripped into saucers.

More people came in and slotted into their accustomed places. Thoughts of the rodeo sharpened Heneghan's mind. He began to count off his preparations.

***

Kate still wasn't sure what a rodeo was, though with only fifteen minutes to go, she had little imagining-time left.

"Don't dress nice," Gwilym had said before going off to work.

She had no idea what he meant. This place was so different from anything she was accustomed to, it was a constant shock to her. The social rules were not yet clear to Kate - and her imagination, in this area, was not strong enough to improvise.

She settled for casual elegance, glad of Gwilym's absence. She'd already discovered how devastating his affectionate laughter could be, and had no wish to invite it now.

Her curiosity about Heneghan had not diminished: she wondered about his face, his voice. She had no idea what she would say to him if, by some unlucky chance, they were left alone. She resolved to stick like a tick to her man. She brushed her hair for the third time and dabbed a bit more scent behind her ears.

Even after only four weeks, Kate was aware that certain neighbours were emerging as individuals from the general cloud. She played games of *'spot the eccentric'* on the bus, making outrageous stories up about the people she saw. She was amazed at how fashionable the teenagers were; somehow, she'd thought they'd all be in animal skins and woad.

A car stopped at the roadside. Kate looked out. She recognised it as Heneghan's Rover, the TR7 being too small to fit them all in.

Gwilym jumped out and called her. She found her legs were shaking, but she walked out slowly, trying to appear at ease.

The boy in the back seat had opened the door for her and was staring. Kate blushed and got in.

"Mike, Tom; this is Kate."

Gwilym slammed his door shut and turned to smile at Kate. Heneghan nodded and muttered something which might have been, "Hello". Tom smiled shyly and went back to the programme of events he was studying.

The two men were looking at a map. Kate heard snatches of their conversation drifting her way. None of it made any sense.

The car's power was a shock to her, after weeks of walking and taking the bus; but she enjoyed the speed and the sense of going somewhere definite. Soon, the interior was wreathed in Woodbine smoke. Gwilym passed his cigarettes around with his usual generosity, even offering one to Tom, thereby producing the first laugh from the silent Heneghan.

Tom had been tempted for a moment, she had seen that, but the reassurance he wanted from his father had not been forthcoming. Kate supposed he didn't dare strike out for himself in these matters.

Having wanted to avoid Heneghan at all costs, Kate now found herself possessed by a perverse desire to hear his voice; but she could think of nothing that would guarantee an answer from him.

Her interest in the countryside waned after a while; bored, she turned to Tom and asked him about the rodeo. His enthusiasm pleased her, though she noticed that he would not look at her while he talked.

"Like father, like son," she thought to herself.

She warmed to the boy: he was like a puppy, she thought, ungainly and eager to please.

They found the place with no difficulty: signs flagged them down for a mile. Heneghan drove up the lane and turned left into a field. The whole area was dotted with land-rovers and horseboxes, leaving the arena just visible. It looked huge to Kate.

She realised that she had worn the wrong clothes straightaway and felt irritated. She hated ruining shoes - and the ground, mined with manure, looked far from promising. She considered staying in the car, but Heneghan's ominous patience oppressed her. She could have coped with the violence her imagination had supplied; it was the faint tapping of his car keys against the bonnet that frightened her.

Everyone seemed to know where to go and the men strode ahead, oblivious to Kate and her thoughts. She was disappointed by the arena, couldn't understand what was so special about log fences and corrugated-iron enclosures. Mulishness rose in her.

The place was heaving with eager-faced people, barging each other out of the way to get a better look. Horses of all shapes and sizes, uniformly terrifying to Kate, were crammed into the enclosure. Their efforts to escape were as vicious as the movements made by the humans.

Kate felt herself being shoved from behind.

"Come on, missus, move. We want to see this even if you don't!"

She was forced right up against the fence before she knew what had happened. The stench of horse was overpowering. She panicked. She couldn't see any of the others. The blast of a whistle produced a ragged silence.

Kate watched without interest as a succession of men leaped around the ring, mainly without their mounts, to roars of encouragement from the spectators. The falling-off spot was usually feet from the start, and the

riders limped out with exaggerated cries of pain and anger.

The whole thing felt barbaric, and vaguely embarrassing, to Kate, especially when a man wearing full cowboy gear, guns and all, appeared, only to hit the dirt seconds later. Kate felt nothing but pleasure when he was kicked soundly in the rear by the horse as it galloped off without him. She laughed so loudly that several people turned round and glared at her.

The microphone spluttered into life again. Kate imagined a wizened old farmer bellowing down it.

"Right! We've got something a bit different for you today, boys, by special request. We're having a race, two men in there at the same time. One of them's a reg'lar here: Gwil, the Viking; y'all know him! He wants the best of three - different horses each time, he says, to let the other bloke have a fair chance of losing. Here they come now: the Viking's on the bay gelding; Mike Heneghan's on the sorrel mare. Get ready, lads! Open that gate, boyo!"

The logs fell away and there an explosion of colourful motion. Gwilym grinned at Heneghan, whose horse was going backwards. The sorrel backed delicately into the arena, swept by a wave of laughter. Gwilym held the mane casually in one hand but it was obvious, even to Kate, that he was good.

The bay leaped towards the fence and Kate closed her eyes in terror. When she looked again, both men were on the ground, Gwilym making a slow "V" sign in the direction of his departing horse. Heneghan's face was grim as he got up.

They were just out of Kate's sight as they remounted, so she saw nothing more until the logs went down for the second time. Bets were hissing round the ring: the man behind Kate offered a round of beer against Heneghan winning. Gwilym, as an old hand, was clearly the favourite.

Tension mounted as the horses crashed round to the half-way mark. Both men were still seated. Kate wondered what it felt like, being on an animal whose one aim in life was to get rid of its rider. She realised that she was starting, reluctantly, to move from boredom to mild enthusiasm.

Just as Heneghan fell off for the second time, closely followed by Gwilym, Tom squeezed through the crowd with two hot dogs in his hand. He gave one to Kate and smiled a little uncertainly. She was touched by this - and the hot dog, though vaguely medicinal in taste, was a welcome source of warmth.

"Did you know this was going to happen?" she shouted.

"No!" he yelled back. "Good, aren't they?"

Kate's boredom returned in full force. This whole thing was going on far too long, in her opinion.

Tom hovered uneasily by her side, aware that her attention had wandered from him, aware also that he liked her.

A vast cheer went round the ring, jolting Kate and Tom out of their separate apathies. Men were stamping their feet and calling out amiable profanities.

Kate, who'd lost the drift of the action, couldn't think what was going on, especially when a different, younger voice came over the air speaking in Welsh.

"What's he saying?" Kate hissed in Tom's ear.

Tom blushed.

"I don't know," he confessed. "I'm in bottom set for Welsh."

"Be quiet!" yelled a man behind.

"Don't be unkind now, Dafydd; girl doesn't understand."

"Shouldn't come here if she doesn't learn the language, should she?"

"Don't pay no mind to him; he's a miserable old bugger," the second man said. "Announcer's saying that the winner of the race was Gwil, the Viking, but the other bloke - can't remember his name - was pretty good for an unknown. There now, he's inviting him back again. *Duw*, he must have been good, mun!"

"Thank you," Kate said, but her mind was still focused on the angry words from the man called Dafydd. She felt hurt and shocked.

"Come on!" Tom shouted. "There's Dad and Gwil. Here! Dad!"

He leaped up and down, waving his arms about. The men around the ring nudged each other and smiled indulgently.

Kate stood face-to-face with Heneghan for the first time. He was smiling; she smiled back.

"Great, Dad! It was really great!" Tom said.

"You next, Tom," said Gwilym. "Just cling on like 'ell and 'ope for the best!"

The boy was holding on to his father's arm. Heneghan turned back to Kate.

"What d'you think of it then?" he asked.

His voice was deep, harsh, with a slight Mancunian accent, very much as Kate had suspected it would be. Honesty battled with the fear of Heneghan's reputation, and won by a short head.

"I thought it was dead boring," she said.

To her surprise, he laughed.

"He's not bad looking," Kate thought. "Only his eyes are a bit shifty and close together."

She tried to imagine him hurting someone.

"It's not really a women's thing," Heneghan said. "I've never seen a female at one of these dos. They don't encourage them around here."

Kate suspected she was being warned. Gwilym laughed and tapped her on the bottom.

"She has other uses don't you, love."

The implied intimacy was faintly alarming to Kate, although she saw no corresponding interest in Heneghan's eyes. She sensed she wasn't the type of woman he went for, and didn't know whether to be relieved or disappointed.

The two men turned to Tom, giving him advice. The boy was clearly nervous: he was biting the inside of his mouth with shaky concentration.

Despite the boredom of having to watch yet more of this deadly event, Kate experienced a certain sympathy for Tom, and imagined that he'd been bullied into this.

The microphone flushed all the young boys out of their hiding places. They ran towards the start.

"Come on." said Heneghan. "I want to get closer, can't see Tom very well from here."

Tom, third in line, fell off as soon as the logs came down. Heneghan laughed. Kate yawned her way through the rest of it, hoping that there was nothing else planned,

A huge farming boy, repellently dense-looking to Kate, won the section. She vowed never to come here, or anywhere like it, again. She was in this area to explore its psychedelic opportunities, not to go tramping through fields in the wake of male egos.

They walked back to the car, the two men and Tom going through each event in minute detail. Kate felt miserable and left out. She wished she'd done something that merited the excitement and congratulations of the others.

Caught up in their own world, they ignored her and Kate, who loathed not being the centre of male attention, sulked, hoping they'd notice her silence.

She stomped deliberately through a vast steaming pile of horse shit, taking a masochistic pleasure in the further ruination of her shoes.

The car, warm after the field, glided away in a gale of laughter. Kate left them to it and cleaned her shoes on Heneghan's back-seat carpet, hoping to leave a permanent stain.

Heneghan dropped Kate and Gwilym at the gate and drove off.

"You didn't like that much, love, did ya?" Gwilym said, putting his arm around her shoulder. He smelt of horses, but it was comforting to be held.

"No," she said dismally.

"It don't matter," he said and smiled. "I like you just the way you are."

They walked into the house.

***

Heneghan knew something was wrong the minute he came into the kitchen. Angela's face was grimmer than he'd ever seen it. She told Tom to go upstairs. The boy looked surprised, but did as he was told.

"I phoned your parents," she said.

"That's nice," he said, keeping his back to her.

"No, it wasn't nice. It was bloody upsetting, if you want the truth. Your mother was in tears."

Heneghan sat down.

"Why? What's happened?"

"Don't say it like that," Angela said, "just don't. I've spent most of the afternoon trying to pacify your mother, feeling a complete idiot because I didn't know what the hell was going on."

"Nobody told you to interfere," Heneghan said coldly.

"For Christ's sake!" Angela yelled. "This has gone on long enough. I'm tired of your silences and your deviousness. Marriage is supposed to be about sharing, you know. You never tell me anything; you keep it all to yourself, like a miser. What are you waiting for: the perfect woman to come along, so you can tell her everything?"

"Maybe she already has," he taunted. "The perfect woman, I mean. You wouldn't know, would you?"

"She must be a brainless, desperate trollop, whoever she is," Angela countered, glad to see Heneghan's face flush with anger.

They sat in silence. She wanted to shake him like a rat. He looked away.

"Why are you shutting me out like this, Mike?"

"I don't like idle chit-chat! People are all gossip, gossip, gossip, letting other folks' secrets out all over the place."

"I suppose I'm included in that category, am I?"

"You? You're the worst of the bloody lot - going to my parents behind my back. I'll bet you enjoyed your little talk with them."

"Oh, come on, Mike," she said. "That's not fair and you know it."

"All right, then, why suddenly phone my parents out of the blue?"

"Because I had a letter from them, that's why! A letter all about you and your pathetic mysteries and how worried your mother is. Ringing any bells?"

"I'll bet my dad had nothing to do with this," Heneghan said viciously. "You bloody women talk too much, have nothing but endless boring chat in your heads. You're as bad as she is: all this deep meaningful stuff, trying to get into people's souls. If I want to tell you something, I'll do just that - and if I don't, tough shit: there's nothing you can do about it."

"But you don't tell me things, do you? That's the whole point. That's why I'm making a fuss."

The phone rang in the hallway.

"If it's my cow of a mother, you can tell her I'm dying!" Heneghan said, walking out.

"If it is her, you can tell her yourself!" she yelled back.

It was Eleri.

Her cool voice eased Heneghan immediately.

"I'm going out," he said, returning briefly to the kitchen.

"Your fancy woman, I suppose?" Angela said, glaring at him.

"No, I'm going cruising in a gay bar."

"About your level," she muttered. "Don't bring anything nasty back."

He went, leaving her with the feeling that she'd made no impression at all. She wondered if he did have another woman – and, if so, who she was. He'd avoided the issue, as always, hiding behind anger and coldness.

She felt guilty for talking about him with his parents. The sense of guilt made her feel angry. After all, how was she to find out what was going on when he never told her?

"Give him up," the voice of her strengthening courage said. "Throw the bastard out."

**

Eleri stood in the lighted doorway, waiting. Heneghan, who had exceptionally keen eyesight, saw her from a distance and his heart beat quickened. He fought, and won, the uncharacteristic wish to break into a run.

Eleri could have been waving or shielding her eyes; Heneghan wasn't sure.

They walked in. The smell of Turpentine was strong. Eleri seemed dazed, remote, though she was friendly enough.

She took him into the studio: already it seemed familiar, a welcoming place to Heneghan. The tension began to leave him.

The easel was covered. Eleri looked secretive, a light smile touching her mouth. A flicker of excitement, half sexual and half something else, waved the skin across Heneghan's belly. He did not know what she wanted; her silence was intriguing.

"It's come through at last," she said. "The thing I've been looking for. You might not like it."

Heneghan watched as Eleri removed the easel drapes. She was right; he didn't like it but, God, it was powerful. He stood, naked, braced against a gigantic hill. There was a faint ghostliness about the central figure and, when he looked more closely, he saw a delicate suggestion of Richard hovering behind. It made Heneghan's flesh creep. Eleri's understanding of his body was uncannily exact. He wondered how she could have known.

He was not shatterproof after all.

He expected her to be disappointed when he told her his feelings about the picture. The fact that she wasn't surprised him. She said honest feedback was all that mattered: that creative artists who took all criticism personally tended to become stuck in a rut of self-pity and fear.

"'*Like*' is such an insipid, meaningless word," she said. "There's got to be more than that: somewhere in the creative process where you can travel beyond safety.

You like what doesn't threaten you - and my painting is threatening because it's about you. I want to jolt people. If I can do that, then I have succeeded, regardless of liking."

Her frustration moved Heneghan. Her hands shaped the things she could not express. He saw what she meant and admired her for it. He could see she was trembling.

"It does things to you, too, doesn't it?" he said, with a rare flash of insight.

Eleri sat down, suddenly deflated, and buried her head in her hands. Her words filtered through in muffled bursts.

"Richard was known as a benign person, Mike," she said. "But his kindness was skin-deep and largely self-serving, only it took me most of our married life to see that. He was a coward; he'd do anything for a quiet life. He was as nice to me as he was to the dog, the cat, the garden, his mistresses; there was no difference, no sharpening. It's as if he dedicated his life to a safe middle course and my passion unnerved him. He was pleasant to everyone, but it was meaningless because he would never come out of his groove to be counted.

"He'd have betrayed me in the name of kindness - and that, to me, is more dangerous than any viciousness or evil intent. I'm sorry; I'm going on, I know that - but it

250

only hit me when he was dead: how angry I am; how I hated the whole softness of him; how I wish he'd stood for what he believed in and put me first..."

"Is that why he only appears as a ghost in your painting?"

"I suppose it is. I didn't want him in it at all, but the anger was there to be reckoned with and I couldn't move on while it was blocking me out - so I included it and painted him as I saw him, a ghost vaguely wandering through a half-life. God, Mike, he was dead even in life - and I've lived so many years with that. It's such a waste, but then people all seem like wraiths to me now - all except you, that is. I think you're the only real person I know. Jesus."

Her head was slowly emerging. Heneghan smiled at her. She shook her hair back.

"Bit ironic really," he said. "My wife's convinced I'm having an affair. God, if she could see us now, she'd laugh."

"Do you? Have affairs, I mean?" Eleri asked.

Heneghan hesitated. Virility fought against honesty.

"No, I don't. I don't like people depending on me and that, from what I can see, is what an affair eventually becomes, however excitingly it starts. My wife knows I'm not carrying on with anyone else, but she needs an

251

excuse, see, for being angry with me - and, I suppose to explain all the things she doesn't like about me; only she's not honest and direct..."

Eleri noted his reluctance.

"You don't have to talk about her if you don't want to. After all, Richard is dead; it doesn't matter what I say about him now."

"No, it's not that," Heneghan said. "I'm not much of a one for words - I think you know that - and I've got out of the habit of talking. I find you easy to talk to because you don't expect me to be open. We were arguing, my wife and I, when you phoned – and I was bloody glad to get away, whatever she thought. I can't stand the way she goes on: she hints but doesn't tell the truth. I think she'd rather believe I was having an affair than face the truth that I simply don't want to talk to her most of the time."

"But why don't you talk to her, Mike?"

"Because she expects it and I hate doing what's expected of me; I hate doing as I'm told. She can't play that game with me. I'm not a bloody idiot. You're a relief, Eleri, you really are. You don't know the half of it."

"I'm a painter, Mike. I resist being anyone's relief because it's inevitably a temporary state of affairs. The greatest security, I find, is in my art. It's the only place where people don't manipulate you for their own ends. Like you, I haven't had affairs, but I've come close. What's stopped me each time is the knowledge that I am only a part-time balm to these men - and, after that's gone, where does that leave me? Nowhere."

"What if a man left his wife for you?" Heneghan asked.

"Don't be naive, Mike. Only one man in a thousand is willing to trade the known secure world for uncertainty - and I have yet to meet that one man."

Hostility had inched its way between them.

"Would you leave your wife for me - or any other woman?" Eleri asked.

Heneghan thought about that one. It seemed important to her.

"I don't know. The question has never arisen."

"Richard vacillated," she continued bitterly. "He was not committed to me, but he certainly wasn't committed to any of his mistresses either. He wanted the best of both worlds - but the agony, the car crash that every affair actually is, he left to us, his women."

"Isn't that a bit unfair?" Heneghan asked.

"Oh, I don't know, Mike. I'm confused about it all. Talk to me about art and I'm as clear as could be, but..."

Her fragile bitterness stirred a gentleness Heneghan hadn't felt for many years. He put his arm round her and hugged her, feeling her initial stiffness give way to desperate need. He could feel her body shaking and he knew, although her face was covered, that she was crying. She felt good to hold, warm and vulnerable.

He kept quiet, sensing that she needed the physical comfort more than any advice. Eventually, she grew calmer and he tensed, expecting her to pull away in a spasm of harsh regret; but she didn't and her watery smile was completely trusting.

Getting slowly up, Eleri went through no compensatory moves. Her body remained soft and relaxed as she made mugs of coffee and brought one to Heneghan. The bond between them shivered out its intensity. They sipped the coffee in silence. There was no need for words and, when Eleri looked at Heneghan, he did not try to avoid her eyes.

"Thank you, Mike," she said as he left, and she kissed him gently.

***

MONDAY 13th

Miriam stared at Heneghan as he walked down the farm track. In her mind, the blood stains, from the rabbit he'd shot all those weeks ago, were still visible. It was for this that she hardened inside whenever she saw him.

It was still mostly dark, and the dullness of the orange walls depressed Miriam. She'd painted them that colour so that there'd be the illusion of sun even in the depths of winter. The failure of her attempt seemed like spite, the underlying harshness of this land and its people.

"Where else," Miriam thought bitterly to herself, "would the pathetic antics of one unpleasant man get so much attention and coverage?"

Miriam was envious: for all his nastiness, Heneghan was at least an accepted member of the community; he had his place.

Miriam heard Flora's footsteps behind her, felt the warmth of the other girl's body pressed against hers. Flora yawned.

"Couldn't you sleep?" she asked.

"No," Miriam said shortly. "I was watching Heneghan."

"Oh, him," Flora said and laughed. "How boring."

Miriam turned away from the window and smiled at her lover: Flora looked absurdly young in the long white nightdress, fair hair out of its usual plait and reaching her waist.

"So are you going to stand there and watch the dawn? You never know, the sight of you might stir Heneghan's baser instincts when he returns. How d'you fancy a bit of early morning sex, Heneghan style?"

"We don't know he's some kind of sex fiend," Miriam said weakly.

Flora giggled.

"You've heard what they've all been saying about him, all those worthy village gossips? O.K, they love to spread rumours, but I reckon there must be some truth in it."

Miriam struggled to be fair.

"Not necessarily, Flora. They hate him around here - I'm not surprised, mind you! - and people will make up stories to discredit those they dislike."

"Granted," said Flora. "But, Miriam, no one calls another human being a sexual abuser for nothing."

Miriam shivered.

"I hadn't heard that one," she admitted. "I know he's supposed to be carrying on with that widow up the road, and everyone says he beats his wife up, but..."

"O.K, listen to this then: I went to the shop the other day. There were about six of the prize gossips in there - took me about an hour to get served, but I'm glad I stayed: they spent the entire time talking about him. That Mrs Jones from the village (you know: the one you call Mrs very tidy!) said that the reason he came here so suddenly was because he'd shown an unnatural interest in some young girl up north and the police were after him. They think he's changed his name too."

"My God," said Miriam.

"Yes, well, have you ever heard a kind word said about him? Even Gwilym has reservations - and he likes, or at least tolerates, everyone."

Excitement flared in Miriam.

"If only we could find something positive out, we could report him to the police."

"I bet that's exactly what the gossips are saying to one another. You wait, Miriam, before long, they'll all be making friends with his wife, getting themselves invited for coffee mornings, having a good old nose..."

"It might not be such a bad thing, Flora. Poor woman; I should think she could do with a few friends. She probably has no one to turn to when he hits her. It's her I feel sorry for in all this. If Heneghan has done something, the chances are he'll get found out eventually, especially with our local ladies on the scent.

"But then, what about her? He sounds like a lousy husband, but at least he's someone. Don't get me wrong: I can't stand the man, and I'd love to see him being carted off, but she's going to be far worse off."

Flora tensed suddenly.

"Sshh, Miriam. There he is!"

It was too dark to see clearly, but it looked as if Heneghan was carrying something.

"You bastard," Flora hissed.

Miriam knew that a large part of Flora's anger was fear: the younger girl felt vulnerable living here, she always had, and Heneghan frightened her more than she was prepared to admit.

Miriam wondered what they could do. Making friends with his wife was out of the question; it was too obvious and, in any case, it sounded as if the poor woman was going to be inundated with new friends in the near future. She was aware that Heneghan and his wife had children – and wondered if any of them were still young enough to be at primary school.

***

Eleri was painting when the front door bell rang, and her immediate reaction was to ignore it. She only moved because she thought it might be Heneghan.

She was unprepared for the two women who stood there. She knew them - they'd both been at Richard's funeral and, further back, in her class at school - but their names, in the shock of seeing them, escaped her.

Relief that she'd locked her paintings away mingled with intense irritation at their arrival; but she invited them in, not knowing what else to do.

They clucked like quail, on the journey down the hall, making comments which Eleri chose not to hear. She wished she could remember what the hell they were called.

As she made the tea, Eleri suddenly remembered: of course, it was that woman who'd plucked at her arm after the funeral - Helydd what not - and Janet Davies. Eleri's spirits sunk.

Those two were the acknowledged leaders of the local gossips; there was nothing they didn't know. For years now, they'd been trying to interest her in their slanderous wares, but Eleri had resisted with ease. Their arrival spelled trouble one way or another.

Eleri's hands shook as she set cakes out on a plate for them. She thought wistfully of Heneghan, who would never have expected this fuss to have been made of him. She wished he was in the room with her.

Finally, when she knew she could put it off no longer, Eleri joined her unwelcome visitors in the stiffness of the sitting room. She noticed how uncomfortably they sat in their chairs, as if enjoyment were a sin. She gritted her teeth.

"Give them a chance, Eleri," she told herself.

Helydd peeled off her gloves and started on the weather. Janet reached for the cakes and contributed her bit on the W.I jumble sale.

Eleri nodded and tried to smile, but, beneath, she was frantic with tension and fear. Their smiles never wavered: Eleri felt as if she were facing a pair of man-eating sharks.

She knew that the moment of truth had arrived, when they put their cups down gently on the saucers. She poured herself another cup, partly out of spite and partly to delay the inevitable. Both ladies declined her mimed offer.

"Well, Eleri," Helydd began, "it grieves me to have to say this to you, but there's been things said - about you and a certain young man."

Helydd looked at Eleri, as if waiting for her to burst into denial.

"Yes, it has been noticed, you may be sure, and it's not seemly, not for a woman your age, with her husband in the ground only a matter of weeks. You have your position within the community to keep up. It's not right."

The two women droned on, perfectly in time, each taking a few lines. Eleri let the expected phrases wash over her, until the word *'sex'* jolted her out of herself.

"What was that you said?" she asked.

Janet, who'd been talking at that point, looked flustered: evidently, it had been bad enough having to say the word once.

Helydd stepped in.

"God, they're like puppets," Eleri thought in disgust.

"Well, *bach*, at our age, that sort of thing isn't important, is it? It's always more a thing for men, anyway."

Her giggle grated on Eleri.

"I was quite glad when my Dai lost interest."

Her look of complicity sickened Eleri.

"Let me just get this clear," she said. "You are suggesting that sex and taking a lover, at our age, is not socially acceptable?"

Helydd looked relieved.

"Oh! I knew you'd understand, Eleri *bach*: I was saying to Janet, now our Eleri, she'll take it in the spirit it's meant. We understand, Eleri; you've just lost your husband, God rest him, and, naturally, you're prey for men; but it'll pass and you'll find other more satisfying things to do."

"Such as the W.I and chapel, I suppose?" Eleri said sarcastically, though she knew sarcasm was wasted on these two.

"Yes," Janet said. "I haven't liked to interfere, but you have been neglecting the chapel these last few years; everyone's noticed. You're not a young woman any more, Eleri. You've got your responsibilities."

Eleri could feel the anger growing, and its habitual inward channelling frightened her. She reflected, as they spoke, on the impossibility of getting intrusive people out. And then it hit her: if she didn't say something, they'd be back - or others like them - time after time with their unwanted advice.

Eleri was terrified. It went against her whole upbringing and life to be deliberately rude, even to those she disliked, but the situation clearly called for decisive action; she refused to be bullied anymore.

Still the women chattered cosily on. Eleri was staggered by their insensitivity. She tried to stay calm.

"When you've finished your tea, I'd like you to go - and I don't want you to come back," she said quietly. "I don't appreciate your attitude or your advice; the whole thing is entirely uncalled for and has nothing to do with me or my life. If I choose to have relationships, it is my business, not yours or the community's or anyone else's."

Eleri had hoped, even as she spoke, that they'd see the point and leave with some grace, but the outrage on their faces told her how wrong she was. It was then that Eleri saw them as the small children she'd known so long ago - beating hell out of any child who did not conform to their world view - and she felt sad.

Helydd put on her gloves. Eleri would not have believed that something so innocuous could be done with such fury: the gloves didn't stand a chance in this particular battle.

Janet, who was the follower in the relationship, started to clear away the tea things, but the glare from Helydd soon stopped her. She hovered, confused and plainly uneasy, while Helydd strung out the preparations for her departure. At any other time, Eleri would have felt sorry for Janet; now, she just despised her for being so weak and stupid.

Nothing was said and Eleri knew that this was quite deliberate.

"How childish," she thought. "I'm being sent to Coventry."

Helydd's attempt at sweeping out disdainfully was ruined by her size, and a minor-collision with the umbrella stand. Eleri would have laughed had she not felt so utterly depressed by the whole thing.

They had gone, but Eleri's former peaceful mood had left with them. She wished, as she stacked the tea things mechanically, that she could have seen them simply as enemies; but, beneath the matronly dignity and stuffiness, she'd seen them as they once were: two pretty blonde little girls, united by drunken fathers and abusive homes against the eyes of the world - and she ached for them. She could no more make friends with them now than back then, however.

The loss, if loss it was, belonged to all three of them.

***

Angela started keeping a diary, for the first time since adolescence. She knew Mike wouldn't look at it - he wasn't sufficiently interested - and it seemed the only outlet she had. It made the loneliness bearable.

Initially, she found it difficult to be honest; she always had the sense that some invisible other person was peering over her shoulder as she wrote - and her early stilted efforts made her smile.

Talking to another human being - other than Mike's parents who were directly involved - was an act of disloyalty too great for her even to consider. She thought of Edwin Russell longingly, but knew she could not tell him this. When the pain was strongest, she disciplined herself to write it down - and, after a while, it helped; she found she was less likely to take it out on the children.

She had always spent a lot of her time alone, especially since moving here. Somehow, in previous years, it had seemed natural. It hadn't upset her; but then, the children had been much younger and had needed her in a very direct, often physical, way. Her time had been filled, and the lack of friends had not registered. Now it was different and it had taken the latest crisis for her to see this clearly. She had no friends, no one she could turn to when she was lonely and unhappy, as she often was. She knew the fault was her own: she could have made the effort, despite Mike's wish not to be socially involved.

The obvious thing, in a way, was to turn to her parents but Angela was loath to do this. For one thing, she'd never been close to them; but the most important factor, to her, was the shame she felt in admitting that her relationship with her husband was deteriorating daily. She felt such a failure even admitting it to herself.

Buying the book had been exciting: it was the sort of pleasure she rarely allowed herself. Exercise books she'd instinctively scorned. Her feeling was that it needed to be both functional and beautiful.

In Galloways, the university bookshop, she'd found just what she was looking for: a hard-back red book with a silk marker and plain red pages. She'd bought it straightaway, and another one just in case.

Her pleasure in using it was always mixed with pain. It seemed sad to be talking to a book rather than a person; often the pages were blotched with tears.

Angela sat in the kitchen. The children had gone to school and she had no idea where Mike was: he'd left the house early after his evening out. A cup of coffee, bitterly-fragrant, cooled by her side. She chewed her pen, not knowing what to say. With Mike the way he was, every emotion she felt seemed a vast indulgence.

The phone did not ring; no one pressed the doorbell; nothing was going to stop Angela getting into the misery of it all - so she wrote because she realised that, at the moment, it was all she had:

'Monday, 13th October 1980

I'm sitting in the kitchen, alone and feeling it. All I can think of is the night before last, although I've tried hard to think of other things. It's impossible; the whole thing's impossible. Take this last bit as an evasion, and what do you get? I feel really depressed by, and uncertain about, my marriage.

Saturday only served to trigger what's been going on for a long time. God, he's a bastard! Now, you see, that's unlike me: I don't swear, by and large; all I can say is there's a time for everything and my time for being quiet, accepting and ladylike is over, in here at least. I've done it and it's got me nowhere, so why bother?

I see myself as a beige person; a person who has drifted, mainly through fear, behind Mike's strength; but what do I get from him? Nothing it seems. Nothing positive anyhow. I told him quite a bit but I might as well have saved my breath. We got nowhere. He's as untouched by me, and what I say, as ever. Can I believe I have rights in this relationship too? No, not really, or I wouldn't be so beset by doubt and fear and sheer insecurity.

My mother would be horrified: "You stick by your husband come what may," she would tell me. She wouldn't understand: "Angela," she'd say, "You take the rough with the smooth!" Oh, God, why do I have to take so much roughness to find a tiny patch of smooth ground? It's not fair.'

Angela cried as she read through what she'd written. She realised that she hadn't smiled, apart from cynically, for days. People had always told her she had a beautiful smile; the loss of it seemed unbearable to her. She rubbed her eyes and tears trickled over her knuckles.

Her crying stopped as suddenly as it had started, leaving her with a faint sense of unease. Yet the thought of Mike's elusive other woman dwelled in her mind long after the page had dried.

The phone rang and she tensed, despite her wish for company. The voice was cultured, not immediately familiar. When the message became clear, Angela's first thought was, "Oh, God, not more! I can't cope."

It was Mr Rees, the Headmaster of Glyndwr School, asking her to come in as soon as she could - some problem with her daughter which he was reluctant to discuss over the phone.

***

Angela ran out to the car. Her fingers, greased with panic, slipped over the ignition key. Once on the road, and knowing she was breaking the speed limit, she just hoped there were no policemen in the vicinity.

To Angela's relief, there was no sign of Rachel in Mr Rees' study. The Headmaster smiled warmly and shook her hand, gesturing for her to sit down. He apologised for the shock tactics straight away; but said he was sure that she, as a parent, would wish to know about any problems as soon as possible.

"Not this parent," she thought to herself, but she smiled all the same.

"It is a delicate matter, Mrs Heneghan," the Head continued. "Now Rachel's always been a good pupil, as you know: hardworking, getting good results, sensible and well-behaved. However, she has changed in the last few weeks: frequent absences, rudeness, careless or missing homework; nothing you could pin down definitely, but worrying just the same."

Angela was stunned. Rachel? Absent?

"She hasn't been absent to my knowledge," she said. "In any case, I have always either rung in or sent a note for both my children at your school. How did you find out?"

"Ah," said Mr. Rees, "I was coming to that. Things came to a head today, I'm afraid."

"What happened?" Angela asked, unable to bear the Head's pause.

"She was found in the girls' toilets this morning by her tutor, Miss Jones, having missed a double lesson of Chemistry, and, when asked to return, became hysterical and, I'm sorry to say, most abusive to the member of staff. Fortunately, Miss Jones knows Rachel and knew this was most unlike her so she talked to her, when Rachel had calmed down a bit.

"Rachel says she's unhappy and afraid at home – that her father hits her whenever she does anything wrong and so she's reluctant to tell him, or you, that she finds much of the work difficult. She says she's scared she'll be blamed if she doesn't get top marks all the time.

"Now I appreciate that girls of Rachel's age are prone to exaggeration so I take what she says about her father fairly lightly; but it seems that she is very anxious about pleasing you both."

"I had no idea," Angela said. "She's not doing that badly, is she?"

"Not as badly as she thinks she is," Mr Rees said reassuringly. "But, there again, her own expectations seem to be unrealistically high. There are some subjects - and Chemistry is one of them - which she doesn't have a natural flair for. Rachel's way out of that particular problem has been to truant. I suppose her reasoning is that she can't fail if the obstacle is removed - and I think Rachel is terrified of failing. Has she shown any signs of strain at home, Mrs Heneghan?"

Rachel seemed to make sense to her mother as a person at that moment.

"She's withdrawn, awkward, inclined to be bad-tempered. I have noticed that she hates to talk about school. I tend to respect that, I'm afraid. Perhaps I should have been more demanding."

The Headmaster stood up. A caring man, she saw, but clearly out of his depth when it came to the emotions of adolescent girls.

"Aren't we all?" Angela thought to herself, as she smiled at him.

Rachel was sitting on a bed in the Medical Room. One of her socks was wrinkled round her ankle. She looked very young and vulnerable to Angela, a far cry from the sophisticated image she worked so hard to portray.

"Mummy," she said.

Angela was touched: the child hadn't called her 'Mummy' for years.

"The guards are letting you out on parole for the rest of today. Lucky girl."

Rachel smiled wanly.

"Are you - very angry with me?"

She sounded so uncertain, Angela nearly wept.

The instinctive joke sank beneath the child's obvious despair.

"Talk about it in the car, ok?"

Rachel pulled her sock up; it fell down again immediately, and she blushed.

Angela felt fiercely protective of her daughter. She wanted to shield her from the stares of the other children as they craned out of the classroom windows.

They got into the car and she turned the heater on, seeing Rachel's body trembling. It seemed an impotent gesture, but it was all she could do.

"Don't push her," she said to herself, as she concentrated on driving out of the school grounds.

They drove in silence for a while. Angela could see that Rachel was nerving herself to speak and she wished she could make it easier for her.

"They're going to throw me out, aren't they?"

"No, darling, they're not, but they are worried about you; we all are. Do you want to talk about it?"

Rachel hesitated.

"I don't know where to begin; I'm all confused. I did want to talk to you, but - I don't know; it seemed disloyal to Dad somehow, so I told only my diary."

"Oh, no,' Angela thought, 'not another one..."

Yet her look encouraged Rachel.

"Tom's not clever at school, yet he seems to please you and Dad anyway. I always feel that nothing I do is up to a high-enough standard, and that I'm always in the wrong. I've tried and tried, but I know I'm going to fail this Chemistry course and then you'll both be ashamed of me."

She paused and looked at Angela.

"Rachel, what does it matter as long as you do your best?"

"But it's not good enough!" Rachel cried. "Tom's bottom set for everything, but it doesn't seem to matter how badly he does. He's the one Dad always takes on special outings - like that rodeo. He never takes me or even asks if I'd like to go. What's Tom got that I haven't got? I just want you to say I'm good and you don't; you say I'm sulky, stupid and difficult - so I don't go to lessons. There's no point: if I get a bad report, Dad will only have a go at me."

"That's silly, Rachel," Angela said. "You'll get into far more trouble not attending lessons. Anyway, why compare yourself with Tom? You're very different and we don't expect the same things of you. Has it ever occurred to you that it might be difficult for him having a brighter younger sister at the same school? He knows he's not academic."

"He doesn't care," Rachel said. "Why should he? He's Dad's favourite, so what does it matter what the teachers think?"

Angela hesitated. She wasn't sure what to say.

"Your father finds it easier to relate to boys," she explained slowly. "But that doesn't mean he cares any the less for you."

"Why does he hit me then?" Rachel asked. "I've never seen him belt Tom even for a joke."

She yanked at her sock again to hide the tears.

"So he *does* hit her," Angela thought and dread filled her.

"Tom's big," Rachel continued. "He's already nearly six foot, almost as tall as Dad. If Dad tried it on with him, Tom would whack him back; but me, I'm small and he knows it. He knows there's nothing I can do to defend myself. Each time it happens, I say to myself, 'This time I'll kick him hard!' but I never have; I'm too frightened to do that."

The irony of it all struck Angela: if this were some bully at school, she'd have no trouble telling Rachel how to defend herself, but against her own father...

"Do you want me to talk to him, Rachel?"

Rachel's face shone with hope for a moment, but then it clouded.

"No, Mum, this is something I've got to do myself."

Despite the tears, there was a strength in Rachel's face which Angela had never seen before. For the first time, her resemblance to her father was unmistakable. Angela felt a surge of admiration for her.

"Good girl," Angela said. "Now, to get back to the school problem: you must be very behind if you've been skiving on a regular basis. You're either going to have to copy up from someone, or risk seeing your teacher and facing his anger. You've caused a lot of worry and he's not likely to view you with favour - and I can't say I blame him!"

Without Rachel's strength, Angela knew she couldn't have approached the subject this directly; but she nearly took the words back when she saw the misery on her daughter's face.

"Come on, Rachel," she said briskly. "1 respect you for your decision to talk to Dad enormously; that's very important - but so is this. Ever since you were tiny, you've wanted to be a doctor. Don't spoil it now because of stubbornness. I want you to decide how to deal with this. I'll help you whatever you choose; that goes without saying."

Rachel laughed. The reference to stubbornness was a family joke.

"The girls' toilets weren't very exciting after a while," she conceded.

Angela looked at her and burst out laughing.

"Well said, my girl, you could have found somewhere more stylish to skulk."

Rachel looked thoughtful.

"It's nice talking to you, Mum. I wish I'd done it before. Who needs diaries?"

Angela felt a lump form in her throat. It was as if she were seeing Rachel properly for the first time in months.

"You don't have to give your diary up, lovey; just don't let it take the place of people. I think privacy is very important. You need it; I most certainly do - but there's a big difference between privacy, which is controlled, and withdrawal, which isn't."

She knew she was talking to herself as much as her child, but Rachel's quiet nods of understanding comforted her all the same. She wished it were possible to tell Rachel the truth. That was her one sadness in the delight of her renewed relationship with her daughter.

* * *

When Tom heard the rumours circulating about Rachel, his first reaction was one of pleasure: creepy, swotty Rachel in trouble? Wow! Great! His elation continued until break, when he was pressed against the form-room radiator, as usual, chatting to his friend, Ifor Jones.

"All those A grades," he was saying. "You wouldn't believe it, Jones; she never seems to put a foot wrong in this place."

Ifor nudged him urgently.

"Shhh! It's Ger and that lot! Watch out..."

The fourth form bully, Geraint Evans, and his cohorts swaggered over. Tom studied the radiator pipes.

"What's all this about your slaggy sister then, Heneghan?" Geraint said, leering openly.

Tom ignored him. The last thing he wanted was a confrontation with Evans.

Geraint moved in closer.

"Oi, farm boy, I'm talking to you! She been doing dirty things? Eh lads, you wouldn't believe it, would ya? Snobby Rachel letting any bloke get into her knickers. 'Bout to be an uncle are you, Heneghan?"

Slimy Weasel from the village poked Tom in the ribs. The gang laughed.

Tom's head came up slowly. They'd been ribbing him for over three years. He wanted to belong. He grinned at Geraint.

"Dunno," he said nonchalantly. "Aven't seen 'er, 'ave I? Stupid tart, always on about 'ow good she is and that..."

Geraint looked at him. Heneghan was always stooped; by God, you didn't realise how big he was. He certainly wasn't posh like his sister. Geraint wasn't a thinker, but a sort of mental rearrangement of Heneghan took place within him.

"Yeah, well," he said. "You comin' out for a fag?"

"Might do..." Tom replied.

Geraint and his gang drifted off. Tom found he was shaking. Ifor, he saw, was red in the face.

"What you looking at me like that for, Jones?" he said angrily. "D'ya want me to get my head kicked in by that lot?"

To his surprise, Ifor's mouth trembled as if he were just about to cry.

"She's family, man," he said. "Whatever she's done, she's your sister. There's often rumours about our Gwawr, but I don't listen, do I? She's my flesh-and-blood. It's all right to tell me; I'm your best mate - but them? That's not nice."

Tom, who'd secretly been thinking exactly this, took exception to Ifor's words.

"Sod off, Jones!" he yelled. "I'm going to the bike sheds!"

From the back, he looked just like an established member of the gang, Ifor thought sadly, as he watched his friend stalk out.

***

Miriam was helping Mrs Roberts with the top class. They were doing creative writing. Miriam watched James with interest: his dark head was bent over his book as he wrote.

Mrs Roberts had told her that he was only nine, but had been promoted because he was so far ahead of his own age-group. The other children, who had been together since Reception, were settling in well with their new teacher; but the older woman was worried about James.

He was such a serious, contained little boy, the sort who gave nothing away; yet he was very talented: Mrs Roberts had never, in twenty years of teaching, seen such an extraordinary writing style in one so young. She'd asked Miriam to keep a special eye on the child.

"All right, children!" Mrs Roberts said, clapping her hands to get their attention. "Miss Forrest is going to come round and look at your stories. Rhodri, come and sit next to Jac, so that Miss can see what James has done, there's a good boy."

When Rhodri, swaggering, had done as he was told, Miriam slotted herself into the seat next to James. He gave her a shy sideways glance. Other than his name, James, Miriam knew nothing about the boy, so it gave her a shock when she saw '*James Heneghan*' printed in neat writing over his book.

"The perfect opportunity to do a bit of fishing," she said to herself, feeling guilty at the thought.

"What's your story about, James?" she asked.

The child looked at her solemnly.

"Well," he said slowly, "it's about the conflict between good and evil, really."

"Interesting!" Miriam thought, impressed by this.

"Do you often write about that?" she asked.

"Oh yes," he said and gave her a quick smile.

For a moment, he looked much older than his years.

"Would you like to see?"

"I'd love to," Miriam said.

James handed her the book. His handwriting was precise, unlike the usual childish scrawl.

Miriam began to read.

'The man on the hill

The man stood on the hilltop. His face was black like thunder and his movements gave out frustrated anger. Sky surrounded him, but he looked elsewhere. His little boy plucked at his coat and opened his mouth in a wail; it was cold. The man ignored him. The boy was a sort of fly, to be swatted off.

The mother saw them and hurried up the hill, flinging new rain aside. She was glowing with love for her little boy. The man snarled; he didn't like things to be light.

He cuffed the mother off, and she rolled down the hill, like a pretty marble.

"That's what happens, boy," he said, "when you take out my power before it is ready. Things roll away. Remember that, son, because I won't tell you again!"

The boy rolled after his marble-mother and was warm again.'

Miriam felt tears in her eyes at the beauty of the story. She wondered if James knew what he was writing about.

"Is that you in the story, James?" she asked.

He gave her a strange look.

"Yes and no," he said. "It's meant to be every little boy who finds difficulty in meeting the two different forces."

"I like it very much," Miriam said.

James smiled openly for the first time.

"Thank you," he said gravely. "I like writing about my mum and dad. They are important to me. Can you see that?"

Miriam was about to answer him when Rhodri came bouncing back.

"He writes real good, don't he?" he said to Miriam. "Gwawr, my big sister, she always says she fancies your Dad, James. Reckon she'll marry him one day, and then we can be brothers."

James looked at Rhodri for a moment. His natural dignity was unbroken. He was more than a match for the other child, Miriam saw.

"Oh, no, you're quite wrong there," he said with total conviction. "They wouldn't go at all. My dad would tear your sister's wings off."

Later, telling Flora all about the incident, Miriam had wondered at the many violent images in James' speech and writing. Yet, despite this, his devotion to his father was clear.

Miriam felt a shift in her preconceptions about Heneghan: what sort of guy was it that inspired such strong feelings in his children?

She knew, with a sudden insight, that James was not operating from fear; it was fascination and an extraordinarily clear-sighted love.

"Leave Heneghan to the gossip-mongers," she said to Flora. 'There's more to that man than meets the eye. It sounds silly, but a man who can produce a little boy like James can't be all bad.'

***

WEDNESDAY 15th

The rain parted gracefully, and a stolen summer day crept through. Heneghan, feeling the early morning warmth, wanted nothing so much as to take Eleri somewhere, anywhere.

Angela lay motionless by his side. He thought of the cryptic note he had received last night from Rachel. It could wait, he thought. She was probably just begging for money.

"That's what kids normally want at that age, ignore you unless they're skint," he thought bitterly.

He got up, careful not to disturb Angela: he didn't want her questions. She'd assume he'd gone out on business. That suited him fine; not for the first time, he was glad he'd been so cagey about his precise work schedule.

Had he known Angela was awake, he might have thought twice; but he didn't know. She was well used to feigning sleep when his sexual demands became too much. Her breathing was deep, even, and Heneghan was not sufficiently perceptive to notice the slight quiver in her facial muscles.

He could hear the children downstairs, making their breakfast before school. For once, he was glad of Ange's determination in that sphere: she had this thing about independence. He'd fought her about it often, accusing her of being selfish, wanting to have a lie-in of a morning, but she'd remained adamant.

He now congratulated himself on giving way. He could do what he wanted without her pottering about below, giving him The Look, as he'd come to call it.

He moved as quietly as a cat, sinking his toes into the landing carpet, alert to the sound of feet on the stairs. The danger time was when they came up to clean their teeth, but he had every intention of being out of the house by then.

His sponge had almost dried out. He held it under the hot tap, careful to let no stray drops fall into the sink. The lower part of his face stood out darkly as he peered into the mirror. He liked what he saw. Superimposing the younger self took little effort: the slight thinning of his hair was the only sign of age.

He peed, forcing his morning erection still so that no harsh sounds broke his bubble of silence. It was painful, almost humiliating, but he grinned, glad of the pain.

He let himself into the spare bedroom and waited, gritting his teeth.

"Come on, you three," he said to himself. "Get a bloody move on!"

Angela, fingers in her ears, felt the tears on her cheeks, and hoped he wouldn't come in to check up on her.

Heneghan heard the tinny sound of Rachel's radio and, simultaneously, the clatter of feet on the stairs. They were arguing, he noted with disgust: "Bound to be Rachel," he thought to himself, "little cow's got a nasty tongue on her."

That he was a major cause of the tension did not occur to him.

At last the children were gone, slamming the door behind them. Heneghan nearly shouted at them, but restrained himself just in time. There was no sound from the bedroom. He chuckled to himself: success!

The car started first time and he drove to Eleri's, full of anticipation.

***

Edwin Russell's voice rang out through the packed lecture hall In the Old College. He was audible even to those seated at the back - though the sea, at this time of year, could be heard quite distinctly, pounding against the walls far below the university building.

Edwin looked up from the notes he didn't need and surveyed the rows of faces in front of him. The students looked back, pens poised, awaiting his next words.

A gentle cynicism settled on Edwin and he sighed. He was deeply gratified to have been invited to do this R.S.Thomas lecture on Anglo-Welsh Literature - but the mindless eagerness of the youngsters depressed him: he could be spouting complete nonsense, for all they knew - and yet they'd write down every word faithfully, whether they understood it or not.

The ones he admired the most were those who took things into their own hands, both literally and metaphorically: those who smoked and talked, or the arrogant ones who sat at the back with crossed arms and looked bored. He was sure that those precious few would at least carry some memory of the lecture, however contentious or distorted, back with them. The rest he dismissed as so many slightly superior secretarial types.

He wound up with the short stories of Kate Roberts, a writer he'd met and of whom he was particularly fond. Professor Dominic Randolph, Head of the English Department, was smiling and nodding as Edwin began to read a lengthy passage from one of the stories - and Edwin let the pleasure of the words envelop him once more.

A fitting end, he thought, even if it fell short of the expectations of these children reared to anticipate concluding paragraphs.

When he finished, he caught them wondering whether to put a full stop or not. A young man in the back row yawned and then laughed, a startlingly rich sound even from this distance. Edwin wanted to applaud this sign of life, but contented himself with a covert wink at Professor Randolph. Feeble claps broke out along the front rows, escalating into full scale applause after a while.

Edwin sat down and wondered what Angela Heneghan would have made of his speech. It was a pale offshoot of other thoughts, but demanded his attention for all that.

After the obligatory speech of thanks, Dominic, Edwin and a few others made their way towards The Cabin. Their conversation reached out and fell away, the issues gently bubbling from a lifetime's application: books published, reviews written, the latest thoughts on particular authors. It was all comfortable, undemanding and familiar to Edwin.

He was brought up sharp at the doorway, however, by the sight of Heneghan, and a woman who looked familiar. It was not Angela. If they saw him, they gave no sign. Edwin let the conversation carry on around him, pitching a few remarks in the direction of the others for good manners' sake, but his mind was on other matters. He felt surprised - and worried.

He wished he'd overcome his reluctance to contact Angela after the accident. His reaction to her distress had been a withdrawal. He'd let himself take on the avuncular role, yet a deep distaste had surfaced. With the safety of the academic world to bolster him, Edwin was far from sure that he wanted to get further involved in the Heneghans' complicated life.

***

Heneghan had been unusually nervous when he rang Eleri's door bell. Used to female adulation, and taking his pick of the ripest womanly figs, he knew that he was at a loss with this one.

Perhaps it was the fact that she was older; perhaps her air of not being quite anchored in the present; perhaps simply the unconventional nature of her beauty. But the chase, which had become boring over the decades, flushed adrenaline and fear through his veins once again, and took him back to the adolescent self – and, most importantly, all of that wondering if one had read the girl's cues right, or was imagining things: the delicious terror and uncertainty so perfectly expressed in Smokey Robinson's 'I Second that Emotion'.

For all that he had come to the song in his twenties, its lyrics had still resonated with Heneghan.

Eleri's slightly distracted air had made him fear rejection, a polite excuse for not going on the proposed adventure – and her warm smile, when it came, had caused both pleasure and relief.

* * *

Eleri's enthusiasm for the trip brought a whole new element into it for Heneghan. He found that he wanted to give her pleasure, make her smile. He decided to drive to Pembrokeshire, after she said it was her favourite place at this time of year. Eleri had been surprisingly firm - she knew what she wanted. Heneghan saw this as one of her oddly masculine traits, and he liked her all the more for it.

Yet, sitting in The Cabin, he had realised that this part of the day had been a stupid mistake, and he felt angry with Edwin for popping up so unexpectedly: he thought the bloke had retired. Heneghan was pretty sure Edwin had seen him, but he thought that he could get away with it by playing things low key.

He was thankful that Eleri had none of Angela's sharpness about people: another point in her favour. Heneghan had no intrinsic objection to comparing the two women; but he also had no wish to spoil his day by obsessing about his wife's recent behaviour.

The road was incredibly clear and he found himself enjoying the drive. It made a nice change. Normally he headed in the other direction, towards North Wales. Eleri, he could see, was absorbed, her eyes fixed on trees and fields. She said little, but there was no threat in the silence. The sea sailed by far below on the right, bright blue and deceptively calm. Mid-morning sun bounced across the fields; raw patches, where the plough had cut too close, shone briefly. Heneghan looked because that's where Eleri's eyes were - and he saw things he hadn't noticed in years.

They swooped up and down. Forests and barb-hedges emerged, with silver tongues of water licking in and out of vision.

Eleri laughed and pointed: two trees - one crimson, one green - huddled together like lovers, startling and magical. The car's whisper along the road gave this just the right exposure.

Heneghan smiled.

Toiling up the steep hill, which wound past the square bay, Heneghan decided to stop in Aberaeron. Hunger was affecting his concentration, and Eleri's eyes were soft with the sight of a much-loved place.

They parked and got out. There were two pubs, one too like a chapel to be contemplated; they made for the other one.

Heneghan chose a corner seat, away from the mock-Tudor beams and copper warming-pans. Sun came in through the window, shocking the artificial fire into life.

Their Ploughman's lunches were delivered by a smiling blonde whose beauty, to Eleri's merciless eye, was make-up deep only.

Heneghan saw no further than her function - though he found himself remembering, for no apparent reason, the pregnant woman he and Ange had seen once. He pushed the thought away because it was an unwelcome reminder of things he wished to forget. Eleri noticed his momentary tension and wondered.

He found he was expecting her to question him, the way Ange did, but she said nothing, appeared entirely absorbed in her food. The comfort he associated with her stole slowly over him, helped by the curiously-unsexual warmth of her body pressed against his. He thought it strange to be with a woman who so obviously enjoyed her food; he smiled at the way she piled butter on the warm brown bread.

"Mike?"

"Yeah?"

"Do you like pickled onions? I can't stand them. You can have mine if you want."

"Waste not, want not!" Heneghan said, imitating his mother.

Eleri laughed.

"Oh, did your mother say that as well? Mine was always reminding me of all the starving children in the world - as if I was going to send all my leftovers to them."

Heneghan speared the pickled onions with his fork, winking at her as he did so.

"Where are we going next?" Eleri asked.

It was a strange moment for Heneghan: she was acceding to his authority and yet her eyes danced. She became, briefly, a teasing older sister. It amused Heneghan.

"Wherever you want," he said.

And that was how they ended up driving through thin country lanes, with Eleri in charge of the directions. Her curious mixture of vagueness and precision astonished Heneghan. She knew, but seemed to swim up to that knowledge from unimagined depths. There was no uncertainty, yet she was detached from the moment. She had an instinctive sense of direction, something Heneghan did not normally associate with women.

He was surprised when they reached their destination, as it suggested a side of Eleri he had not suspected. It was a hut, a simple wooden shack to be more precise, standing at the edge of the cliffs. Dark wood fences surrounded it and Heneghan could see a thin line of smoke coming from the chimney.

"Richard was an enormously keen and proficient climber," Eleri explained, as they walked over to the gate. "He used to come down here to practise. It's a sort of elementary climbing hut - not as much used as the ones in North Wales, but quite popular with people working themselves up to a big climb."

"And you went along too?" Heneghan asked.

"Oh yes." Eleri smiled. "I loved it. I was never up to Richard's standard, but I got to be quite good on simple climbs by the end. Richard was like a monkey: he showed no fear and would swarm up the sides of the most terrifying cliff faces. His hero was Dougal Haston; he was devastated when Haston died back in 1977.

"He always wanted to try some of the really difficult climbs but he never got around to it. I think that was his major sadness: he didn't mind his heart problems from any other point of view; but the climbing - God, he'd get so frustrated. It was awful. I didn't know what to do or say."

He looked down at the cliffs and tried to imagine Richard Morgan edging up them. He found his preconceptions of the man got in the way: Richard had always seemed so placid and sedentary to Heneghan. He was aware of jealousy, jealousy because the quiet, unassuming Richard had done something he'd never been able to do.

"Lucky bugger," he said.

Eleri looked at him.

"Lucky? Yes, I suppose he was really. He always did what he wanted to do. That's one thing I can say about Richard: he was never one for wasted chances, where his pleasure was concerned. He didn't make excuses. I admired that in him. But, it can have its negative side too, Mike."

The wind took some of her last words away, so quietly did she speak. Heneghan had to bend close to hear her.

He opened the gate and took her hand without thinking. She smiled.

The grass looked as if ruminant teeth had been at it. Coarse curtains flapped in the open window. Eleri's hand was alive like a small animal.

Inside, a man knelt by the fire. He was huge. Heneghan felt puny in comparison. It was not a pleasant sensation. Anger rose in him.

"Won't be a moment," the man muttered. "D'you want to stay?"

He turned round and looked hard at Eleri.

"Hey!" he said. "Don't I know you?"

"Geoff?" she said softly. "God, Geoff, it must be six years."

Heneghan stiffened.

Geoff smiled broadly and stuck out his hand. Eleri took it.

"Eleri, isn't it? There, I never forget a name! Where have you been? Haven't seen you or Richard in years! Is he still thinking of trying K2 one of these days?"

"Richard is dead," Eleri said quietly.

"Oh, Jesus, I had no idea. I'm sorry. He was a fine climber. Good guy, too."

"Yes," said Eleri. "Yes, he was..."

She sounded so forlorn that Heneghan's anger diminished. He gripped her hand tighter.

The big man's discomfort was obvious.

"Yeah, well look, make yourselves at home - you know where everything is, Eleri. I've got to go and take over from a colleague who's supervising kids on the rock face below. I'll see you later."

He rushed out, tangled in unfamiliar shame.

Eleri had gone very quiet and Heneghan regretted bringing her here, even though it had been her idea. It occurred to him for the first time that Richard must have been years older than his wife. Eleri looked ageless, but she couldn't be that much older than he was.

"Maybe..."

"I'm..."

"Go on, Eleri, you say..."

She turned to face him.

"I fear I know what you're thinking, Mike: that we shouldn't have come here, but I needed to. I'm sorry that I involved you, but I had to see this place again. It's a place I love and it has good memories: Richard was at his best here, or places like it, and ignoring that side of things doesn't help.

"Can you see, that I've got to have some good things to hang on to? It's like I was saying before: Richard was most himself here. He seemed powerful, and I needed that then, or thought I did. God knows, I need it now.

"Your wife's still alive, so there is still hope and time to mend things, to make a better stab at the marriage if that is what you want to do. I don't have that luxury anymore. When Richard died, he took that potential future – and all it might have been – with him. Do you see? He has left me a box of jumbled memories and a haze of anger and regret."

Heneghan sat down and lit a cigarette.

"Yeah, good memories are important," he said, but he would not meet her eyes.

There was an awkward silence.

"I've mucked things up, haven't I?" she said.

He wanted to say yes; he wanted to say no; he didn't know what he wanted.

He watched her hair: incredible hair, though he'd never looked at anyone with a touch of grey before, not in this way. He warmed to every pause, despite his uncertainty.

"I'm glad you're here," she said. "I can't imagine bringing anyone else. Despite everything."

"You've got great hair, Eleri, and you haven't ballsed anything up," he said.

"Me? Oh, God, Mike, I'm far past my best, if I ever reached it. I drag you here, get you into all this..."

"No!" he said violently. "I've already told you: it's all right. I don't want you to sound like Angela. Come here."

Bemused, she did as she was told. He ran his hands through her hair. She smelled sweet, natural, and, when she looked up at him, he noticed that she was trembling slightly. He wanted her but, for the first time in years, he was not certain of being wanted in return.

**

Angela cried until the damp bubbling of her nose shamed her into silence. The inner soreness was back, she realised - and wished she could return to her former easy acceptance.

Mike had not changed. She had known what he was like when she married him. Knowing that the change was in her, it did occur to her to wonder why she'd suddenly grown disillusioned at this stage.

For the first time, she was not seeing herself simply as *'daughter of'* or, more relevantly, *'wife of'* - and Angela, who was not naturally assertive, found this transition difficult.

She was experiencing bursts of restlessness, and a worry too close to panic for comfort. She tried to list all the things she'd done, with apparent satisfaction, over the years - and, to her horror, the overriding sense she had was that she'd been travelling, in a metaphorical hearse, at very low speed, possibly in reverse. She'd never actually been interred, but it struck her forcibly that she'd never been fully alive either.

She tried, without success, to shut out Mike's self-satisfied smile. She'd known he was deceiving her in some way, but his enjoyment of the situation had been a blow. It hit Angela quite suddenly that he had always needed the element of secrecy to function. She felt, in that moment, profoundly disillusioned. He didn't keep things from her as an act of kindness; on the contrary, it was all about him and his needs.

She wished she could block him out of her mind. Yet memories of their old life in Manchester came back in warm detail.

In retrospect, the first two years, before Thomas's birth, had been the best time in their relationship. Mike had been a keen fisherman in those far-off days and he used to take her with him from time to time. She had been happy. She'd loved him and had made endless excuses for his odd nature. Friends and relatives had sounded warning notes even then, but she had convinced herself that they were wrong, that she knew him best and was good for him in a way these others could not understand.

Strangely, the greatest opposition to the marriage had come from Mike's older brother, Padraig. At the time, Angela had dismissed it as evidence of jealousy. She had met Padraig first, gone out with him briefly before becoming fascinated by his younger brother.

Now, looking back, she wasn't so sure that he had been motivated solely by jealousy. She remembered meeting him in the pub to tell him that she and Mike had just got engaged. He had been astonished, angry - and, she could now see, worried.

"My God, Angie," he'd said. "You don't actually want to marry him. He's my brother and I love him, but he's a cruel sod, always has been. You may think his silences and moods are evidence of a deep, sensitive nature, but it's not like that. I wish I could tell you that, beneath it all, you were going to find a gentle, caring man - but I don't think you are."

Angela, certain in those days that she held the key to Mike's soul, had laughed this off.

She had treated him, in her blithe innocence, as a wounded human being, a man damaged by life; the fact that he caused most of the damage had passed her by completely.

She cursed herself now for wrapping something so simple in complex psychological terms. In attempting, as she saw it, to save Mike from himself, she had missed the most important point: that she was in greater need of saving than he.

When had the mists of romantic love begun to clear? And, more to the point, why had she buried all the little dark hints and red-flag signs?

Mike had always told her that her tendency to over-react was the problem – and, for years, she had believed him accepting, docilely, that she provoked his anger.

***

Rachel knocked on the Staffroom door and asked for Mr Thomas, before her courage deserted her. She knew she couldn't expect kindness, but still the man's chilling glare frightened her.

"Yes?" he barked.

"Can I talk to you for a moment, Sir?" she asked.

He brought his coffee out into the corridor and stood, glaring at her.

"I'm very sorry for missing your lessons, Sir," she said in a rush. "It won't happen again, I promise."

Mr Thomas gave her a look as if to say, "I've heard this one before!"

"You've got behind, due to your appalling attendance," he said angrily. "Do not expect any help from me. I am not putting myself out for one truanting pupil. You're going to have to copy up everything you've missed from a friend. It won't be easy, but you only have yourself to blame."

"Yes, Sir," said Rachel. "I've already started actually and I'm going to work hard till it's done."

Mr Thomas looked slightly mollified by this.

"Yes, well, just make sure you do."

Then he smiled briefly, a mere twitch of the lips, but like gold to Rachel.

"Thank you for coming to see me, Rachel. You have made a bad impression, but that took some courage."

***

Gwilym came home from work. The house smelled enticingly of fresh cawl. Good cook, his Kate. Good in bed too. Gwilym grinned happily. Everything was working out fine in his life.

"Hey, love, load of miserable ol' buggers around 'ere, aren't they?"

"Yes," said Kate. "Have you noticed how everyone seems to be either arguing or cracking up? It's really quite depressing. I sometimes think we're the only normal people living in the village."

"Too right, love. I've 'ad this great idea, came to me at work today. Time's getting' on, right? Soon be winter. Cold'll make 'em all even worse. Why don't us 'ave a party - cheer 'em all up!"

Kate smiled with pleasure.

"Ooh yes," she said. "I'd love that. We could invite everyone, make it a real community occasion."

"Not everyone, Kate: I'm not 'avin' them old biddies from the village sniffin' around 'ere. I know, what say we make it a Hallowe'en party, yeah? Get 'em all to come dressed up as witches and that, 'ave a whole load of games. We'll get the Miriam and Flo to help. They've got good ideas."

"Who shall we invite?" she asked.

"Right, love, let's get down to it. Bryn, of course; 'e's me best mate - and Iestyn, reckon 'e'd like to let 'is 'air down a bit. What about Edwin, you know that teacher bloke I told you about, and the Heneghans."

Kate tensed.

"Do we have to? I don't know her and I can't see him being a bundle of laughs at a party."

"He's all right, Kate, not a bad bloke when 'e's 'ad a few! You don't 'ave to talk to 'im, if you don't want to. Now, 'oo else? Yeah, Eleri. She's just lost 'er 'usband. I reckon a party's just what she needs."

"Isn't she supposed to be having it off with Heneghan?"

Gwilym laughed at this.

"Not 'er, love! She'd 'ave more sense."

"It'll end in tears, just you wait and see," Kate said darkly.

***

Heneghan wanted to get back while it was still light. Eleri was quite happy to go along with this. The painting beckoned.

Geoff had not returned when they made their way out to the car. Sea, like a vast dog, placed its forepaws over the top of the cliff. The sky, sullen now, waited.

Heneghan turned the ignition. Nothing happened. He tried again. Nothing. Eleri stood by, fear stealing over her. She didn't want things to become concrete.

"Fucking car!" Heneghan shouted, and kicked the nearside front tyre.

He lifted the bonnet and peered inside. The greasy inwards stared back inscrutably. The game edged into seriousness.

"Looks like we'll have to stay," he said.

A baby thunderclap burped in the background.

"Not another storm," Heneghan said. "As if we didn't have enough to worry about. Is there a phone in the hut?"

"Yes," said Eleri. "What are you going to tell your wife?"

Heneghan's smile was unpleasant.

"Business, Eleri. I've been detained on business."

Another wave rose threateningly. Rain took over. Heneghan and Eleri ran for the hut.

Eleri turned to the fire, which they had put out before leaving. She could hear voices, flattened by the rain. The door shot inwards with startling force and the place was suddenly alive with teenagers and Geoff.

Heneghan's back was to Eleri as he dialled. His shoulders stiffened at the sound of the laughing newcomers. He turned round, glaring.

"Shut the fuck up, will you!" he yelled. "I can't hear a bloody thing!"

He tapped angrily on the wall. Waves of tension emanated from his stiff figure. The telephone receiver was ominously silent in his hand.

The children, stunned into silence, crept about the hut, tidying away their belongings. Heneghan crashed the phone back and turned to face the room. Eleri had never seen him so furious. Geoff was trying, tactfully, to ignore the unspoken rage in the room.

The rain's attack intensified. Lightning played a brief stark tune over the landscape.

"I can't get through!" Heneghan said. "Jesus!"

"If you're staying," Geoff said calmly, "how's about having some food with us?"

Heneghan looked at the big man. Geoff smiled, an open friendly smile. Heneghan began, slowly, to unwind.

"Yeah," he said. "Good idea."

The fire began to draw, sending a weak heat out into the room. Geoff started to prepare food.

***

Eleven pm came and went and there was still no sign of Heneghan. Angela's terror mounted. He'd given no indication that he'd be away overnight. Despite his love of secrecy, she had never known him to disappear without explanation.

"He's finally left me," she thought - and, despite the ambivalence of her recent feelings, she experienced a terrible sadness.

The children, protected by a simple lie, had long since retired. Angela felt horribly alone. She tensed every time a car drove by outside.

The rejected stash of whisky had been broached with guilt an hour ago. Aware that the alcohol was accentuating her mood of depression and rising paranoia, she none-the-less took a masochistic delight in getting drunk. She felt she had no one she could turn to.

The shrilling of the phone shot Angela out of her chair. It had to be him. There'd be some simple explanation; everything would be all right again. Her hands trembled.

"Mike?" she said. "Oh, thank God you've called. I was so worried."

"Angela?"

The voice was not Heneghan's. She began to wail with terror.

"Angela? It's Edwin. What's wrong?"

She started to cry openly, choking her words out.

"He's gone, Edwin. He's left me."

"Stay right where you are," Edwin ordered. "I'll be with you in ten minutes or so."

The telephone receiver, falling from her nerveless hand, crashed against the wall. She poured herself another whisky.

***

Sudden storm light flickered through the window of the hut, painting, with silver fingers, the slumbering forms of the children as they lay on the long bench bed.

Heneghan rested on his elbow, unable to sleep. The smell of bangers and mash was strong. Acidity, from the rough lagers drunk with Geoff and Eleri, lined his mouth. Geoff's big blonde head moved slightly in sleep across the room.

Eleri lay curled like a child in the wooden cot next to Heneghan's. Worry gnawed at his mind, just out of sight of the anger.

He had tried Angela five more times: the last two times, an ominous flat sound indicative of blown-down lines had reached him. He didn't want her to know what was going on. The fear that she would contact Edwin pulled at his guts.

He raked at his lower face, a nervous habit he was unaware of. Veins stood out against the brown surface of his hand. Wind, from a crack in the window, pulled at Eleri's hair. Watching it, he felt full of restless energy. He wanted to burrow into her cool soul and shut out the world.

He lay down and closed his eyes, in search of calming images of Eleri. Slowly she rose before him, but it was an Eleri he had never seen before. Naked she stood, not soothing but almost unbearably erotic. He got hard just thinking about her. He licked his lips, a hot sweat breaking out. Quietly he removed the jeans he'd kept on for warmth; they constricted him painfully. He bit his fingertips.

He swung stealthily out of the cot and pressed shaking fingers on the wooden support of Eleri's bed. She slept on, unaware, her back to him.

He climbed in next to her and stretched his legs down beneath the quilt. Her body, next to his, was warm and relaxed. He moved as close as he could, hardening still more at the sensation of her soft bottom against his cock. The thought of the others in the room - the possibility of them waking - turned him on hugely. His throat felt dry. He swallowed continually. His body quivered.

Eleri's hair was cool and fragrant. He cupped the top of her head gently. Her nakedness was arousing. He molded his hands to her breasts, feeling their soft weight. He ran a hand down her belly. She stirred and moved slightly so that there was more room for him. Her legs opened a tiny way. He wondered if she knew what was happening. The drifting of her hand to alight upon his underpants could have been a reflex action. He tensed. Her fingers were inside the waistband. She knew what she was doing all right.

One of the children coughed and cried out in his sleep. Eleri's fingers were pulling the thick white material down Heneghan's legs. She had turned round. Her face was hidden on his shoulder.

The child got up, stumbling in the dark, and wandered over to the sink.

Eleri was wet.

The child filled a glass with water and drank slowly.

Heneghan was overwhelmed by the illicit excitement of it all. Eleri was undoing the buttons of his shirt, gently removing it. They clasped for a moment, breath jagged, then he pulled her on top of him. Her long hair swept his body, filling him with a strange delight. Her eyes were cloudy. She pushed him slowly into her body - and, when Heneghan began to thrust urgently, she pulled herself up and away slightly, smiling mysteriously. Oh God, but she was clever, he thought through the tightening of his balls.

She rode the tip of him teasingly, contracting her own muscles, until he could feel the waves of her climax breaking over him. He was bursting, he was outside of himself, as he thrust into her faster and faster.

The child was coughing again.

Heneghan could feel a great cry rising up in his throat, a cry which came out as a long moan, almost of pain.

He came, his body arching and shivering with the power of it.

***

Edwin walked up the path, feeling deeply concerned. If Heneghan really had left, he wondered how on earth Angela would cope. He rang the bell, thinking of the woman he'd seen with Heneghan earlier.

Angela looked dreadful, blotched and undermined. Edwin's heart beat with her distress. She smelled of sweat and whisky, an uncanny echo of Heneghan's collapse. Her hands fluttered uselessly.

Edwin walked into the living room and sat down. Angela hovered, touching things absently.

"It's late...I'm sorry," she said at length. "I..."

"Sit down," he said. "Tell me what's going on."

"You must think me totally hysterical," she wailed. "But I have this dreadful feeling that he's gone for good. He's often gone on mysterious trips but never this late, never at night. It looks as if he has got some woman after all. I can't bear it...the thought of it... all those years, thinking I could...I dunno...save him, I suppose; thinking that, whatever else didn't work, I was enough for him in that way."

"What can I do to help?" Edwin asked.

"You can tell me I'm wrong; that's what you can do!"

Edwin reached for the whisky bottle and took a swig.

"Oh heavens," Angela said, half laughing. "Don't do that. Let me get you a glass, otherwise you'll think all my standards are dropping."

She circled the kitchen like a panicked moth, brushing tears on harsh wool.

Edwin drank the whisky gratefully. She sat down.

"Has he ever been unfaithful to you?" he asked.

She laughed, a bitter ugly sound.

"Him? Huh! He could've been sodomising school boys for all I know. I don't know a damn thing about him. How does that strike you after seventeen years of marriage? Pretty good, eh? I've always thought that, secretly, he hated women - but they always say the wife is the last to know. The way I'm feeling right now I wouldn't put anything past him. Oh, Edwin! Why did I have to fall for him of all people? That's what I ask myself. Why him?"

"Maybe he brought out your maternal instinct," Edwin suggested.

"Oh, he did, he did," she said, leaning forward. "You wouldn't have believed the charm that man had in the early days. He was like a hurt little boy and I just loved him and wanted to protect him. He seemed so lost in life somehow. Now I think it was all a clever act which he dropped as soon as he'd got what he wanted.

"No doubt his new woman will get some other variation of the *'Poor little Mike'* act - and she'll be sucked in just as I was. I could almost pity her if I didn't feel so angry. Edwin, I don't need all this on top of everything else."

"Angela, my dear," said Edwin gently, "let me say a few things. Firstly, my impression of Mike accords with your early one. He is hurt; but, he also hurts others. You've got to think how far you are prepared to go on putting up with that. Remember, in the final analysis, only Mike can help himself - and that's if he's willing to accept that there's a problem.

"The other thing that occurs to me is this: I don't think his unfaithfulness - be it theoretical or actual - is the point. It's more to do with what your relationship with him is about; whether you are getting what you want out of it, never mind him for the moment. You say you love him, and I'm not doubting that for one moment, but do you really accept him as he is - or are you just hoping that, one day, you'll make a new and better man of him?"

"You don't pull your punches, do you?" she said, but she was smiling for the first time. "Padraig, Mike's brother, warned me about that very thing years ago. He accused me of reading more into Mike than was there. Maybe he was right. But he's not a total rat, really he isn't! The children adore him, even Rachel - and funnily enough, he's always been good with them in his own way."

Edwin looked at her.

"We're back to what you want, Angela," he said.

"I want to be loved. I want him to demonstrate that he loves me. I don't want to be in doubt all the time. I want him to say that I'm the most important person in his life and to mean it. Perhaps that's asking too much."

"Perhaps," Edwin replied, "but are you prepared to go on settling for less? And what if he has been unfaithful?"

"I'll kill him," she said quietly. "No, that would be too quick and easy. I want him to suffer. I'd throw him out. Let him know what it's like to feel rejected and uncertain all the time."

TUESDAY 21st

October continued to unfold slowly. Leaves stole out of the trees, packing the pavements with a red-gold mosaic. All the students returned. The life of the town altered subtly. The seat of learning was waxed and polished once more.

Grass grew on the raw wound of Eleri's soul. The painting surged ahead. She followed it nervously, netting colours as they floated in front of her. Grief stole the occasional day. At such times, she would lie curled up in her bed, weeping, unwashed.

Richard's grave became one with the earth gradually. Eleri trailed up there often, and then hung back, watching magpies and jackdaws alighting on the hedge.

She felt she had no right to Richard anymore. He had become common property. During this time of adjustment, Eleri saw no one by choice. She ignored the doorbell, took the phone off the hook for hours at a time. She thought occasionally of Heneghan – but these thoughts were no more than flickering images, insubstantial as dust.

The incident at the hut had pulled no great holes in the fabric of Eleri's life, as far as she could see. She had enjoyed the sex, but felt too fragile to start a relationship, especially with a married man.

Yet, at odd times, something elusive about it bothered her. She had no wish to be troubled, so she ignored it. She had no idea how much, if anything, Heneghan had told his wife. To her surprise, she found she didn't care.

Already it was a remote memory. For her, the intensity between them had burned fiercely up to that point before flaking away to cinders – and that was the way she wanted it to remain.

Eleri took to walking long, unseen miles in an attempt to clear the fuzziness in her head. From time to time, she came out of herself with a start, to find that she had wandered too near the middle of the road. Fear shaved her to skinless panic on these occasions. The world seemed huge and threatening, coming at her with a force she could not avoid.

One day, in a state of acute physical anxiety after hours of painting, she blundered down a track near the estuary. Heneghan's face, stared at in the painting all morning, seemed to glow in her mind. The figure walking fast in the opposite direction turned out to be Gwilym.

Eleri jumped back. Gwilym's roaring laugh centred her.

"Ullo, Mrs Morgan! 'Ow's it goin', then?"

She remembered her liking for him, and smiled.

"Gwilym," she said. "I think you should call me Eleri. I no longer feel I am Mrs anybody."

"Right you are, love, Eleri it is. I was goin' to call on you, got a favour to ask."

"Not tea for the worthy village wives, I sincerely hope!"

Gwilym laughed.

"*Iesu mawr*, not bloody likely, 'scuse my language, love. No. You're a painter, aren't you?"

"Yes…" Eleri said warily.

"No need to panic. Nothin' posh needed 'ere. I don't want no genuine reproductions. See, me and Kate's 'avin' this party, for Hallowe'en. Should be great. You wanna come? I can't draw to save me life and paint like a fuckin' cart'orse! We need these invites, right, with pictures of devils an' that, whatever you think."

Eleri laughed and nodded.

"I get the idea! When do you want them for – and how many?"

"Jus' do the one. We'll get copies in town. A few days? Ten days till 'allowe'en, so that'll give us time to 'and 'em out."

"Fine," said Eleri, "thanks, Gwilym. I'd love to come and this would be a good way of keeping my mind busy."

"Great!" said Gwilym. "It's a dress-up do. See what you can come up with..."

"Ooh, I will. Just you wait and see."

Gwilym sat down on a nearby log, and took out a Woodbine.

"You 'eard the latest gossip, then?"

Eleri shook her head, knowing Gwilym's love of scandal and feeling slightly wary.

"Well! Seems like there's been 'igh drama up the Heneghan place. Oh, two weeks ago, it must be. Everyone's sayin' that 'is missus threw him out, over some bird 'e's been knockin' off. I think 'e's back 'ome again now, but she's not talkin' to 'im or summat. Bit unexpected, eh?"

Eleri, who had stiffened at the start, now relaxed. If Gwilym didn't know the identity of the '*bird*', it couldn't be common knowledge.

"People say these things," she said vaguely. "It's probably exaggerated – you know how people talk round here."

Gwilym started moving again.

"Yep!" he said. "See ya, love!"

***

Miriam was tired. All morning, she'd been pestered by Arianwen Jones, Rhodri's twin, Gwawr's little sister and the most insecure child in the top class. She felt she would scream if she heard the girl's voice once more, and was thankful that Half Term was only a few days away.

There was the party to look forward to, for starters. She and Flora were going round to Gwilym's house that evening to plot and plan. She smiled at the thought.

"Miss Forrest!"

"Yes, Arianwen. What is it now?" Miriam asked wearily.

"James is crying!"

"Oh God," Miriam thought. "I do not need this..."

"All right, Ari, go and sit down. I'll sort it out."

Miriam was getting used to this. They were a volatile bunch. There was always someone in tears or sulking.

She walked over to James, wondering which friend he'd broken up with. The little boy was hunched over his book. He made no sound, but tears were streaking his carefully-written work.

Miriam sat next to him. He looked small and lonely, sitting there in his grief.

"What's wrong, James?"

He looked up at her.

"You won't tell?"

Miriam smiled.

"No, James. I won't tell. I'm not the telling sort."

"I want to whisper," the child said. "No one must hear but you. They'd only laugh…"

Miriam bent her head down.

"I think my mum and dad are going to get divorced," James said, tears breaking out again.

His obvious fear moved Miriam.

"What makes you think that, James?"

The child was agitated, rubbing his hands together.

"I shouldn't have been listening, I know," he said. "It's not good to listen to other people talking, is it?"

"Not usually - but maybe you couldn't help hearing," Miriam said, wanting to put his mind at rest.

"Oh no," he said. "I crept down the stairs when I heard my dad come in – and hid in the cupboard. They'd be mad if they knew. My dad didn't come home all night. I could hear my mum crying downstairs, so I knew something bad had happened. When he came in, really early, six, Mum was waiting for him and she screamed and screamed and screamed. It was horrible.

"My dad didn't say much, but he was furious. I kept thinking they'd hear me breathing and drag me out. Mum was saying about a bit of stuff – that's a woman; I asked Rachel – and Dad kept saying, 'You're being a stupid bitch!' to her. And they went on and on, getting quieter, till I heard the door slam and Mum shouted out, 'And don't ever come back!' I don't want to tell you what she called him."

Miriam was stunned. She hadn't believed the rumours that circulated freely around the village. It was all true, then.

"Poor James," she said. "It's really upset you, hasn't it? I'm sure they'll get over it. People often have stupid arguments, say things they don't mean, but then they make up and say they're sorry. It doesn't necessarily mean your parents are going to split up."

"You don't know them," said James, dully. "Mum meant it. I've never seen her so angry. He was gone for two weeks. We didn't see him at all and Mum wouldn't speak, just shouted at us all the time. He came back yesterday and they're not talking to each other. I hate it. I keep thinking about running away."

Miriam sighed inwardly. She was aware of a conflict of loyalties. She knew she ought to pass this information on to the Headmaster, but she had told James she would keep it a secret – and she didn't want to lose his trust.

"I'm sure things will get better," she said. "Come and talk to me if you feel sad or scared, though, won't you? And don't run away. It's getting very cold, you know!"

James smiled at this. His dark hair stood up in wet tufts.

"Thank you," he said.

***

Telling Flora about it later, Miriam had found herself in tears, memories of her own parents' volatile marriage resurfacing.

As eldest child, she had felt she had to keep everyone else safe – and, as a nine year old, had even written out detailed instructions on how she would protect the rest of the family if fire or violence came their way.

The prospect of an evening with Gwilym and Kate cheered her up, to Flora's relief.

***

Flora pushed Gwilym's gate open. She felt an odd sensation, almost like jealousy, at the thought of meeting Kate again.

Miriam, whistling by her side, had no such reservations.

Trees, weighted by their burden of colourful death, stood all around. Laughter spilled warmly out under the front door. Nipper, pottering about under the trees, cocked an ear and trembled at his exclusion. Smoke wrote poems in the air.

The front door opened, bringing a slice of evening sun in with it. Nipper shot in, banded briefly in purple.

The house smelled of wine, dope, sheep and Gwilym. The girls went into the front room. Kate shone with a new light. Flora admitted grudgingly to herself that the girl was pretty.

Gwilym busied himself with a bottle of dark crimson wine, while Kate rolled a joint.

Miriam held her glass to the window, fascinated by the unfolding of the garden in blood.

"So, what's happening then, Gwilym?" Flora asked eagerly. "Tell all!"

Gwilym took the joint from Kate, inhaled and smiled.

"We told you we was 'avin' a party, yeah? Right, well I decided it wasn't goin' to be the usual stuff – everyone getting' drunk and snoggin' in corners and cryin' and runnin' away and all that. Keep the buggers busy; that's my idea!"

"Hallowe'en?" Miriam asked.

"Yeah. 's'right, love. Got any good ideas?"

Miriam grinned.

"Millions," she said. "When I was living at home, we used to have a Hallowe'en party every year. There's loads of wonderful games. Ever played Pass the Unmentionables?"

Gwilym bellowed with laughter.

"You what, love? Only Kate gets a grip on those!"

Kate blushed. Gwilym's openness still had the power to embarrass her.

"No, not that! Honestly, Gwilym, you've got a mind like a sewer. Everyone closes their eyes – then you pass round all these revolting objects and people have to hold them while you describe what they are meant to be in ghoulish terms. A raw sausage always works well. You can have great fun with that, especially if it's one of those really long and thick ones!"

"Yuk," Flora said. "Hey, how's about getting a real sheep's eye from that butcher in Bow Street? You know, Miriam, the one we refer to as the obsequious toad?"

"Great!" Gwilym said. "I knew you two'd get into the mood of it. Make a list, will ya, Kate – your writin's better than mine."

Kate grabbed a sheet of paper.

"We'll have to decorate the whole house, Gwil," she said. "You know, cobwebs everywhere, masks, skeletons, rats, bats..."

Flora clapped her hands together in excitement.

"I've just had the most brilliant idea," she said. "We're all dressed up, right, waiting for guests to arrive? Well, I reckon we should just sit there, looking creepy, in a kind of tableau, and have some really weird music on...leave the door open...keep silent, so, when they come in, they get into the mood straightaway."

"Yeah!" cried Gwilym. "You got it, Flo! Then we have this treasure 'unt, yeah? Leadin' to them trees on the knoll. Just 'ope to God it doesn't rain!"

Miriam inhaled deeply on the joint. It was affecting her smoothly this time. Kate, laughing, was writing their ideas down.

"Who've you invited?" Flora asked.

"Well…" Gwilym paused and grinned wickedly. "Right collection of odds and sods – should be real 'ell. There's Mike 'eneghan and his missus – get some fireworks there, I reckon, if all the stories goin' round are true."

Miriam was serious for a moment.

"But they are true, Gwilym. I teach their youngest child. He told me. I shouldn't be saying this probably, but what the hell. You're taking a bit of a risk inviting both of them, aren't you?"

"You 'aven't 'eard the best bit yet, love," Gwilym laughed. "I've also invited Eleri Morgan – remember, the widow?"

"Not the one…" Flora said, aghast.

"Yeah, that's the one! She's supposed to 'ave been away with 'eneghan somewhere. Mrs H. found out and went ballistic. Should be an interestin' party, eh?"

"Gwilym, you're a devil!" said Flora. "'*Interesting*' isn't the word I'd have used; I think '*explosive*' would be better!"

"Pass us that joint, love. Come on, Flo. It's a party, not a funeral. It's just what they all need. Get 'em goin', bit of fun; they can forget it all…"

"Well, as long as the Heneghans don't start divorce proceedings in the middle," Flora said.

"What if Heneghan starts one of his famous rages?" Miriam asked nervously.

"Won't 'ave time, will 'e?" Gwilym replied. "Ere, there and everywhere they'll be: out in the woods, down the road; won't have time to scratch 'is arse never mind get stroppy. Look, it's like this, see, them older ones are makin' a bit of a cock-up of it all, right? Up to us younger ones to show 'em what's what!"

Gwilym went to the stove and ladled out huge bowls of cawl. Miriam's stomach rumbled in anticipation. They all laughed.

"What say we go swimmin' in the sea later?" Gwilym said with a grin. "It's great when you've 'ad a bit of dope."

***

Angela heard the bang of the letterbox and jumped.

"Strange time to get post," she thought.

Heneghan had gone for a walk. She was glad he was out of the house. His brooding presence unnerved her.

She had expected some sort of explanation for his absence, but he'd said nothing – had pushed it all onto her and made it her problem.

Angela frequently wished that she had never let him come back. They were living a half-life, passing one another with snarls. She was aware that the situation was having a bad effect upon the children, but she could not bring herself to back down. This time, she was damned if she'd let him win.

She remembered with horror the early morning when he'd returned. There had been something different about him; even in her anger, she had sensed that. He had seemed softer somehow – and this had bitten deep into her shaky confidence. That this unknown woman – and she was now sure that there was one – had affected Mike more in a few weeks than she had been able to in seventeen years of marriage was a blow more devastating than the actual fact of infidelity.

Faced with the probable end of her marriage, she had to deal with the possibility that she had never been right for him – and somewhere out there lived the perfect woman he should have been with in the first place.

She made her way to the front door. A large envelope lay on the mat. She did not recognize the writing.

Shaking with tension and fear, she opened it. A painted card fell out. It was strikingly unusual. Angela wondered who the artist was.

It showed a silhouette landscape, with twisted trees and a strange figure, like a demon, in the foreground.

Angela smiled as she read the message: from Gwilym. She might have known somehow; only he would think of having a Hallowe'en party for adults. She faltered when she saw it had been addressed to both of them, then thought, "To hell with it! I'm going anyway. He can please himself."

Over the past three weeks, she had felt things becoming clear in a way they never had before. She realized that she had been too eager for Mike's taste. She sensed that he preferred remote women, women he had to chase.

She was, she realised, a classic people-pleaser, and this trait made her low on the scale of assertiveness, and very easy to manipulate both physically and emotionally.

She had offered herself up on a plate – and had been consumed then vomited out.

An end seemed inevitable now. The question left in Angela's mind was whether she actually had the courage to break up the marriage – and the subsidiary fear that no other man would want her.

***

Heneghan strode along the beach, his mind jammed with blackness. He had no hat and his hair, longer than he normally allowed it, dipped into his eyes, annoying him. His teeth were locked, cheekbones sharp with a fury he was only half aware of. He could not walk fast enough to outpace the inner darkness.

Frothy white form pinked the sand edges; gulls mourned overhead, melting into the wind. Hills, in the distance, broke up into segments of evening colour.

Heneghan was aware of none of it. The ache in his head was a cry for Eleri, a scream of vulnerability which he hated and resisted.

He'd called on her, ringing the doorbell with certainty – only to be confronted with silence. He'd tried again every few days – still nothing.

Her disappearance was devastating in a way he had not expected. Angela's anger, and later tears, became like a meaningless dirge at the outer reaches of his own grief.

Heneghan, normally the epitome of control, was edging towards a danger point. The rigid barrier he maintained between his feelings and the world was starting to waver. Confused images whirled in his brain, Eleri, his mother, dark places – and, behind it all, the horrifying sense that a blanked-out part of his past was creeping back. He was not sleeping well. The swollen hands of nightmare grabbed at him repeatedly, trying to leave their imprint of sloughed skin.

***

In Gwilym's front room, the preparations were complete. A lightness fell upon them, as they drifted in the peaceful tides of wine and dope.

Night's claws were digging in, after a day of unseasonal warmth and sun.

Gwilym got up and stretched. He looked round, grinning, at the three girls. Kate had one leg over the armchair; Miriam, eyes closed, appeared to be in a world of her own – a nice one, Gwilym thought, if her smile was anything to go by.

It was Flora who made him laugh, however. She was crouched on the carpet, talking to the dog. Gwilym was almost reluctant to disturb them.

"You up for a swim, then, girls?" he said.

Nipper barked, and Flora sat back in shock. Miriam opened one eye.

"Why not?" said Kate. "You're only young once!"

"That's my girl!" said Gwilym. "Come on, you two. It'll be warm after all that sun today – and you're always tellin' me how you leap into pools and whatnot. A little sea'll do you no 'arm!"

The harmony and adventure of their four-square relationship prevailed once again. Miriam wondered if she could remember how to drive the car.

Half way there, Gwilym delved into his tobacco pouch and brought out a chunk of dope, which he divided neatly into four.

"One for the road!" he said.

They drove with all the windows open, Jethro Tull's 'Acres Wild' blasting out of the car's speakers.

The sea, bisected by a thin red line, appeared to suck the sun into its giant mouth. They watched for a while in silence. The shingle was wet from an earlier high tide. Gwilym jumped over the sea wall and ran with his arms outstretched, whooping.

"Gwilym, shut up!" Kate called. "You'll get us arrested!"

But his high spirits affected them all – and the girls found themselves taking off, whirling and twisting, in a strange dance. Flora felt as if her body had become air. Happiness filled her.

They held hands, the four of them, and flew round in a dizzy, stoned circle. Faster and faster they went, the lights out at sea blurring into a continuous golden line.

They stopped as abruptly as they had started – and Kate began slowly to peel her clothes off until, clad only in bra and knickers, she turned and ran for the water, the other three following suit.

The sea was warm. They ducked and splashed, licking salt off their faces. Gwilym began to run his tongue over his arm with a seriousness that had Flora, who was closest, convulsed with laughter.

"This is what you do when you get scurvy," he said gravely.

"Not scurvy, you idiot!" Flora laughed. "It's for cramp!"

Miriam sat down and mentally placed the pieces of her world in front of her, like shells. She was sure she could communicate with the sea, that its warm whisper was a message especially for her. The perfection of the waves dazzled her, the way they bunched themselves up, like muscles, and then let go.

She could hear Gwilym and Flora laughing and splashing one another.

"I'm stoned!" she thought – and a warm, uncaring stream of laughter flowed from her mouth.

Kate squatted down by her. The two girls looked into one another's eyes and started giggling. They rolled in the warm sea, laughing and laughing, not knowing quite what was so funny, until the waves pushed them gently to the shore line where they lay, letting the water wash over them.

Miriam came out of herself with a great shout of pain. Something had banged hard into her left arm.

"Agh!" she screamed, and looked up.

A man was crouched in the sand before her. As Miriam stared, the figure rose up and she saw it was Heneghan. She backed away instinctively.

"Oh, it's you," he said. "I might have known."

His blank tone surprised her. She had expected a mouthful of abuse at the very least. Heneghan just stood there, staring at something Miriam could not see. The warm pleasure was evaporating, and she shivered. It unnerved her, the way he stood still, saying nothing.

"Come on, Kate," she said. "Let's go back and join the others."

"He makes you nervous too?" Kate whispered. "Jeez, I thought it was just me..."

"He makes everyone feel on edge," Miriam replied. "I don't know what Gwilym was thinking of when he invited that man to our party."

Kate and Miriam stood on the sand near Gwilym and Flora. Heneghan's dark shadow, now yards away, seemed to loom over them.

"Ullo! You two back then?" Gwilym said.

"We banged into Heneghan," Kate said. "'*Banged*' being the operative word. He almost fell over Miriam."

Gwilym got up.

"Might as well go see if he's comin' to our party," he said, and wandered over to where Heneghan stood. The older man had his back to Gwilym. There was something forbidding about the way he stood, even to Gwilym who rarely felt fear.

"Oi, Mike!" he called.

Heneghan turned round like a robot. Gwilym stepped back, shocked, at the look of utter despair on the other man's face.

"Men don't let their feelins' show," he thought, "especially not this one."

The man made no attempt to smile, and Gwilym, fiery and warm-hearted, was appalled by such open misery. He did the only thing he could think of under the circumstances, took out two Woodbines and offered one to Heneghan.

"You wanna be left alone, Mike?" he asked.

Heneghan looked at him for a moment and then sighed.

"No," he said, "don't think I do…"

He inhaled deeply, holding the cigarette with fingers that did not shake. Gwilym was amazed by the other man's control.

"Gotta get changed, man – it's turned fuckin' cold – can't leave the girls."

"Gwil, look, I'll give you a lift back – fact is, I could do with some company."

"Right you are, Mike. I'll go and tell the girls."

Gwilym walked back and changed quickly.

"Miriam, love, you all right to drive these two drunk buggers back? I've got to sort out a fishin' trip with Mike. Sorry it's a bit short notice and that, but we're thinkin' of goin' tomorrow."

343

Miriam smiled.

"God, men and their bloody fishing," she said without true animosity. "Yes, I think I can just about manage that. Great evening."

Gwilym put his arm around Kate and hugged her.

"See you later, love, keep the bed warm for me!"

***

The girls had gone. Gwilym felt a small twinge of regret at the loss of their sparkling swim, but something of liking for Heneghan had come to him during the rodeo. Gwilym was loyal. You didn't desert your mates. He pulled his jacket on and went back to the other man.

The two men walked in silence up the beach towards Heneghan's car.

"Great," said Gwilym. "Never been in a TR7 before."

They set off.

"Pub?" Gwilym asked.

"Yeah," Heneghan replied. "Town."

Heneghan drove the way he did everything, with barely-controlled savagery. Gwilym enjoyed the speed, the sense of power.

They parked in a back street and Heneghan led the way to the pub, a tiny building set back from the road.

The place was packed. Gwilym saw one or two women he knew. He grinned at them and waved, then wandered over to a corner seat and waited until Heneghan arrived with the drinks. The older man's momentary loss of control might never have happened.

While Heneghan busied himself with his pint, Gwilym studied him.

"God, he looks rough as a badger's arse – 'asn't shaved, eyes like piss-'oles in snow, the full works," Gwilym thought to himself.

"Thanks for that, Gwil," Heneghan said.

Gwilym licked a globule of froth off his moustache.

"'S all right, man," he said.

Heneghan looked uneasy.

"Don't like all that emotional stuff," he said, "opening myself up and all that. It's not fucking typical, tell you that for starters."

Gwilym shrugged.

"Didn't see you as the weepin' and wailin' type, some'ow."

Heneghan smiled faintly.

"It's difficult," he said. "I've met this woman – doesn't matter who..."

"Eleri?" Gwilym said.

"Oh Christ!" Heneghan said, dragging his fingernails over his jaw. "If you know, that means everyone must know. Shit!"

"Calm down, man," Gwilym said, "jus' a guess, that's all."

The agitated scratching continued.

"Come on, Mike. We're mates, remember? I'm not gonna send this to the local paper."

"All right, all right. This – Eleri, then – she's...important. Yeah, that's the word. And she's disappeared, gone somewhere, I don't know..."

"What d'you mean she's gone? She 'asn't gone nowhere. I saw 'er out walkin' only last week."

"She's hiding from me, isn't she?" Heneghan said bitterly. "They always do, don't they? Fucking women. The ones you really want, they go..."

"So, find someone else," Gwilym said.

"It's not like that," Heneghan said harshly. "I don't even like women usually. They creep. They cling. None of them are worth the price of a condom. Look at my wife. Typical! She's always moaning on about something. Eleri's different. She respects herself, knows who she is, what she wants..."

Gwilym turned away from the renewed desperation on Heneghan's face.

"Jesus, 'e's got it real bad," he thought.

"Nothin' wrong with bein' upset about it, man! I've been cut up to fuck by a few girls in my time, I can tell you!"

The fingers were scratching once more. It occurred to Gwilym that Heneghan was not aware of this.

"Christ! You don't get it, do you? I fucking hate being like this. You open the door – and you don't know what's going to come in. Bad things; things you don't want to see. My life is how I want. I don't need all this, people squirming their way in when there are gaps. My life's tight. Intruders are not welcome."

"People are gonna think we're a pair of queers 'aving a tiff," Gwilym thought, but his compassion was stronger than the fleeting embarrassment.

347

"Back down, mate. I'm not getting' at you. You wanna talk about Eleri, or any other chick, go ahead, just don't get complicated about it. God, you should'a seen me when Tania left, cried on me mam's shoulder like a baby, I did. No shame in it."

Despite his light tone, Gwilym was beginning to find the other man's determination not to feel anything irritating.

"I've got tight boundaries, Gwilym, there for a reason, to protect. I don't let anyone fuck me about, especially women. I am in control and they know where they stand because they need that strength."

"Bollocks," Gwilym said roughly. "That's total crap, Mike, and you know it. If you wanna be a bastard, go right ahead; no one's gonna stand in your way - but don't give me all that boundaries and protection rubbish. That's just an excuse for keepin' others out."

He paused for breath, took their glasses and went to the bar.

"He'll 'ave gone when I get back," Gwilym thought. "Good bloody riddance! Disappear up 'is own arse, that one..."

Gwilym chatted to the woman behind the bar. He knew her from years back. She was soothing after the conversation with Heneghan.

When he finally drifted back, the man was still there, his face hard, closed.

"Don't trust anyone, do ya, Mike?"

"Nope!" said Heneghan. "Damn right I don't. People always betray you in the end. Best to depend on no one but yourself."

Gwilym thought of the interrupted swim, and exploded.

"Fuck you!" he hissed. "I might as well go 'ome, to my girl, 'oo I do depend on, yeah! She's warm an' she's soft an' makes me feel good. There's no talkin' to you: you don't listen to a soddin' word anyone else says, just go your own way and to hell with the rest of us. Right? I dunno what you're on, but I don't want any part of it."

Gwilym slammed his beer glass down and walked out, too angry to stay any longer. He'd get the late bus back; anything was better than another second in that man's company.

Outside, he cooled down as he walked. He had a quick temper – but, once it was over, that was it; he didn't bear grudges.

Whistling, he thought of Kate and walked faster.

By the time the TR7 drove up beside Gwilym, he was quite calm again.

Heneghan stopped and got out. He faced Gwilym on the pavement.

"You didn't deserve that shit. I'm angry – and other things. You're a good mate. I apologise."

"It's all in the past, man," Gwilym said. "Let's get back!"

***

FRIDAY 31st

On the last day of October, Flora and Miriam walked down the road to Gwilym's house early in the afternoon. There was a great deal to be done before half past ten, when the various guests were expected.

A thin brightness of autumn remained, ready to be swept away by November's weather-related caprice. Miriam had a sense of things coming to an end. This time next year, she would be teaching elsewhere; the carefree, dope-dancing days would be gone forever. She felt sad, wondered if Flora would come with her.

Kate opened the door, a huge towel wrapped round her head.

"Come in," she said. "You wait till you see the costumes Gwil and I have got from town! They're amazing!"

Flora held her bag of material tighter and laughed. The house was unusually tidy. Nipper was wandering around, obviously worried, not sure where to put himself with all these clean surfaces.

Flora and Miriam sat down. Gwilym appeared. Excitement bound them.

"This is it, then," said Flora.

"Yeah, 's'right, love," Gwilym said. "Our chance to knock 'em dead with our party! Great, eh?"

"Gwilym's made some dope cakes," Kate grinned. "We're not going to tell the others what they are, just say they're special Hallowe'en cakes – then we send them out looking for treasure, blitzed out of their brains!"

Miriam laughed.

"Now, then, girls," said Gwilym. "Nough of this yakkin' – loads to do. Me and Flo'll nip up and put the clues along the trail. Kate, you and Miriam get going on the decorations. C'mon, Flo; shift your arse!"

"Aye aye, Boss," Flora said.

Gwilym tapped her on the backside. She yelped.

"See you later!" Kate called.

Gwilym shut the door behind him and walked to the end of the garden, looking for a suitable tree. The first clue, in its plastic coating, dangled fluorescently from his hand. He reached up and secured it to a low-lying branch's fork.

"Just in case Bryn's going out with a midget!" he explained.

Flora giggled at the thought.

They wandered companionably along the road, placing three more of the clues in bushes and hedges. The skeleton of the knoll rattled before them, touched with milky-silver light. Flora picked red berries off a bush and squashed them between her fingers, enjoying the stain and the cool, clear air.

Gwilym opened the gate leading to the knoll. A tiny rabbit zig-zagged across their path, its tail bobbing ridiculously behind it. Gwilym kicked out at it and roared.

"Aw! Poor little thing. You are cruel, Gwilym," Flora teased him.

"Food on the hoof, love! Catch us a few of these, put 'em on sticks for tonight!"

A shiver of light, uncertain in its intensity, caught the trees in a slim line of gold confusion. Lines of grass lit up briefly. Hills glowered grey above everything.

Flora and Gwilym sat down at the highest point, sheltered by gently-waving limbs, and pondered. Flora's happiness was complete. Gwilym was a curiously restful person to be with, for all his bright energy.

"Now," he said, "we want 'em to end up here, right? But not too easy, like – don't want to spoil the fun. What d'ya reckon, Flo?"

Flora thought a bit.

"A wide circle leading down to the stream and back up again?"

"Good girl!" said Gwilym and smiled at her.

They set off again.

***

In Pwll-Coedwig, children in home-made costumes gathered on the village green, an instinct older and wilder than they leading them by its bony hand.

Small witches, devils and werewolves formed a big circle and began to dance. Slowly at first, and then gathering pace, the little ones – mesmerised by music only they could hear and sensing the unseen presence of Gwyn ap Nudd – wove the ancient and enchanted Samhain circle.

***

Miriam gouged a gigantic eye in the pumpkin she held between her knees. Bits of flesh flew all over the room. The two girls howled with laughter. Kate tied a last piece of black wool to the complicated spiders' web they had entwined, then hung all over the ceiling and walls. Plastic bats and skeletons completed the macabre effect.

"Hurry up with that lantern, Miriam. I want to put the red light bulbs in and see what the place looks like."

"Can't you use the ones we've already done?" Miriam complained. "This is hell's delight. I think I'm down to the second epidermal layer and never want to set eyes on another pumpkin, turnip or swede as long as I live!"

Kate bustled about, replacing all the light bulbs with red ones. She pulled the curtains and switched on the lights.

The room flared eerily, a vast wound sutured with protruding black 'veins'. Miriam shivered. It was even better than she had expected. Kate lit the tiny night lights inside the lanterns. Malevolent faces grimaced at them. Miriam began to believe in the magic they had summoned up: the room seemed to throb with a power quite at variance with the cheap wool and Woolworths' red bulbs.

"Done it!" Kate announced with satisfaction. "God, I'm looking forward to this. The waiting's going to be the worst part."

Miriam consulted her watch.

"Only half three – we've got hours and hours!"

"Keep digging, woman!" Kate said, laughing. "That thing looks ridiculous with only one eye…"

***

Heneghan lay in bed. His eyes were closed. He did not want to go to this party: load of kids farting about in fancy dress. Not his scene. Keeping up appearances,

Angela had said. Jesus! What would she know about that, screeching away like a demented harpy!

He wondered if Eleri would be there, and his jaw tightened. She could crawl to him; he wasn't going to make the first move. He congratulated himself on keeping his cool with her. In retrospect, her temporary absence seemed like a good thing: meant he could do what he did best- erect a barrier of indifference; play mean to keep her keen.

"More likely to get her that way," he thought, smiling thinly.

He did not realise the extent to which his feelings were in conflict. Similarly, although he knew that, "...the little session with Gwilym..." as he'd come to call it, was a bit out of character, he failed to recognize how far he had wandered towards the point of no return.

He had battened it all down, nailing the boards into place with a mixture of viciousness and contempt.

He felt supremely confident that nothing could touch him now. But the blackness returned, night after night – a symptom he put down to the bang on the head – leaving him shaken and helpless.

It was a closed area, even in the privacy of his own mind.

***

Eleri had the sewing machine out. Great swathes of white material billowed out in front of her. She smiled gently. She was coming to realise that Richard had been rather a stuffy man in many ways: she could never have done anything this frivolous when he was alive.

She was excited. The only parties she had ever been to with Richard had been tedious affairs, with people standing stiffly around making polite conversation.

She was opening out gradually, timidly, accustoming herself to the freedom of the big house. The studio had always been her special place, but the rest of the house had been theirs – which had meant Richard's. Not an overtly aggressive man – at least not in the physical sense - he had still ruled each room with the quiet barbs of his personality.

Eleri had been astonished, and dismayed, to discover how little of her own character had been reflected in the place. She made minute alterations uncertainly, the shade of her husband still blocking out most of the light.

The ghost of the painting had left her alone, for which she was grateful. Much as she loved the creative process, the intensity of it all threw her into a state of anxiety, even paranoia. The peace was welcome. She knew – with a blend of excitement and dread – that the flame would burn at her again; but, for the moment, the soothing movement of her hands over the white silken material was enough.

**

Edwin frowned, worried. He did not see how this party could end anything but disastrously. He feared that Gwilym was mischief-making; that the young man, with the impetuosity of youth, had got himself – and everyone else – into a situation more serious than he realised.

He poured himself a stiff drink and smiled wryly. This damned party was going to be quite bad enough without the additional disadvantage of sobriety. Besides, alcohol soothed the stomach pains he had noticed increasingly since summer's end.

"For two pins, I wouldn't go," he thought to himself. But there was a part of him which was charmed by the freshness and lunatic spontaneity of the whole idea. There was something essentially young and hopeful about it: the way Gwilym thought he could make a party from so troubled a collection of individuals was intriguing.

"And perhaps he can," Edwin said to himself. "If anyone can do it, Gwilym's the man!"

**

"Yes, that's the way it looks, Mairead. I'm afraid divorce may be the only way out. Yes, I know it's horrible and sad – and against all your religious principles. Dear God, I've done nothing but mull it over – but I can't go on like this; really I can't.

"Well, you can try talking to Mike if you want; but I don't think it'll do much good. No. He won't discuss it- refuses. Please don't tell Rory for the moment. I'm going to keep trying. Yes. Goodbye."

Angela put the phone down, shaking. Mairead had rung when she was at her most vulnerable – and it had all come flooding out.

She lit a cigarette, glad of something to occupy her hands.

She admitted to herself that she was feeling stronger these days. A part of her had hardened – but telling her mother-in-law had re-opened the wound. She blinked back tears impatiently.

"After this party," she thought, "I'm going to have to talk to him: tell him what I've done, go through the options."

***

Darkness gripped tight, grudgingly allowing the bright half-moon room to wander. Pale lunar rays lurked behind a cloud, waiting.

Gwilym's front door was open. Crimson squares gave the night-black house distorted features. In silhouette, it resembled a skull, mouth open in a silent, blood-drenched scream. A deep slow beat rumbled down the garden.

Inside, a transformation had taken place. The hilarity of earlier had given way to the stillness of serious role-playing. The hosts sat, immobile, on chairs set in a circle.

Gwilym broke the mood.

"This fuckin' wig," he moaned, "itches like 'ell."

Nervous laughter fractured the tension.

"I don't feel this music is quite deadly enough," Flora said. "It's too fast!"

"Well, put on that 'orrible medeeval rubbish, then!" Gwilym replied. "*Iesu mawr!* 'Ow the 'ell did blokes get about in these poncy leggin' things? My balls are goin' numb!"

"Do stop moaning," Kate laughed. "You insisted on wearing that ridiculous Witch Finder General's garb. The black wig looks vile with your moustache. Should have dyed that black too!"

Miriam fiddled with the stereo. A truly depressing sound rolled towards them.

"Hell's bells! What have you done?" Kate cried.

"Put it on at 16. Sounds suitably macabre, doesn't it?"

"Bloody awful," groaned Gwilym.

Miriam, dressed as a vampire, bared her blood-stained fangs at him. Laughter fought with *The Agincourt Carol* played at hearse speed.

"Sshhhh!" hissed Flora. "They'll be here any second!"

"No chance," Kate replied. "They'll all be holed-up in the pub for hours yet. Hey, get an earful of that bit, chaps – sounds just like someone's head being cut off!"

A resounding crash, in slow motion, broke through the melody. Flora settled her devil's tail more comfortably.

"There goes the head!" sniggered Miriam. "It's…it's…falling down a steep flight of steps. There! It's landed. Shhh! I hear footsteps. Keep quiet, you lot. Don't move."

"I think we're supposed to go inside," someone said, outside the window. It sounded like Angela Heneghan, though none of them could be sure through the gruesome caterwauling of St George's Canzona.

Miriam bit the hem of her dress to stop herself from snorting with laughter as the footsteps came into the room.

None of them looked up, or said a word.

"Heavens," Angela said. "Look at this!"

Heneghan laughed, despite himself.

A particularly cacophonous medley of sounds came from the stereo. Miriam burst out laughing. She laughed till tears rolled down her cheeks.

"Welcome!" said Gwilym in deep, sepulchral tones. "Oh shit! Me codpiece is slippin'!"

This started them all off.

"Nice one, Gwil," Heneghan said.

"I thought you had red hair," Angela said to Miriam.

Flora giggled.

"She dyed it specially – only the stupid fool failed to read the label: it's permanent! She'll have black hair for weeks!"

"Come and join our witching circle," said Kate. "We've got to sit like this till the others arrive, you see..."

"This is a brilliant idea," Angela said.

In that moment, the possibility of enjoying this party broke through. She sat down next to Miriam. Heneghan took up position near the stereo. Just in time, as it transpired.

More people came in – and soon the small room was milling with strange figures. To Gwilym's surprise, Heneghan was the oddest of the lot. God knows what he had on his face: it looked like dried sick.

Kate and Flora poured wine into the glasses. An Egyptian mummy figure, whom they hadn't yet identified, bent to pin up a few trailing yards of material. Heneghan's face began to peel off. Half of it dropped into Kate's wine. He winked at her.

The four of them converged in the back room. Miriam's face was pink with excitement.

"S goin' brilliant, girls!" said Gwilym. "Kate, get them cakes. We'll get this lot organized in a minute."

"I just can't believe Heneghan's face!" Flora whispered. "He's the last person I'd have thought would get into the ghoulish spirit."

"Let's hope Eleri doesn't turn up," said Miriam.

Gwilym smiled wickedly.

"Too late, love. She's already 'ere. That's 'er in them windin' bandages, what d'ya ma call it?"

Flora giggled.

"Heneghan's going have a bit of trouble getting those off her!"

Kate reappeared, and they drifted back to their guests.

"Cakes!" Gwilym announced to the room at large. "Come and get 'em! Special family recipe passed down from my great-grandma 'oo was a witch!"

They surged forward. There was friendship in that room — and something more: excitement and a willingness to enter the fantasy world created for them. Miriam was so happy, she almost cried. People were talking, laughing, drinking. Edwin, revolting in red, wandered in.

"If I don't take my head off, I shall suffocate," Eleri said to no one in particular. Everyone cracked up laughing. Kate, who was nearest, helped to unwind the silken bandages.

Heneghan had retrieved his face from the wine and was trying, in vain, to mold it back into place.

"Right, folks!" yelled Gwilym. "Over to my gorgeous girl now. She's gonna tell you what's next."

"Whatever else they've been expecting, it wasn't this," Kate mused to herself as she unfolded the details of the treasure hunt. A few people laughed and Bryn, who'd arrived as one of the undead in black Y-fronts and not much else, looked comically horrified.

"Ok," Kate finished. "There's twelve of you – you can go in three groups of four. We'll send you off at intervals: first lot to return win the prize. One of us will go with each group, to make sure you don't get lost, but we're not going to help you! Anything I've forgotten, Gwil?"

"No, love," Gwilym said. "Now, then, Mike, you can be leader of group one: that means you get to hold the torch. You take Edwin and Bryn and Bryn's girl."

While Gwilym finished sorting out the groups, Miriam took Heneghan outside and lit one of the big candle torches for him. It cast weird shadows. Heneghan's eyes shone.

"He's really enjoying himself," Miriam thought in surprise.

The groups set off along the road, at five minute intervals. Group three, led by Eleri, took ages searching for the first clue. In the end, Gwilym pointed to the tree and hoped that none of the others could see his cheating. He had a soft spot for Eleri.

Torch light heightened everything, made the normal grotesque. A spirit of competition was abroad. Excited shouts and laughter broke the stillness of the night.

The half-moon stole out, bathing the macabre procession in silver. The vast weaving dragon, with its three grotesque yellow eyes, meandered down the road.

Gwilym, arriving at the knoll with his group, found Heneghan's crew wandering drunkenly about, clearly lost. Their torch, half burned down, flickered from side to side, as Heneghan poked in yet another tree. Gwilym could hear him muttering to himself.

"Takin' the scenic route, are ya, Mike?" he asked, laughing.

"Sodding great tree on the left, it said in the last clue," Heneghan replied. "All wizened little bushes here. Where's that tree gone?"

"Try goin' back!" Gwilym said airily, and walked off.

"Never see 'em again!" he said to Eleri, who was getting good at this game. She smiled happily back.

Moonlight floated peacefully down the little stream. Iestyn, dressed as a zombie and abandoned by his group, sat on the grass and communed with a particularly vacant-looking Jacobs ram. Gwilym, passing this touching pastoral scene, could hear fragments of the conversation. He laughed unkindly.

A sense of unreality pervaded everything. The groups straggled back. The remainder of Heneghan's face fell down Bryn's girl's cleavage. She threw up in the garden. Gwilym sent out a search party for Iestyn. The man, clearly stoned out of his skull, had to be restrained from bringing the ram back with him.

They sat – those still capable of so-doing – in a circle on the carpet. Eleri was unwinding at an alarming rate. Gwilym put a blanket tenderly over Iestyn and left him to sleep it off in the back room.

The plate of unmentionables was passed round. People nodded sagely and made outrageous suggestions. The music droned on. The sheep's eye was never seen again. Gwilym suspected Owain. Bryn accused the dog. Nipper ate the raw sausage and seemed none the worse.

The room emptied slowly, like a giant glass of silvery wine. Heneghan spoke briefly to Eleri. A few ears, at sluggish half-mast, twitched, but no one heard what was said.

The party spirit crept gently out.

PART THREE: NOVEMBER 1980

FRIDAY 21st

Gwilym's party became the talking point of the village. Those who had attended it agreed, unanimously, that it had been an outstanding success. Those who had not been invited conjured up visions of extreme licentiousness for the delectation of their more gullible friends.

Helydd and Janet spent several thoroughly enjoyable coffee mornings telling everyone exactly what had gone on between Heneghan and *'that tart, Eleri Morgan'*, in Gwilym's garden. The rumour hive buzzed.

Eleri finished the painting. It hung in front of her, in the dimmed November sun, shining with a light of its own. She was pleased, though her critical eye picked out loose threads in the taut weave.

She usually dreaded the end of a picture. This time she felt full of energy. A collection of images from the party were coming together in her mind. She felt that, initially, they had stood outside the magic of that night as cynical adults; but had gradually been swept in despite themselves. Gwilym and the three girls had created something more than a party: they had fashioned a gate through to the landscape of childhood. Eleri felt that, in truth, no one had remained untouched by this.

Carrying a cup of coffee, Eleri wandered over to the studio window. The winter bleaching had begun, though long necklaces of red-gold bryony still lay draped along hedgerows.

Heneghan was supposed to be calling round. Eleri had agreed to this, though she did not know what she was going to say to him.

She was having to confront her reluctance to get involved with this man. She liked him; she had enjoyed the sex – but she shrank away from further commitment. As long as he had been bound up with her painting, Eleri had felt safe – for it meant she had a sense of control, of limits.

Now, stripped of her artist's role, she felt naked.

"Maybe it's simply too close to Richard's death," she reasoned to herself, as the doorbell rang.

It was Heneghan.

He looked strange to Eleri, slightly out of focus.

"He's not going to influence me in any way," she thought fiercely.

"Mike," she said calmly, "come in. I've finished the painting."

Heneghan followed her. He winced, trying to shake the sense of blankness growing inside his head. He reached out for the comfort of the studio, sinking into his usual chair.

"Coffee?" Eleri asked.

Heneghan nodded.

While she was out of the room, he looked at the painting. It made him feel as if he had been flayed. It was terrible in its beauty. The light hurt.

Eleri returned with coffee, and then sat gracefully on the floor. She looked sorrowful but determined – and Heneghan, used to her more dreamy moods, felt a sense of shocked warning.

"We have to talk, Mike," she said. "Not something you enjoy, I know – but..."

"It's not going to work?" he said harshly.

She sighed.

"Oh, it would work all right. That's the awful thing. It would work too well. We'd destroy one another."

"I doubt it," he said.

"Listen, Mike — please. We're too alike, you and I. We are both distant, not willing to open up. Can't you see? There'd be no space, no hiding place, on that shared frequency. It's to do with the habits of a lifetime, needful masks and keeping others at bay. You can't distance yourself with me, Mike — and that, in the end, would lead to hatred."

"So?" he said bitterly. His voice changed, softened. "You're good for me, Eleri."

"Mike! Get real! You don't want anyone to be good for you. I know you because, whatever wavelength you are on, I share it. Your habit of hiding is too deep. You wouldn't thank me. It would become a trap, a cage. You'd be hemmed in by that shared knowledge. Life isn't like the idealistic illusion of the twin-soul stuff. Where would you go when the harsh lights intruded?"

Heneghan's head was pounding.

"You're wrong!" he cried. "Jesus, Eleri, you are more perceptive than most — but on this one you are way off."

"No," she said quietly. "Don't think I haven't noticed the way you've been during the last month. It was clear as clear at that party: all that anger dammed up; that raging stiffness. Oh yes, you think you can hide that from me — some hope. Your whole body was full of fury, fury that I hadn't contacted you; hadn't let you in. But that's not the worst of it. The really awful thing is the way you kick it all out, deny it. I can just imagine you saying to yourself, 'Well, fuck her! I don't care anyway!' And do you know what frightens me, Mike? I can be exactly the same! I tried to warn you when we first met. My painting comes first with me. I don't want to be in love. I don't want emotional complications in my life – not after thirty years with Richard."

Eleri trembled with the bitter violence of her thoughts. She glanced up at Heneghan. There was a new quality to his silence. His face was whiter than she had ever seen it. He looked ill.

"You need to go, Mike. I can't stand it."

And then Heneghan seemed to break up into pieces in front of her. Eleri was horrified. His teeth were clenched tightly and he was shaking. To Eleri, it looked as if something of immense and elemental power were flooding him, and he was fighting it grimly.

She wanted to comfort him. She wanted to kill him. Most of all, she wanted her own unwilling perception of the deep bond between them to disappear.

The intense trembling stilled – and Heneghan seemed to hunch deep into himself.

"No one has ever seen him like this," she thought suddenly, "not since childhood, at any rate," – and she was torn between dismay, compassion, and a dread recognition.

"I have been lying to myself," she thought. "This man means more to me than Richard ever did. Oh God."

She knelt at his feet then, and put her hands gently on his knees. She could feel the energy pulsing through him.

Eleri limped across the bridge of her own reluctance.

"Mike," she said. "Talk to me! Shout at me! Don't go into silent mode. What's going on?"

He was vaguely aware of her light touch. She felt like a point of safety and light in a wobbly world. Tears welled. Ashamed – after all, boys don't cry – he blinked them back as best he could. He held Eleri's hand tightly.

"Fucking terrified, Eleri. You're cruel, very cruel. Hurts, that does. Pain, hope and light – that's you. Opened a door, it seemed like, and let me in a little way - then slam! Banished as a bloody emotional complication. Never mind all that conventional bollocks – husbands, wives, being faithful, all that biblical detritus – what is it that really counts, eh? Vibrating wire of connection, that's what. We're dead a hell of a long time. If two people slot into place, that's the true love."

Eleri, transfixed, felt that pulse between them; experienced the pain-pleasure of its electrical shortages and tremors; felt the joint arrival at the connective mains and the gasping anguish of shocked instinctive pairing.

"No wonder he hides behind anger, and I in the guise of the eternal outsider," she thought. "Social rules teach us to deny this: to follow the fairy story scenario, or the purely sexual route. There is no place for something so peculiar in the annals of human romance, and so we fight it with rage and despair."

Eleri had married Richard, in part at least, in order to avoid that part of herself which undulated away from the conventional wisdom on pairing-up with another human being: the part that wanted to delve beneath it and find the mind-spirit source; the locking together which, once achieved, could not be picked apart, by key or violence, this side of the grave – and maybe not even then.

That Heneghan recognized this, in his own way, was both terrifying and thrilling – and she realized that, whatever happened next, there was nowhere else for him to go. He'd climbed as far as he could – and the process of falling had begun.

Heneghan's eyes opened. He looked around the room, dazed, as if unsure where he was. Reluctant tenderness rose in Eleri. She moved so that she was sitting on his lap and put her arms around him, stroking the dark hair.

"Mike?" she said.

"Eleri."

His voice sounded gentle.

"I didn't want to hurt you," she said, "and, by God, I did too. I was fighting my own battle – not wanting to trust any bond, any connection. Didn't recognize the blindly bloody obvious and was raging against it. Love is a word. Spirits in synch a rare state. Do I love you? Probably – but the word seems thin and inadequate as a way of describing something that doesn't need the sanctity of marriage, or even sexual contact, to exist and flourish."

Heneghan rocked them both in the chair, the creaking so reminiscent of millions of sex scenes - and yet so bewilderingly other.

"I'm not a child, Eleri," he said at length. "I've never been a child. It's not easy. I've always prided myself on being a survivor- and am happy to be cruel and hard if that keeps people at a distance. Don't like to be seen as weak. This last month, though, the dark things took over – and you're right: I didn't want to know.

"People have always expected me to be strong, certain, in control. Angela thinks she'd like me some other way, but she wouldn't.

"It's you, Eleri – you, with your lack of fear and your – how can I put it? – reading the whole of the book that I am and not flinching. I can't go back..."

Eleri experienced an utter longing; her solar plexus contracted with its muscular insistence. She wanted to cry, to bury herself in this man's arms, to follow the dictates of the spirit's yearning – but, as a woman betrayed in the name of love herself, she could not pull the marital rug out from underneath another woman's feet.

Climbing off his lap was one of the hardest things she had ever had to do. The desire to claim him, to roost, to seduce him away from his family was enormously powerful.

"You must go back, Mike. There is no option. You need to sort things out with Angela and your children. No good you pretending they don't exist – are an inconvenience in your chaotic inner life. Be honest with Angela – but, most of all, be honest with yourself.

"I want both my freedom and the connection I have with you. Classic cake and eat it scenario. Greedy, probably; unrealistic, almost certainly. The world doesn't work like that. Other people exist. Our actions can wound deeply. I want the best of both worlds: to avoid domesticity, while keeping open the door to sex and mental/emotional bonding. Masculine mind, I daresay. Marriage? No, thank you. Never again. Once was enough. I just wish the ideal state I dream of between men and women could be made reality in this realm; that the bonding goalposts could be shifted, and the definition of a love goal changed out of all recognition."

He smiled.

"Idealistic Eleri! You'd take the world on, wouldn't you?"

"I'd fight, yes, fight tooth and claw to shake the flower of romance until all its false petals flock to the floor and only the true, the real, the strong and lasting remained. Meanwhile, you need to tell Angela what happened between us. If you don't, the sanctimonious cows in the village will – and she will be made a laughing stock. She doesn't deserve that. I probably do – but she has done nothing wrong."

"Fucking hell, Eleri – they wouldn't, would they?"

She looked sadly at him.

"Not only would they; they probably already have. They've had a go at me – but, getting no joy there, Angela is the logical next step. I know how this is played out, ironically, because I went through it with Richard countless times."

Heneghan got up and hugged Eleri briefly.

"You're right. Thanks for the warning."

Once he had gone, Eleri curled in the chair and cried, knowing that her views – however honest and heartfelt – would give Heneghan, essentially a conventional man, the escape clause he needed.

***

The grey car stopped opposite the gate. Angela, looking out, did not recognize it – and, shrugging, went back to chopping vegetables. She felt calm, almost hypnotized, by the soothing nature of this job.

When the doorbell rang, she jumped, slicing her finger. Blood dripped on to the carrots as she rushed to the door.

Two women she knew slightly from the village stood on the doorstep. Having seen no one all day, Angela was pleased to have visitors.

"Maybe," she thought, "this could be the start of a new friendship..."

She smiled warmly at the women standing outside, and invited them in.

"Apologies, ladies. I am sure I recognise you, but your names have slipped my mind."

The larger of the two stepped forward and held out her hand. Surreptitiously wiping gore onto her apron, Angela shook briefly and let go before causing an inadvertent Lady Macbeth moment.

"Good morning, Mrs Heneghan. There's lovely, isn't it? I'm Mrs Jones and this is my friend, Mrs Davies. Not disturbing you, are we, dear?"

"No, no, not at all. Do come through to the living room – and I'll make a pot of tea. Sorry about the chaos: three children. You know how it is?"

Mrs Jones and Mrs Davies sat down – and Angela, grabbing a plaster from the medicine cupboard, went back to the kitchen.

In her loneliness, and anxious desire to make friends, she failed to pick up the slightly menacing aura seeping from the two visitors – and felt, instead, absurdly excited, child-like, as she carried the tea tray in and joined them.

"I'm really pleased you called actually," she said. "I don't know many people around here, and my husband works away a lot."

The look exchanged was spikier this time – and Angela felt confused, a sense of dark fear passing over her.

"Something's wrong, isn't it?" she found herself blurting out.

"Now then, why should you think that, *cariad*? Janet and I thought we'd come and have a nice cup of tea, seeing as we're neighbours. Did you say Mr Heneghan was out at work?"

"Yes," Angela said wildly. "Yes, he's gone up to Manchester on a business matter – we used to live up there, and he still has work connections in the area."

"You must have misheard him, dear. Why, we saw him, not half an hour ago, didn't we, Janet, coming out of Mrs Morgan's house – and her husband only dead a matter of weeks! He wouldn't be doing some business for her, would he? Only he seems to be over there all the time just lately – and you know how people misinterpret things like that – such silly stories we hear being passed round!"

Mrs Jones laughed insincerely. Angela's heart was beating so fast, she felt faint.

"Mrs Morgan?" she said. "You mean Eleri?"

Mrs Jones's voice slid briefly into bitterness. Angela registered this, despite the shock of it all.

"Yes, Eleri," the woman spat. "Thinks she's too good for the likes of us, dressing like a hippie and never socialising. It's disgraceful. She's lowering the village tone."

"Oh, yes!" Mrs Davies chipped in. "Terrible woman, that one. You wouldn't believe some of the things she's done. Well, her daughter – lovely, tidy girl, Catrin – won't speak to her at all, never comes here. Dreadful, I call it."

"What are you implying?" Angela cried out.

Mrs Jones gave a smile so false that Angela almost vomited on the spot.

"Not trying to say anything, dear. Oh dear me, no – just making a little observation, you might say. Just being a good neighbour; but then, I'm sure there's a perfectly good explanation for it. All I can say, though, is I wouldn't let my Dai anywhere near that woman. She's got a reputation, you know…"

Angela felt her world descending into a steep-sided pit.

Mrs Jones stood up and glared at Mrs Davies until the other woman moved hurriedly.

"Well, Mrs Heneghan, we mustn't keep you, must we? Such a lot to do when one is a wife and mother, isn't it? I have enjoyed our little chat!"

Angela let them out in a daze. She couldn't believe what she had heard. Eleri? No, surely not. Mike, for all his dark moments, had never struck her as the unfaithful type – and, surely, if he had been, she'd have known, it being someone so close to home.

But, into her mind, came a picture of Heneghan and Eleri huddled together at the party. She ran to the toilet and was violently sick, then knelt over the bowl, trembling with shame and fear.

"How could I have been so naïve?" she thought. "Imagining they came in friendship, when all they were doing was laughing at me, laughing at my lack of awareness."

She got up slowly – knew she had to see Eleri and find out the truth. Eyes sore from weeping, she walked away from the house.

***

Heneghan drove home as fast as he could; but he knew, as soon as he got there, that he was too late. He recognized Helydd Jones' car from the funeral.

"Oh, Christ!" he said out loud. "Fucking hell!"

He was so angry that he was tempted, for a brief moment, to burst in and kill that interfering old cow. He knew, however, that his arrival would only make things worse – and so, reversing, he shot down the road, way past the speed limit and not giving a damn.

He felt the need to get right out, away from the present claustrophobia of this place – and he knew exactly where to go: a castle, on a remote hill in North Wales, he had discovered soon after arriving in the area. He told himself it would be better to see Angela when he had sorted a few things out in his own mind.

The sky seemed to be gathering in, as if a mighty hand were pulling on a vast piece of elastic. Grey folds draped over the mountains; metallic-sheened waves arched and spat white plumes in the distance.

Heneghan could feel the wind boxing at the car as he drove along. Rain, netted by mist, broke through in a fine spray.

The town vanished. Tiny villages, swallowed whole, whipped past in a new frenzy of rain. Heneghan felt his anger give way – and the glory of the elemental day caught him once more.

On an impulse, he indicated right and joined the mountain road. The day was right for it. Rocks jutted out; miners' cottages, long-abandoned, stood like a mouthful of decayed teeth. There was sorrow in the air, and loss. The roots of the land dug in deep here. Time might never have penetrated the darkness of this place.

King Arthur was reputed to have set his mark up on one of the mountain ranges. Looking up, seeing the birds circling, Heneghan found this only too easy to believe.

Nothing gave way. He drove through unremitting greyness. He saw no one. Loneliness haunted the echoing spaces. The gloom increased, enveloping everything. Nothing could be anticipated: mist closed doors and distorted even the calls of the birds.

Heneghan drove up the rough track leading to Castell Morgause. The fortification rose, dark and forbidding, from the hill. Grass withered in a vain attempt at softening the place.

He began to climb. Echoing whispers from the castle and its bloody past surrounded him. The problems of Pwll-Coedwig seemed far below, mute as sharks.

The drawbridge, stretched stiff as death across the moat, was blasted with a sudden bolt of silver. Heneghan walked over it, under the menacing spikes of the portcullis, and into the castle grounds.

A sense of long-ago times and ancient people assailed him immediately. He could smell the huge boars roasting on the spit; hear the raucous cackle of servants going about their tasks. Music rose from imaginary tabors, rebecs, viols and crumhorns.

He was filled with a savage happiness. He could easily imagine himself as a king of old, lord of this castle.

"Henry V111 had the right idea," he thought, "He just divorced or beheaded the unwanted spouse and moved on to the next one. Good bloke, old Henry!"

He climbed the worn steps to the tower. The vertiginous drop held a delicate mirage of bustling floors and huge log fires.

Heneghan's thoughts turned to the two women in his life. Out here, surrounded by the wild places, the balance between them seemed equal – and he realized that he wanted both of them. Part of Eleri's charm was the aura of mystery which enfolded her: he had a horror of her becoming normal for him.

He knew, in his heart, that his need for order, control and stability would not be met with Eleri. Her magic did not encompass such things as regular meals and a tidy house. He knew then that, vital as Eleri's life-force was, he could not live with her. He had also recognized, in that moment of seeing Helydd's car, that he felt protective of Angela: she frequently annoyed him; his anger had been known to explode into violence – but the thought of her being chewed up by others gave him as strange pain and sense of sadness.

Heneghan walked along the battlements. Mist gave way to brilliance so suddenly that his eyes watered. The moat moved, languorously green-gold. Huge spears of sunlight pierced the stone cornices.

Hundreds of feet below, the fringe of trees was combed with light.

Heneghan's love for this place knotted his throat in a sensation almost like tears. He knew he had to go back; knew there were things, and people, to be faced – but, for a space of time, he just stood there, letting the warmth shift a few lingering black shadows.

***

Angela walked away from Eleri's house. There had been no answer when she'd rung the bell. Eleri was either out or not prepared to see anyone. Angela was relieved. She had feared Mike would be there.

She felt faintly embarrassed by her impulsiveness: *'Wife confronts mistress!'* sounded like a scene from some awful novel.

She knew that Mike, and not Eleri, was the one she needed to talk to.

***

Eleri saw Angela through the frosted front door, but she was unable to deal with another emotional scene.

***

Strange slats of sun continued to break through the stormy sky. The sea blackened. Worried fishermen double-checked the mooring ropes on their boats. There was unease in the air. Men lined the shore, watching with dread. It didn't look good. Highest tide tonight and already giant veins of water curled, pulsed and gathered in on themselves far out at sea. Time to get the sand bags out; time to get behind doors and hope to hell that the worst of the storm passed them by.

**

Edwin Russell, exhausted by pain, slept through the time of safety.

**

Heneghan, driving back along the sea front, felt fear – and a curious exhilaration. The dark power out there was unmistakable. He was glad he lived inland.

The place was deserted. This was unusual. The booming out at sea deafened him. Water was coming in fast: already the bottoms of the groynes were covered. Heneghan drove on.

**

Angela heard the sound of the car pulling up outside. This was it, then. She braced herself.

Heneghan leapt into the room, a creature larger than life for a brief moment. His energy crackled between them. He seemed entirely unfamiliar. Angela stared, noting the odd light in his eyes.

High wind smashed the wood of the outhouse. Granite cloud creaked apart to let rain through.

Heneghan and Angela looked at one another. Honesty trembled in the gap between their bodies. She did not falter. She had a sense of communicating fully with Mike: the pared-down essence of recent experiences passed wordlessly from one to the other. He smiled at her.

"I'm not going to change, Ange," he said.

"No," she agreed. "Me neither."

"And I can't leave," he added. "You know that, don't you?"

They sat down on the carpet, facing one another, a strange position for both but oddly appropriate under the circumstances. Angela rested her chin on her hand.

"No. I didn't know that, Mike. These last few weeks have been so horrifying that I have thought almost exclusively in terms of divorce. Isn't that what you really, secretly, want?"

"No," he said roughly. "Look, I'm not going to pretend to be a particularly pleasant person: I've got a fucking awful temper, and I don't suffer fools (or anyone else) gladly. Truth be told, almost anyone else would be better for you – but that's not what it's about, is it?"

"What about Eleri?" Angela asked.

"What about her?" Heneghan countered. "You want me to apologise? Promise never to see her again? All that women's magazine crap? Think again, Ange. That's not written into our contract. You'd despise me if I did. You don't like weak, soft men – and you know it. That's why you married me instead of my dear considerate, gentlemanly brother.

"Your problem is that you feel guilty because you enjoy being dominated, at some level. You love feeling powerless and like a little girl, don't you? And all your feminist friends are telling you that's wrong. Face it: it's got bugger-all to do with Eleri. She has no influence on whatever it is that keeps us together."

Torn between terror and arousal, Angela sat still.

"You're completely unbending, aren't you, Mike? I should just leave you and have done with it."

Heneghan laughed.

"But you won't, will you? You can't. Jesus, Ange – you're as stubborn as I am in your own way. You like being a victim too much – and I'm the one you chose to punish you. So don't fucking blame me for being what you most needed and denied wanting."

Despite herself, Angela realized that there was a dark grain of truth in what Mike was saying.

"God, Mike, we could just go on tearing one another apart for the next thirty-odd years. Great example to set the kids, I don't think!"

"Yeah!" he replied. "That's the real world for you. No doubt if some romantic author were to write the story of our life, I'd be neatly paired off with Eleri and you'd marry Edwin or some such nonsense, thus getting your father-fixation sorted once and for all. It's a shitty fact, Ange, but people can only take so much happiness and contentment before breaking out into rage. I reckon people are happiest being thoroughly miserable and resentful most of the time!"

She laughed.

"You're a bastard, Mike – but there's something about you..."

"Yeah," he said, complacently. "There's something about me!"

SATURDAY 22nd

Edwin woke suddenly. The pain was back, worse than ever, stabbing at his guts. He felt clear-headed, however – and happy in an odd sort of way.

Things sounded as if they had come loose from their supports outside. Edwin imagined rocks being torn free from the sea bed and smashed through windows. It was that kind of night.

He poured himself a large whisky, found alcohol helped more that any number of pain-killing tablets.

Edwin disliked doctors; refused, on principle, to consult one – but he knew, instinctively, that something he did not want to think about had taken over his body. He found the whole business deeply offensive: it reminded him too much of the sick, and embittered, old man his father had become. He had no intention of letting anyone else take control of his life. The thought of such unwanted intimacy repelled him.

The storm sounded unusually vicious to Edwin, but that suited his purpose well enough. Smiling, he drank the rest of the whisky – then put on the black overcoat he habitually wore and went downstairs.

On the bottom step, he paused and looked about in disbelief. The sea had come in and was now washing up and down the hall in an indolent manner, carrying all manner of things clasped to its salty bosom.

Edwin felt a great flood of mirth breaking from him. He stood there, surveying the incongruity of sea-borne detritus, and howled with laughter.

He waded through the mess and opened the front door. It was lighter than he had expected, nearly morning. The sea was retreating. Seaweed hung from gate posts; patches of sand lay in the road.

Edwin made his way down onto the beach. The sand appeared blotched. He walked closer and stopped, a sense of awe stealing over him: hundreds of starfish lay before his eyes, stranded by the storm. It felt like stepping on the rough weave of a vast orange and pink carpet. Edwin kept walking. He felt as if he and the emerging light were going to meet somewhere in the middle.

**

The sea, gentle and cleansed now, carried on its tidal business. Fishermen untied their boats and stretched into the brief warmth of a beautiful day, relieved that the damage to themselves had been minimal.

The starfish were swept out again. A small boy brought one home in a bucket. His parents laughed at his claim that the beach had been full of them.

Doorsteps were scoured and gates repainted.

Mountains softened with early snow.

PART FOUR: DECEMBER 1980

TUESDAY 2nd

Gwilym saddled the stallion. He did not normally bother. Taking the big animal through traffic was a different matter, however: Rameses had become increasingly restless over the past few days. Gwilym knew that the change in the weather was affecting him: the merest hint of snow made the stallion skittish and uneasy. He needed a good long gallop – and the beach was the best place for this.

Gwilym set off down the road. He held the reins loosely and smoked a cigarette as the stallion walked along. Few cars passed. The air was cold.

Rameses' great head came up when they turned into the dune-way track. Sea-mist dampened Gwilym's hair. He leaned back as the horse picked his way down onto the sand. The stallion needed no urging. He took off, galloping close to the waves. The animal's speed and grace always surprised Gwilym: Rameses jumped the groynes with no trouble.

The powerful pleasure of it all took Gwilym over. The jolt, when it came, shocked him. The huge animal skidded sideways so suddenly that a less-experienced rider would have been thrown.

Gwilym looked around automatically. Something had frightened the horse. A bundle of rags lay to his right. He was intrigued, and puzzled: Rameses normally took such things in his stride.

Gwilym jumped off and walked over. The smell warned him before he reached the object. He was not a squeamish man – but something of reluctance gripped him.

It was, as he had feared, a dead man.

"Been in the sea a few days by the looks of things," he thought.

He could cope with the smell of death. It was fear of the unknown that caused Gwilym to squat in the damp sand and take a closer look. He straightened up in shock.

"Jesus Christ!" he said. He felt out of his depth here – and wanted someone else with him to bear witness, someone who had known the man.

Gwilym took the stallion up the beach and, stopping at the phone box, made two calls.

The police arrived, and a man Gwilym presumed was the District Pathologist. They gathered round the body. Gwilym soothed the stallion, and answered the inevitable questions. Mist clung to the corpse's black coat.

The shingle crunched and clattered. Gwilym looked up. Heneghan stood before him.

"Thank Christ you're here, Mike," the younger man said.

"What's going on, Gwil? You were a bit vague on the phone."

"It's Edwin, man. He's dead. I found him down there."

The two men looked at one another. Heneghan felt anger and grief rising in him.

"Fuck," he said. "Better get over there quickly. You know what this means, don't you?"

"Nope," admitted Gwilym.

Heneghan started walking down the beach.

"Tell you later!" he called.

One of the men crouching on the sand looked up when Heneghan approached. His face was guarded, suspicious.

"Yes?" he said. "What can I do for you?"

"I know this bloke," Heneghan said.

"He's already been identified by Mr Thomas, thank you. Let us get on with our job, will you? I'd rather not have members of the public hanging around and contaminating the site at a time like this."

Heneghan's patience, weakened by shock, snapped.

"Look, you bureaucratic bastard, don't try that heavy shit on me. Edwin was a friend of mine and I've got some information you should know."

The man stood up. For a moment, Heneghan thought he was going to punch him. Anger and violence simmered between them. Then the other man shrugged.

"All right," he said. "Let's hear it, then."

"He always wore this bracelet thing round his left wrist. You found anything like that? It's got an object attached to it – bit like one of those barrels used for dogs' names and addresses, I imagine. He's got something written inside it."

The man looked sharply at Heneghan for a moment – and then barked an order at one of his subordinates. A young policeman came over with something in his hand.

"This it?" the man asked.

Heneghan nodded.

"Well, don't just stand there, Constable! Open it!"

"Yes, Sir," the young man said, blushing uncomfortably.

Heneghan tensed. The little barrel was green from the sea's salty lick, and tightly-jammed. When it burst open, a tiny sliver of paper floated on to the sand. The older man picked it up and read it. He looked at Heneghan.

"Your name?"

"Mike Heneghan."

"How did you know about this, Mr Heneghan?"

"Jesus!" snapped Heneghan. "I didn't murder him, if that's what you're thinking! He told my wife about it."

The man cast an impassive eye over Heneghan.

"Thank you, Mr Heneghan," was all he said.

Heneghan walked back to Gwilym. They watched as the men, carrying a long zipped-up black bag, moved up the beach.

"Do you want to come back to my place, Gwil?" Heneghan asked. "Wouldn't mind having you around when I tell Angela."

"Ta, Mike. Bit shook up by this, I am, man. Different when it's a mate."

"Yeah. You take the horse back. I'll see you later."

***

Angela let Gwilym in. The bounce had gone out of him, and she felt a fleeting concern. Heneghan poured three shots of whisky. They sat down. Gwilym closed his eyes briefly.

"Bad news, Ange," Heneghan said. "Edwin's dead. Gwil found him on the beach."

Angela started to scream. Heneghan sat helplessly. Gwilym got up and slapped her round the face.

"No, no, no..." she wailed, her face buried in Gwilym's shoulder.

"Sorry, love," he said gently. "There's no nice way of sayin' it."

Heneghan pressed the shot glass into her hand.

"Mike, you know more than I do about this, man. You'll 'ave to tell her the rest," Gwilym said.

Heneghan hesitated.

"Yeah. You're right. You know what he told you, Ange? About how he'd deal with things if it got too much? Looks to me as if that's just what he did. You've got to admire the guy. Must have taken a hell of a lot of courage."

"Why didn't he tell us?" wept Angela. "We were his friends! There must have been something seriously wrong – and I didn't know. I feel as if I just used him when I needed someone to talk to, and never gave anything back."

"He was a proud man, love,' said Gwilym. 'Dignified, like. He wouldn't 'ave wanted people fussin' over 'im."

"I suppose you're right," Angela sighed. "But it seems such a desolate and lonely way to die. No friends, no comfort, nothing – God, what must he have gone through? I didn't say goodbye. I'll never see him again, and I never told him how much I liked him..."

Separate griefs silenced them.

Gwilym, looking at Heneghan over Angela's head, thought with horror of the things the sea had done to Edwin. Heneghan, having seen the shock and sickness on the other man's face, thought it just as well Angela would never see Edwin again. Angela, remembering the old man at the party, sobbed.

***

Edwin Russell's death hit with great force. Even Pwll-Coedwig's nest of gossips could find nothing bad to say about him. After exhaustive inquiries, and a post mortem – which concluded that, although the cause of death was drowning, Edwin had had inoperable cancer – the police decided that the old man had known what he was doing, and prepared to release his body for burial.

No relatives could be found, however, so the villagers stepped in, headed by Gwilym and the Heneghans.

The reluctance of the police turned to relief. Someone had claimed the man. He was out of their hands. Angela started a fund. People gave generously. Plans drifted towards reality.

***

Angela found she could cope as long as she kept busy. Then the letter arrived, on a winter-thin December day. She knew, at once, that it was from Edwin.

Heneghan walked into the kitchen just as Angela was finishing the letter. He saw the tears on her cheeks – and was aware of a surge of protectiveness. She handed him the sheets wordlessly. He put an arm around her as he read:

'Angela, my dear –

Remember a conversation we once had regarding the sea – and the planned end of my life? I am sure you do. I always had the delightful feeling that you were listening to me most attentively. When you receive this letter, you will know that I have had to make that unenviable decision.

I have known for some time that something serious was amiss. The name does not matter. Suffice it to say that I have assessed the quality of life likely in the next few months – and know things can only get worse. I do not relish endless pain – and feel, therefore, that I may have to take matters into my own hands rather sooner than originally anticipated.

This letter is partly in the nature of needful back-up just in case the bracelet I wear for this purpose fails in some way. I want the authorities to understand the truth: this is not suicide while the mind was unbalanced; but a carefully planned conscious choice. Water sustained me in the womb. I like the thought of my life closing in the great uterus of the sea.

You have been through much in recent months, Angela. I think of you often. Had I been twenty years younger...

There may not be a permanent solution to your situation; but I have every confidence that your honesty, openness and integrity will keep that door open as long as possible.

There is one last thing, I'm afraid – and I am going to have to be very blunt here. I will be found. I hope not by you. I have no wish to be buried or cremated. What I want is to carry through my original plan and end up in the sea.

I do not want you and Mike to haul me down there at dead of night. You might well be arrested on suspicion of murder. I might float back ashore once more!

Go through the proper channels, will you? It might well be difficult. I served in the Navy during the war – and know a bit about this, have left money for you so that the financial side of things will be problem-free.

The major difficulty will be finding a ship prepared to take a body on board. The big warships are not likely to be interested. The man to contact is Rear Admiral Colin Roberts. He lives in Penarth and he'll know what the options are. I have already written to him, so he will be expecting to hear from you.

Thank you for this, Angela.

Yours, in deep affection,

Edwin Russell.'

Heneghan was stunned. He looked at Angela. She was shaking.

"I'll contact this guy of you want, Ange," he said at length. "Get it all set up."

She looked at him gratefully and nodded.

"I'm sorry about all this," he added. "I know how fond you were of Edwin. I liked him too. You stay there. I'll go and phone."

"Will they let us, his friends, be there too?" she asked.

"Dunno. I'll see what I can find out."

She waited, running the sheets of paper through her fingers. She thought of how the village had closed in tightly, protecting Edwin from outsiders. She reflected, with a smile, upon the way *'The Englishman'* had become *'Our Edwin'* in death, and knew that they'd all want to be involved if possible.

Heneghan returned.

"Seemed a pleasant bloke," he said. "Helpful, down-to-earth. Edwin was right, though. This Roberts says he'll see what he can do – but out best bet will probably be to find someone we know who's got a boat and do it privately. Edwin had a distinguished service record, apparently, got to be captain before he left. I had no idea, did you?"

"He never talked much about himself."

"No," Heneghan said. "He didn't. You sure you want to go through with this? It's going to be upsetting. We don't have to take charge."

"It's what he wanted, Mike. He has no living relatives. He trusted us, knew we'd enter into the spirit of it."

Heneghan sighed.

"Yeah, sure. Going to have to be soon, though. He's been dead at least a week already."

"Mike?"

"Yeah?"

"Do you know what to do?"

"Roberts told me all the details, Ange, and I've got it written down. I was thinking of getting Gwilym to help with the nasty bits. Unless you really want to see the body, of course."

"No. I've been thinking about that. I don't think I could bear it."

"Right. I'll get on to Gwil, and see if he can help with the boat problems. You let all the people who are going to be there know the details. We'll make it Wednesday week, if possible."

WEDNESDAY 17th

Wednesday morning dawned cold but clear. The forecast said there would be sun later. Gwilym had found a boat. It waited for them near the estuary. The others were meeting them at midday.

The Rear Admiral had pulled a few strings. A ship had agreed to take the body and to launch it from its deck. Edwin's corpse had to be ice-packed and weighted first, however. Heneghan had told Angela what he and Gwilym needed to do. She shivered at the thought. Tears gathered.

Heneghan and Gwilym drove along the road to Aberystwyth. The tide was coming in slowly.

Heneghan had used part of the fund to buy a hammock. It lay in the back of the Rover, a mute reminder.

"Cigarette, Mike?"

"Yeah. Not looking to this bit. Are you?"

"Christ, no, man! Gonna be 'orrid whichever way you look at it. 'ow's your sewin'?"

Heneghan laughed.

"Crap! I was hoping you'd do that bit!"

"You've gotta laugh, Mike — else we won't get through this. Can't be any worse than findin' him in the first place."

They drew up at Bronglais Hospital, and parked outside the mortuary.

Heneghan got out, carrying the hammock.

"This is it, then, Gwil. Find out whether we're mice or men!"

Gwilym followed him with the weights.

***

Rear Admiral Roberts looked at the sun, then at his wrist-watch. The ship was sleek, grey, a deft porpoise in its movements. Sea thudded against its sides. They should be here soon.

Roberts sighed. This whole business took him back to the war — and the one sea burial he had witnessed. Difficult and expensive though it was to organize, Roberts privately felt that it was the best way to go.

***

Water lapped gently at the estuary bridge. Pale gold streaked the snow on top of the mountains. The boat bobbed up and down. A man, clearing river silt with a long pole, stared in astonishment at the people approaching down the road: three young women, two older ones and a teenage boy, all clad in black.

The pole stuck and went unnoticed. The faint slap of water against wood was the only sound.

A car drove up and the silt-clearer watched as two men, also wearing black, got out. They were carrying what looked like a long rough sack. It appeared to be heavy. The men's faces were strained. Pole-man scratched his head. Odd people you met around here.

***

Angela watched with a feeling of terror. That bundle was Edwin. Heneghan and Gwilym stepped carefully on board. They placed the body gently on deck, resting upon a thick plank Heneghan had found on the beach. Then Heneghan secured it with rope.

Gwilym looked unfamiliar in black, his tawny hair, freshly-braided, was neatly slicked down. Heneghan straightened up and turned to look at the others. They clambered on board fearfully.

"Right!" said Gwilym. "You all set? Tom, come an' 'elp me, will ya? I'm not brilliant with motors."

Edwin dominated the boat.

Heneghan led the others below. There was a fairly big cabin, with a few chairs and a bed. They all sat stiffly while the boat coughed its way into life. Miriam could see a corner of the body-sack from where she sat. She shivered and edged closer to Flora. Kate felt sick. She just hoped the water wasn't going to be choppy once they got out to sea. The boat rocked. A spray of water caught the sun, fanning a rainbow into brief existence. They began to move out, slowly. Aberdyfi glittered with cold light.

Gwilym steered the craft round the headland – and they were out into open sea. Heneghan prowled, trying to calm his mind. Eleri noted his agitation. She looked at Angela. A moment of silent communication passed between them. They both moved to the drinks supply. Gwilym had insisted on bringing some of his home-made wine with him. Angela was glad he had now. His girl was looking pretty ill, she noticed.

Eleri passed tumblers around. Kate began to cry.

"Come on, you take it, my love," Eleri said, kneeling down by the weeping girl. "It'll make you feel better."

Heneghan strode up the steps and out on deck. The sea was all around them, heavy and dappled as petrol in a sun-warmed puddle. He could hear Gwilym cursing in the engine room. Kate suddenly sprinted past and was violently sick over the side.

"Don't worry about it," Heneghan said to her. "You'll settle down."

Kate turned round, saw the body bag and retched again.

Eleri had followed the girl. She joined Heneghan. They leaned over the rail together.

"Angela told me what you and Gwil did this morning, Mike. I thought that was very respectful and caring. How did you stand it, though?"

Heneghan looked at her and smiled slowly.

"I couldn't have done it by myself," he admitted. "Funny that. But Gwilym's down-to-earth. He was cracking jokes all the time – not disrespectfully, you understand, but just because he's Gwilym and he knows how to cope in most situations. The worst bit was sewing up the hammock, knowing that was it, our last chance of seeing Edwin. We did half each. It was bloody hard. That material's thick as hell. Freezing cold too. They had to put him in this transparent iced container to comply with the ship's regulations. Jesus!"

Eleri touched Heneghan's arm briefly.

"How far have we got to go, Mike?"

"Gwil says he knows the spot. I dunno. We'll know when we see the big ship. She going to be all right?"

He pointed to Kate.

"I'll keep an eye on her," Eleri replied. "I think it's particularly hard on the young ones. They haven't got as many defences as we have, and I suspect this is her first encounter with death. I'll see you later."

In the cabin, sea lurched against the window. Flora looked frightened. Angela wanted to drift forever so that she did not have to face that final leave-taking. Eleri returned, supporting Kate.

Tom joined Heneghan. The ship appeared, tiny at first. Soon, though, it felt as if they were about to swoop right up underneath it. The size of the thing fascinated Tom.

The boat stopped. Gwilym came below.

"This is the place," he said.

They moved up the damp steps. The air was cold. Angela's whole chest ached with the grief, and finality, of it all.

A large dinghy took them to the ship. Rear Admiral Roberts shook hands gravely with Heneghan and Gwilym. The ship's deck shone white.

"Round here, Mr Heneghan," Roberts said. "You can attach the plank to our system. You've done a good job. Just as it should be. Difficult to get chaps buried at sea, y'know? Unless they die on board. Stretch a point from time to time."

His smile was kind.

Eleri held Kate tightly. Tom moved towards his mother for comfort. Miriam wept in Flora's arms.

Gwilym and Heneghan moved forward. Roberts bent down and attached the plank. The two men listened to his instructions.

The Rear Admiral stood to attention.

A lone gull, bathed in gold, wheeled above. Heneghan's sight was blurred.

Gwilym nodded at him. They bent and, in unison, started to activate the pulley. The plank rose slowly in the air.

"Go, then, Edwin!" Heneghan shouted, his voice thickening. "Whatever you want, I hope you find it! Let go, Gwil!"

Their hands moved in a blur of speed and tears.

The plank reared upright into the sun.

Briefly, they were blinded.

The hammock slid gracefully towards the sea.

The bulge that was Edwin disappeared from sight.

Gwilym lowered the plank back into place.

There was a faint splash.

Roberts saluted.

Heneghan's back flowed down the railings.

He buried his face in shaking hands.

The clouding of the mountains began.

Snow softened the air.

The boat drifted back to shore.

The drinking began. It seemed a good way of filling the gap where Edwin's body had lain. The eight survivors dipped tentative toes in a new intimacy. Chairs were piled up. They sat on cushions or leaned against the bed.

Tom operated the boat, proud to have been trusted by his father and Gwilym. Heneghan sprawled on the bed. He had removed the black jacket and rolled up his shirt sleeves. Angela, looking at him, realized she had rarely seen him so relaxed, so open.

"These are my friends," she thought. "These five people here," and she was overcome with the wonder of it.

Gwilym's hair flamed in the evening light. He raised his glass and grinned.

"This one's for Edwin!" he said. "We did it, man! *Iesu mawr!* I wouldn't 'ave thought it possible!"

His laugh rattled the windows. Glasses clanked together; soft voices stumbled over Edwin's name. A few tears mingled with the rough wine. No one minded. They felt reckless, outlaws from the society in which they lived.

Angela cupped her chin in her hands.

"We're all risk-takers, aren't we?" she said. "I mean, each one of us here is the target of rumour and gossip. They need us, but we don't fit in. They are wary and uncertain: get close enough to gawp at the Freak Show and then skitter away. Very interesting the number of people who suddenly had something more important to do this afternoon."

"Yeah," said Heneghan. "I noticed that too. They could have coped with the trek up to the graveyard, but this? No way!"

Flora giggled. She decided Heneghan wasn't too bad, quite fanciable really – if you liked that sort of thing, she added quickly to herself, and smiled at Miriam.

Heneghan grinned to himself and flexed his muscles. He felt the power flooding back into his body. He winked at Gwilym. Alcohol had calmed the earlier agitation. Leaping from the bed, he made his way to the engine room, to see how Tom was doing.

A bolt of dark silk hung over the boat, sea and sky stitched so close together that no seam appeared. Tom turned and saw his father. Heneghan stood there, glancing around him, a strange expression on his face. Tom had never admired him more.

"All right, son?" Heneghan asked. "You coping?"

Tom smiled.

"It's great, Dad! Really enjoying it! Can we get a boat?"

"Hmmm. Yeah. Might do just that. I could teach you how to fish. Good time for sea fishing now – reckon we could catch some cod, flat fish, perhaps a mullet or two!"

The boy's face was full of wonder.

"You carry on, Tom. See you back on land!"

Tom could see the lights of Borth getting closer. The headland loomed ahead, a dark creature waiting to pounce. Tom steered carefully.

An ambulance screamed along Aberdyfi's main street. Tom stopped the boat, jumped out and tied the rope to the wooden support by the bridge. Seagulls quarrelled loudly in the darkness. He could hear laughter from below. He was glad the grown-ups were happy; it made him feel safe. Gwilym joined him, and put an arm companionably around his shoulder.

"Good one, Tom! Don't think I could've got us back in this – not with my eye-sight. Your dad's right proud of you."

The others emerged, drunkenly. Tom laughed.

Heneghan got out the car keys, looked at Gwilym and shrugged.

"Not much to choose between us, Gwil! I'll drive. Get in, you lot!"

A mood of madness hit them. After all, home was only just up the road. Eleri got in the back with Flora on her lap. Angela held Miriam. Kate sat next to Heneghan. Gwilym and Tom perched on the bonnet.

"For Christ's sake drive slow, Mike!" Gwilym yelled. "And don't stop sudden!"

Heneghan drove at a stately ten miles an hour.

"We ought to be grieving," Miriam thought.

"Found a peanut, found a peanut, found a peanut last night..." Gwilym warbled loudly and tunelessly.

The car crackled with laughter as everyone joined in.

"Edwin would have been the first to sing something utterly vulgar," Angela said, recalling his wine-drinking toast – and they all knew it was true.

The car rattled up the road, filled with wine fumes and alight with song. Gwilym rolled a joint, lit it and passed it to the emptiness on his right.

"There ya go, Edwin! Take a toke of ya first post-death ganja! Enjoy, man!"

It had become a crazy kind of party: a celebration of the passing they had eased, the life they still had left – and the glory of meeting like-minded souls in this harshly-beautiful and hostile land, under Cader Idris.

Printed in Great Britain
by Amazon